D1426360

MORAY HOUSE
AND
PROFESSIONAL EDUCATION

MORAY HOUSE AND PROFESSIONAL EDUCATION

Papers to mark the college's
150th Anniversary

Edited by
Gordon Kirk
Principal, Moray House College of Education

1985

SCOTTISH ACADEMIC PRESS
EDINBURGH

Published by
Scottish Academic Press Ltd,
33 Montgomery Street
Edinburgh EH7 5JX

SBN 7073 0455 5

British Library Cataloguing in Publication Data

Moray House and professional education.
   1. Teachers, Training of—Scotland
   I. Kirk, Gordon
   370'.7'109411   LB1725.G6

   ISBN 0 7073 0455 5

Printed and bound in Edinburgh, Scotland
by Clark Constable   Edinburgh   London   Melbourne

Contents

Preface

This collection of papers has been planned to appear during Moray House College's celebration of its 150th Anniversary and as a way of recognising that landmark in the history of the institution. It is natural that these papers, all of them written by staff in the college, should reflect the professional concerns and interests of a college such as Moray House. However, in no sense has the book been envisaged as the kind of 'in-house' publication which concentrates, introspectively, on the internal politics and activities of the institution. On the contrary, the brief to which the authors worked stressed the importance of undertaking a theoretical analysis of issues, and of examining how the college is both responding to change as well as influencing developments in the professional education of teachers and others. In writing to that brief the authors have certainly taken account of changes and developments within the institution but they have sought to locate these firmly in the wider context of professional education. The papers should therefore be regarded as contributions to the continuing debate on professional education. While the book will therefore be of interest to past and present staff and students of Moray House it addresses those issues and problems which a much more extended readership will find of relevance to their professional activities.

The structure of the book is straightforward. After two contextualising chapters, the first on the broad historical background and the second on the current retrenchment and institutional responses to it, there follow five chapters, each of which deals with a major area of professional education — teacher education, the professional preparation of community educators and social workers, education overseas, the professional development of teachers, and research. Chapters 8 to 14 focus on more specific aspects of professional education in which there has been very considerable development in recent years and in which there is widespread professional interest. These relate to placement, special educational needs, educational management, guidance and counselling, multicultural education, educational television and computing. Finally, Chapter 15 considers some of the possible changes in the context in which professional education may be conducted in the years ahead.

The authors are all deeply involved in the developments which they describe and analyse, and the views they express are entirely their own. Readers may therefore expect the papers to reflect a wide diversity of views. It is to be hoped that they may also encounter evidence of that capacity for self-criticism without which an institution committed to professional education has very little to celebrate.

Acknowledgements

The preparation of this volume relied on the willing co-operation of very many individuals. Dr. Edmund Ewan, Vice-Principal of Moray House, made many helpful suggestions on the book's structure. The contributors themselves are to be thanked for working to deadline at a time when, as busy people, they had more than enough to keep themselves fully occupied. The typing and retyping of drafts and the final preparation of the text was carried out by many of my colleagues on the secretarial staff of the college: Margit Hall, Nan Herd, Georgie Hunter, Elaine Marshall, Maizie McBeth, Hannah McKie, Carole Milligen, Helen Robertson, Karen Rosie, Margaret Russell, Vera Saunders, Mary Swinton, Norma Tennant and Christine Walker. Dr. David Jenkins devoted many hours to the correction of proofs. My secretary, Mrs. Mary Bradly, also contributed in numerous ways throughout the whole operation. Finally, Douglas Grant of Scottish Academic Press is to be thanked very sincerely for responding so positively to the idea of a book of this kind and for his generous advice and help in translating the idea into reality. To all of those mentioned I gladly record my sincere gratitude and also that of the college.

1

The historical perspective

Wilson H. Bain

In the 20th century there have been two celebrations of the college's history. The first, in 1935, commemorated 100 years of formal teacher training in Scotland,[1] while the second in 1948 marked the centenary of Moray House's official opening in 1848.[2]

Systematic training, however, was first offered in the Market Street Sessional School in Edinburgh as early as 1835. That school, supported by local Kirk Sessions, adopted new approaches which attracted 'visitors ... in droves'[3] to see the methods of teachers such as the school's director John Wood, who explained points to pupils and created a basis of understanding on which the learner might build. In 1826, the General Assembly's Education Committee sent teachers to Wood for a brief, unsystematic instruction before they began work in Highland schools. By 1834 the Church of Scotland was convinced of the need to give improved methods of instruction a more general and rapid diffusion throughout the country, and stated that this could be accomplished in only one way, by schools for training teachers, because 'there is an art in teaching in which every schoolmaster ought to be instructed'.[4] The Church pursued its policy vigorously and in 1835 formally asked Wood for further help. Based on a considerable achievement over a very short time span, the Assembly's 'normal school' came into being in 1837, as a college where the 'norm' or rules of teaching could be demonstrated and imitated.

At the same time, in Glasgow, inspired by Dr. Chalmers's Tron Church ministry, David Stow created interest with his Drygait infant school. In 1829, for example, his colleague, Mr. Caughie, took 12 children by coach to Edinburgh, to speak and demonstrate their work over several days. As with the Edinburgh Sessional School, teachers came to observe Stow and his colleagues; in 1836 the new Dundas Vale College was begun.

Before the two institutions in Edinburgh and Glasgow could

consolidate their position as Church of Scotland colleges, the Church split apart in the 1843 Disruption. Almost all staff and students of the Edinburgh college became Free Church members and had to leave their college. Thomas Oliphant and his community proceeded to temporary accommodation in the Whitefield 'Chapel', Carrubber's Close, and later to Music Hall rooms in Rose Street. Plans for a specially built Free Church college in Lothian Road were abandoned when Moray House became available, and Church representatives (led by James Moncreiff, later Lord Advocate) arranged the purchase of buildings and grounds between Canongate and the present Holyrood Road. By 1847 the House had known many occupants over two centuries, including its founder, the Countess of Home, Charles I, and Cromwell, to a paper mill and the North British Railway Company, who sold it to the Free Church. After considerable alterations, Moray House College welcomed its students officially in 1848, and the Church's education scheme now had the Edinburgh and Glasgow (Cowcaddens) colleges at its apex.

The new colleges faced important changes in teacher training, initiated by the highly influential Secretary of the Education Department. Sir James Kay Shuttleworth introduced the pupil-teacher system in 1846 and, although it 'was badly conceived' because 'it assumed a child could do two exacting things'[5] at once, it continued for 60 years despite criticism. Each pupil-teacher served a five-year 'apprenticeship' in schools, helping, and receiving extra lessons from, his or her teacher, before facing an examination at 18; those who passed received a Queen's Scholarship for their maintenance at college. The Free Church Committee quickly adapted Moray House to train more students, including many new pupil-teachers, whom Kay Shuttleworth hoped would meet the increasing demand for trained teachers and raise the standards of students' work.

Initially the Churches and, especially, David Stow had wanted colleges to concentrate on methods of instruction, but the annual government examinations (stressing subject content), and many students' lack of essential knowledge, altered this. In the 1850s new subjects, such as music and drawing, were introduced, with science encouraged. Indeed, the increasing number of students had to cover a 'formidable array'[6] of subjects, by attending five and a half days each week and studying in the evenings. The Church opposed a 'monastic' hall of residence for men, who stayed with relatives or in lodgings; young women who could not travel home daily lived in boarding houses. All were carefully supervised by the Rector and the Lady Superintendent.

This expansive period ended suddenly with new government regulations, whose purpose was largely to reduce public expenditure and concentrate funds on elementary education. The Revised Code, which affected Moray House from 1864, awarded grants to a college only for those teachers who gained the government certificate after two years' work in an inspected school. Fortunately, that year also brought Dr. Maurice Paterson as Rector. He led Moray House for 43 years and represented the college over two generations from the days of Palmerston to Churchill's early career. His written statements and recorded speeches are those of a good teacher: individual, to the point, serious without undue solemnity and with the condiment of humour.

Those qualities can be seen as early as 1866 in his reply to the Argyll Commission,[7] which asked for views on the previous system governing teacher training and on how the Revised Code was changing matters. Paterson quickly pinpointed the central issues. The Free Church had to ask each scholarship student for a surety to repay sums received, if they gave up the profession. In two years, however, the deaths of four students, six others' illnesses, and four ladies' marriages meant government grants were lost for 14 students.[8] Cash limits reduced the college's income, and students had to contribute more to their education. Young men, especially, found this hard, since most came from labouring or artisan families, while others had fathers who were small farmers, clerks, or shopkeepers. Female students came more often from shopkeeping families. In 1863 104 men entered Moray House but only 52 in 1865, while trained teachers were 'in greater demand than ever'.[8]

In 1883, Paterson described the 1860s as 'The Dark Ages',[9] although the Free Church strove to fund higher learning. 'Classics, French and Science were still at Moray House, though they gained no marks in the Government examination.'[10]

A clear picture of the college, as it was in 1866, emerges from Paterson's description. 'The number of students in attendance is 115, 52 males and 63 females.'[11] Most received maintenance aid from the Free Church Committee of £11 to £12. 'The teaching staff consists of a rector and five lecturers' (three of them part-time) and 'a lady superintendent and governesses for the female department.' As to the relevance of the curriculum, 'The work in all its parts is so arranged as to have the most direct bearing on the future duties' of students. 'The theory and practice of teaching engross a large share of attention, and even the instruction of a more general kind' fits them for their profession. Strictly professional education in the first year concentrated on 'best methods of teaching the elementary branches.' 'During the second' the student 'is occupied with the subjects of moral discipline and school organisation.' 'As for crit lessons, nine per week are given to pupils of the practising school at various stages by male students in turn'; these 'are afterwards criticised by their class-fellows and the teacher who presides.' Female students had similar tasks and also spent a week or two 'in the infant department of the school, partly observing and partly putting in practice, the methods recommended by the teacher'. The college's long established link with rural schools continued with a 'model village school', illustrating the best method a single teacher could use to instruct pupils of different stages and capacities. Paterson believed 'that professional education is absolutely indispensable to a teacher' and his argument has a timeless quality. No one 'who reflects on the difficulties always experienced by young teachers, in so interesting children as to bring them to attend to and understand their instruction, can maintain preparation can ever be dispensed with, or that mere experience can ever compensate for it'.[12] Yet 'in addition', said the Rector to his students, 'we give you something of the higher education as in University classes. Knowledge is a well of water, teaching power is the pitcher.'[13]

The late 19th century saw a growing feeling of community in colleges, and in 1877 former students, foregathering for the EIS annual meeting, formed a Moray House Club 'to testify their regard for their Normal School'.[14] The addresses of those who breakfasted in the Café Royal that day stretch from St. Boswells to Glasgow, with many from Edinburgh and Fife, two from England and at least one from Cape Town. This fellow feeling extended to Aberdeen College, whose Rector, Alexander Ramage, became Vice-President.

As well as providing a forum for ideas and social gatherings, the Club worked for their successors, awarding prizes, establishing travelling scholarships, and setting up a free kindergarten in Canongate. At Dr. Paterson's suggestion, they expanded their Club Library to form a circulating library with 2,000 volumes for serving teachers. Any Club member could also draw upon its Benevolent Fund. At its peak, in 1907 there were 1,600 members, and, referring to the Club as 'one great community', which provided hundreds of friends for a few shillings subscription, Paterson challenged the stock market in 'Glasgow 'Change to parallel an investment that pays like that'.[15]

Moray House students also worked directly for the community of Edinburgh. A Children's Church brought 100 to the practising (demonstration) school, where students sat as monitors, 'perhaps the most educative factor in their College life'.[16] They also took clothing and other gifts to poor families.

After the 1872 Education Act, most students went on to posts in Board schools, and it was important that colleges such as Moray House should 'enjoy the confidence of School Boards throughout the country'.[17] In 1888 the Parker Committee, including the SED Secretary, Sir Henry Craik, believed that they had this confidence and 'were undoubtedly efficient'.[18] In addition they were 'entirely free from sectarian intolerance',[19] including staff and students of various denominations. Moray House work also gained 'a powerful stimulus' in 1901[20] when colleges were allowed to decide their own courses and examinations, and to issue their own diplomas. However, by 1905 Scotland still trained only 700 student teachers per year, whereas the SED judged demand as 1,100. 'The root of the problem was a shortage of places at colleges.'[21] After college representatives met Sir John Struthers's Department officials, the 1905 Minute recommended Provincial Committees for training teachers and four city training centres, including Edinburgh's at Moray House. Churches were not forced to transfer their colleges, but the Presbyterian Churches did so, with guarantees that Religious Instruction would continue.

This was such a fundamental change that Club members feared the identity of Moray House might disappear. The Club itself was centred on Maurice Paterson's students and took no new members after he retired, when he received the portrait of Henry Kerr, ARSA, which now dominates one wall of the Board Room. He had played a central role in keeping the college alive and flourishing, with his strong influence on his own Free Church committee and on other colleges' developments through informal joint Church committees. He had overseen a gradual widening and strengthening of the curriculum, closer links with the University of Edinburgh and increased freedom from external control – all causes which he championed. He saw the transition through but 'you cannot bid the shadow go back on the sundial'.[22] He did, however, help his successor Dr. Alexander Morgan carry over 'much of the old Moray House tradition into the big new college'.[22]

Since the change of 1907 was meant to increase teacher supply, new and extended buildings were required. The new junior students (replacing pupil-teachers), and school leavers who took a full secondary course, came in large numbers to the training centres. Main Building in 1913 replaced the old premises, including the 1876 building with its examination hall. This new accommodation, added to the drawing facilities and science laboratories built in 1900, fitted the new role of one of Scotland's four centres and blended well with neighbouring buildings, partly through its ivy-covered quadrangle. Quiet and

discipline were insisted upon. According to one former junior student from Dunfermline 'We would not even dare whistle in the corridor.' Female students sat in alphabetical order during their lectures.[23]

Teaching practice in local schools expanded after the 1905 Minute required School Boards to facilitate this, but even in 1910 the practice was only 'one afternoon a week'. 'The teacher watched, we taught. The teacher criticised. There was no observation. Occasionally a tutor came and listened.'[23] In 1912 that former junior student gained a Chapter 3 qualification (as did ordinary graduates) to teach in primary schools, part of the 1906 Regulations which were little changed until 1965. The other main divisions were Chapter 5, for honours graduates to teach higher subjects in intermediate and secondary schools, and Chapter 6, for those teaching practical, aesthetic and technical subjects. Non-graduate students trained for two years until 1931, when this was extended to three years. From 1924 male entrants had to be graduates, while women required a minimum of the Scottish Leaving Certificate. For all students, whatever their courses and the qualifications they aimed for, the demonstration school (which as early as 1877 had 1,100 pupils[24]) remained an important part of Moray House, with new buildings in 1930. In 1946 the Advisory Council Report regarded such a school as essential to each college so that students can see methods not in use in other schools.'[25] However, it gradually became one of many schools with which the college had a close relationship as students' school experience lengthened and became more systematic. When the demonstration school closed in 1968, the work of head teachers such as George Mowat, Grace Fleming and William Pickard was still remembered.[26]

Certain features of the training system, such as demonstration schools, pupil-teachers and junior students, eventually disappeared. Sir John Struthers, Secretary of the SED, had been a pupil-teacher, and his first Act in 1905, 'was to publish regulations ... which abolished the system he had trained under'.[27] In a later generation, one junior student was George Barclay, later Vice-Principal in Moray House and 'miracle worker with board room business'.[28] Although the junior student system lasted only until 1924, the new arrangements had helped raise the numbers of trained, certificated teachers from 9,000 to 15,000 by that decade.

Nevertheless, the problem of balancing supply and demand has remained over 150 years. In the 1920s and early 1930s, the National Committee for Training Teachers was beginning to 'regulate the inflow of graduate students, now the great majority of applicants'.[29] Because the number of all graduates was decided by Universities,

'outwith the province of the Committee ... there always remains an element of disparity between the needs' of the Education Authorities (and their schools) and Universities' output.[30]

In 1946 the Advisory Council's Report, usually coupled with Professor William McClelland's name, described what a training institution should include. The description is very like Moray House. It 'should have its own nursery school and demonstration school'. It should be the focal point of educational activities and yet still have a community life and individuality of its own. 'In co-operation with the Scottish Council for Research in Education' it should 'be a centre for educational research, training research workers and organising large scale investigations with teachers' co-operation'.[25] This virtually portrays the work of Godfrey Thomson and his staff.

Professor Thomson gave Moray House an international reputation, after Maurice Paterson had established its national influence through his long participation in Scottish Church committees and his views on college courses. Combining the Principalship with Edinburgh's Bell Chair of Education, Thomson led research teams who studied human ability, testing and selection, and by 1948 Moray House tests were given to two out of three British pupils, to help decide their secondary school. This experimental work, much of it centred in Main Building Room 70, maintained Moray House as 'the home of the newest ideas in education'[31] at a time when many countries were concerned with selecting pupils as accurately as possible for secondary courses. While the Principal continued his meticulous attempts to measure ability in this research, he delegated much of the college administration to his colleagues.

From 1940 'Moray House was run by' Dr. W. B. Inglis, Depute Director of Studies and subsequently Principal (after 1951)[32] at a time when the war and an acute teacher shortage made unprecedented demands on colleges. Student numbers expanded greatly for a decade, before falling back, and general education courses were provided for servicemen such as RAF crews. (The college community's contribution in two wars is recalled by the memorial within the quadrangle of Main Building, opened only one year before August 1914.) As the Advisory Council recommended, Selection Boards selected candidates from the Forces, and other work, who did not have the usual admission requirements and in the late 1940s 3,300 entrants were accepted throughout Scotland.

Moray House welcomed these men and women. There was a clear sense of purpose about their work, as Professor Ruthven recalls.[33] In addition, Dr. Inglis, a founder member of the Scottish Youth Leader-

ship Association, encouraged training of social workers, which cul-minated in the establishment of the School of Community Studies. His Glasgow University years with William Boyd,[34] who set up the first Scottish child guidance clinic, were a formative influence for the Principal who had 'a vision of a new role for Colleges of Education. His determination to see education as a whole found expression in a nicely tempered scepticism about fashions in education.'[35]

When Dr. Douglas McIntosh became Principal in 1966, the colleges had trebled their student numbers in a decade. Many more pupils, especially girls, stayed on at school to take SCE, and mature students joined the Special Recruitment Scheme, but colleges such as Moray House were 'running at full blast merely to keep the supply position steady.'[36]

Dr. McIntosh, a student of William McClelland and of Godfrey Thomson, had served on the Advisory Council which produced key Reports such as that on 'Further Education'. His research background was coupled with long administrative experience as Director of Education for Fife, where he combined a statistician's approach to staffing and school building programmes with a keen personal interest in individual schools and districts. Both qualities were essential at Moray House, as it strove to meet the Government's demands for more teachers and to develop new courses.

In a 1967 statement to the College he noted 'accommodation problems' while 'the work by the College steadily increases.'[37] The watchwords of the time were 'continuous building' and 'rolling rebuilding programme'. Charteris Land teaching block, St. Leonard's P.E. building, St. Mary's science and technical education complex, Chessels Land for visual arts — all were built as a new Moray House rose to 'the drumming decibels of a thousand pneumatic drills'[38] playing Stockhausen against the new music rooms' harmony.

Moray House in 1970 was 'large, complex and rapidly expanding', reaching 3,000 students the next year, close to the total Scottish figure for 1939.[39] With a centre for computer education, the Scottish centre for training teachers of the deaf, new overseas students' courses, and a major in-service timetabling course for senior teachers, Moray House continued to meet the needs of those working in the field. 'The profession must regard themselves as part of the training system' while 'the College must undertake research of a practical nature',[40] as Dr. McIntosh pointed out when he was Chairman of the Scottish Council for Research in Education.

When another Principal of national stature and broad interests took office in 1975, times were changing once more. Professor Baillie

Ruthven led Moray House in a period of economic and educational challenge perhaps greater than any since the Revised Code years. With experience of teaching in Borders, Highland and Central Scotland he chaired the first CCC group to review secondary education overall, when the 'Ruthven Report' rethought the meaning of a general education.[41] His work in Stirling University involved new approaches in teacher education, such as microteaching and the Stirling BEd courses. To Moray House he brought a blend of experience, which led him to emphasise co-operation between different sectors. This was especially valuable when ever-increasing numbers of students soon became a memory, and falling school rolls combined with economic constraints to produce a potent compound.

One of the new Principal's first actions was to develop a Regent scheme, and almost all secondary schools in four Regions appointed Regents, several years before the Sneddon Report, 'Learning to Teach', supported such initiatives. Teachers joined in-service courses, discussed Moray House work and helped devise more effective assistance for students and for their own colleagues through in-school in-service. He also developed close links with the University and remains a strong advocate of concurrent courses as part of his philosophy that all the contributors in education should work together to produce the right atmosphere and facilities for learning. Those facilities included Scottish schools broadcasting, which the BBC reprieved after Professor Ruthven campaigned with his Broadcasting Council to save it.[42]

The college did not stand still while it and many others were waiting for the Secretary of State for Scotland's decisions about teacher training, but the undercurrent of tension was unhelpful to a system which, that Minister declared, 'is working well and which is served by . . . highly dedicated staff'.[43] Even so, the colleges had 'taken a pounding', as Baillie Ruthven expressed it in 1979.[44] Public attention was caught by meetings of the Scottish Grand Committee in 1977 and 1980 when 'capacity' and 'costings' were the constant themes; but the painstaking negotiation and presentation of arguments depended on college staff, led by the Principal and his Vice-Principal, Bernard Thompson, before Professor Ruthven handed over to Gordon Kirk.

In 1981 the number of colleges was reduced from ten to seven, and one college ending its short separate existence was Callendar Park, in Falkirk, which then amalgamated with Moray House. Opened in 1964, Callendar Park was one of three new colleges of education which hoped to do 'more than fill a temporary need for teacher supply'.[45]

None had known the titles of 'training college' or 'training centre', which were removed in the 1958 Regulations, nor the power of the Central Executive Committee for Scotland. Although all colleges now had Boards of Governors and more freedom over appointments and curriculum development, the Secretary of State for Scotland could still control college funds, student numbers and course innovations, and he increased this control again in the 1970s.

The peak year for the college, set in Falkirk's historic Callendar Estate, was 1971 when it had almost 900 students, more than some 19th-century colleges saw in a decade. After 'an equally notable fall in intake',[45] the figure was 300, just when 'Teacher Training from 1977 Onwards'[46] raised so many issues. As late as 1980 the Principal of Callendar Park, Tom Rae, described 'exciting developments', such as the Associateships for Early and Upper Primary Education. Within a year, however, there were only seven colleges. During its 150 years, Moray House has merged with several bodies such as the Edinburgh Church Colleges and St. Georges's College, but the link with Callendar Park clearly brought most valuable expertise and skills to the college, especially when it was losing experienced staff. Development of the new primary degree has shown a remarkable harmony of contributions from staff who quickly became one community.[47] The presence of the Scottish Curriculum Development Service and neighbours Scottish Council for Research in Education was also a valuable addition to the campus.

That feeling of community, in a large college serving the nation and many other lands, is perhaps best expressed in the Staff Bulletins which John T. Low edited between 1966 and 1978. In one of his learned and humane articles, often drawing upon several languages, he tried to sum up 'the spirit of Moray House'. Above all, it was that 'ye ken the pleisures there hae been, lernan along wi the young fowk here and gaun out tae the schules an meetan aa the bairns'.[48] John Wood and Maurice Paterson would have agreed.

References

1. Scottish Education Department (1935)   Committee of Council, Report, p. 35. HMSO.

2. Malcolm, C. A. and Hunter, J. N. W. (1948)   *Moray House — A Brief Sketch of Its History*. Moray House.

3. Gunn, J. (1921)   *Maurice Paterson, Rector of Moray House*, p. 63. Nelson.

4. Morgan, A. (1935)   *Two Famous Old Edinburgh Colleges*, p. 8. Church of Scotland.

5. Wilson, J. D. (1967)   'The Junior Student System', in Bone, T. R., *Studies in the History of Scottish Education*, p. 195. ULP.

6. Cruickshank, M. (1970)   *A History of Training of Teachers in Scotland*, p. 64. ULP.

7. Argyll Commission (1867)   'Schools in Scotland': Appendix to First Report, pp. 124-130. HMSO.

8. Argyll Commission (1867)   'Schools in Scotland': Appendix to First Report, p. 127. HMSO.

9. Gunn, J. (1921)   *Maurice Paterson, Rector of Moray House*, p. 259. Nelson.

10. Gunn, J. (1921)   *Maurice Paterson, Rector of Moray House*, p. 230. Nelson.

11. Argyll Commission (1867)   'Schools in Scotland': Appendix to First Report, pp. 125, 127. HMSO.

12. Argyll Commission (1867)   'Schools in Scotland': Appendix to First Report, p. 128. HMSO.

13. Gunn, J. (1921)   *Maurice Paterson, Rector of Moray House*, p. 191. Nelson.

14. Gunn, J. (1921)   *Maurice Paterson, Rector of Moray House*, p. 223. Nelson.

15. Gunn, J. (1921)   *Maurice Paterson, Rector of Moray House*, p. 229. Nelson.

16. Gunn, J. (1921)   *Maurice Paterson, Rector of Moray House*, p. 284. Nelson.

17. Wilson, J. D. (1967)   'The Junior Student System', in Bone, T. R., *Studies in the History of Scottish Education*, p. 193. ULP.

18. Scotland, J. (1969)   *The History of Scottish Education*, Volume 2, p. 110. ULP.

19. Gunn, J. (1921)   *Maurice Paterson, Rector of Moray House*, p. 109. Nelson.

20. Scotland, J. (1969)   *The History of Scottish Education*, Volume 2, p. 110. ULP.

21. Wilson, J. D. (1967)   'The Junior Student System', in Bone, T. R., *Studies in the History of Scottish Education*, p. 193. ULP.

22. Gunn, J. (1921)   *Maurice Paterson, Rector of Moray House*, p. 309. Nelson.

23. Pearson, Anne (1978)   Interview with 'Mrs. F', in *Moray House Staff Bulletin*, 29, pp. 9-10.

24. Cowan, C. (1878)   *Reminiscences*, p. 400. Edinburgh.

25. Advisory Council in Education Report (1946)   'Training of Teachers', p. 59. HMSO.

26. 'J. D. B.' (1973)   *Staff Bulletin*, 18, p. 5.

27. Wilson, J. D. (1971)   *Staff Bulletin*, 15, p. 4.

28. Keith, G. (1970)   *Staff Bulletin*, 11, p. 3.

29. Scottish Education Department (1935)   Committee of Council, Report, p. 33. HMSO.

30. Scottish Education Department (1937)   Committee of Council, Report, p. 53. HMSO.

31. Malcolm, C. A. and Hunter, J. N. W. (1948)   *Moray House — A Brief Sketch of Its History*, p. 30. Moray House.

32. (1984)   The author's conversation with Dr. Douglas McIntosh (13-11-1984)

33. (1984)   The author's conversation with Professor Baillie Ruthven (14-11-1984).

34. Bell, R. E. (1983)   'The Education Departments in the Scottish Universities', in Humes, W. M. and Paterson, H. M., *Scottish Culture and Scottish Education*, p. 167. John Donald.

35. Peter McNaught   As Vice-Principal, in *Staff Bulletin*, 13, p. 4.
    (1971)
36. Scotland, J. (1969)   'Teacher Training', in Nisbet J. and Kirk G. (ed.) *Scottish Education Looks Ahead*, p. 191. Chambers.
37. McIntosh, D. (1967)   *Staff Bulletin*, 4, p. 2.
38. Low, J. (1971)   *Staff Bulletin*, 15, p. 1.
39. McIntosh, D. (1969)   *Staff Bulletin*, 10, p. 2.
40. McIntosh, D. (1970)   *Staff Bulletin*, 11, p. 2.
41. Curriculum Paper 2   'Organisation of Courses Leading to the SCE'. HMSO.
    (1967)
42. Ruthven, Baillie   'The Unkindest Cut', in *Times Educational Supplement, Scotland*, 14-3-1980, p. 16.
    (1980)
43. Hansard (1980)   Scottish Grand Committee, 9-12-1980, paragraph 8.
44. Ruthven, Baillie   *Staff Bulletin*, 32, p. i.
    (1979)
45. (1980)   Callendar Park College of Education Prospectus (1980-81), p. 11.
46. Scottish Education   *Teacher Training from 1977 Onwards*. HMSO.
    Department (1977)
47. (1984)   The author's conversation with Bernard Thompson (14-11-1984).
48. Low, J. (1978)   *Staff Bulletin*, 31, p. 22.

Rectors and Principals

1835-1840 John Wood, Rector
1840-1848 Thomas Oliphant, Rector
1848-1855 James Fulton, Rector
1855-1863 James Sime, Rector
1864-1907 Maurice Paterson, Rector
1907-1920 John King, Director of Studies
1907-1925 Alexander Morgan, Principal (and Director of Studies, 1920-1925)
1925-1951 Godfrey Thomson, Director of Studies
1951-1966 W. B. Inglis, Principal
1966-1974 Douglas McIntosh, Principal
1975-1981 Baillie Ruthven, Principal
1981   Gordon Kirk, Principal

2

The contemporary context

Gordon Kirk

Introduction

From the mid-70s Moray House, like the whole college of education sector in Scotland, entered a period of sustained contraction. The progressive shrinkage of the student population and of the number of staff has persisted into the mid-80s. Such an extended period of retrenchment might have induced a degree of institutional inertia and a disinclination to embark on fresh initiatives. However, particularly since 1981, the college has undertaken a major series of institutional and professional developments which have resulted in a transformation of its whole mode of operation. This chapter describes the constraints that operated during the period of contraction and against that background charts the steps taken by the college to revitalise its activities and to respond to a new set of professional challenges.

The climate of contraction

The contraction of the system was the direct result of the dramatic decline in the number of pupils in the nation's schools, with a corresponding reduction in the number of teachers required. Each year the Scottish Education Department undertook an analysis of the required level of intake to colleges, on the basis of wastage from the profession, the size of the school population, and of other factors. Following consultation with interested bodies, the Secretary of State for Scotland fixed the total number of students to be admitted to training and allocated an intake quota to each college with the clear instruction that these quotas should under no circumstances be exceeded. The effect of these intake directions on the student population at Moray House was as follows:

	Teacher education students	*Total students*
1975/76	2,241	2,707
1978/79	1,005	1,554
1983/84	670	1,121

The annual fixing of intake quotas to individual colleges of education had a direct effect on college staffing, since the level of staffing was very largely determined by the number of students enrolled. In addition, then, to the annual fixing of student numbers, there was an annual calculation of each college's authorised staffing entitlement — the official staffing level agreed with SED following the application of recognised staffing ratios and allowances for research and development, in-service activities and other matters. The calculation of the authorised staffing entitlement was crucial because it determined the level of funding the college would receive for staff salaries. Consequently, there was enormous pressure on colleges, if they were to avoid serious financial difficulties, to ensure that the staffing complement — the number of staff actually in post — was in line with the authorised staffing entitlement.

Inevitably, with the progressive reduction in intakes, staffing complement exceeded the staffing entitlement: there were more staff than were required and reductions had to be effected. Fortunately, the Crombie compensation regulations proved sufficiently attractive financially to induce members of staff to seek voluntary redundancy. Naturally, before a request for voluntary release was granted it had to be established to the satisfaction of SED that a clear case of redundancy existed and that that redundancy was directly attributable to the Secretary of State's directions on intake. Across the system hundreds of staff were released in this way. At Moray House the number of academic staff released between 1977 and 1982 was 94, a reduction of approximately one-third.

As student and staff numbers continued to decline and as a diminishing total number of students was year-by-year being allocated in ever-decreasing numbers among the various colleges, the viability of a ten-college system became increasingly questionable. In 1980 the Secretary of State intimated that from September of 1981 the total number of colleges would be reduced from ten to seven: the two Roman Catholic colleges would form a new St. Andrew's College; Hamilton College of Education would be incorporated within Jordan-hill College of Education, and Callendar Park College of Education in Falkirk would be transferred to Moray House. While every effort was made to ensure that there was minimum dislocation to students' programmes of studies and detailed discussions took place to ensure a rational and sensitive transfer of responsibilities, the closure of three colleges of education in 1981 marked the most public and definitive evidence of contraction. As it was, the contraction did not end there; for reductions in intake to the colleges continued into the 1980s. In these circumstances there were some who felt that even a seven-college system was more than the country required or could afford; and there were widespread fears that further mergers and closures were imminent. Fortunately, SED responded to the decline in pre-service student numbers by making a generous allocation of staff for all forms of in-service activity and colleges were able to exploit this provision to strengthen the support they were able to provide for the professions. Unquestionably, without that increased provision for in-service activities the contraction of the system would have been even more pronounced than it was.

The college's response

How, then, did Moray House respond to these conditions? As has been made clear, the college could not respond to contraction by diversification and by venturing into new areas of academic and professional activity. On the contrary, its sphere of operations was precisely delimited by SED and that meant a continuation of its established functions — the provision of courses for those entering the professions of teaching, community education and social work, the provision of ongoing professional support for members of these professions in post, and the undertaking of research and development work into effective professional activity in these areas. Since the door to diversification was closed the only avenue of institutional development for the college lay in improving the quality of its established professional activities. The strategy adopted to effect that qualitative improvement is considered under the following five headings:

> The reassertion of institutional purposes and values
> The strengthening of links between the college and its professions
> External validation of courses
> Academic restructuring
> Institutional policies and procedures.

These are examined in the following sections.

The reassertion of institutional purposes and values

Teaching, community education and social work are commonly regarded as the 'people' professions or the 'helping' professions: they involve action with and on behalf of others; they are concerned to equip others with the skills, dispositions and understandings that will enable them to assume increased responsibility for the ordering of their own lives and the realisation of their own purposes. In an increasingly complex and rapidly changing society, in which people are more than ever driven back on their own resources and are faced with a bewildering range of choices, these three professions have a critical contribution to make to human well-being and to people's capacity to cope with the demands that contemporary life imposes. These professions, therefore, while they are practised in very different social and institutional contexts, have many characteristics in common and the most significant of these is a commitment to professional activity. What are the values which underpin that kind of commitment?

First, professional activity implies a commitment to action that is principled, in the sense that it is based on a properly elaborated and defensible theoretical framework. Professional activity is not reducible to a restricted set of routines and practical manoeuvres; nor, on the other hand, is it simply a form of cerebral virtuosity. It is the kind of activity in which performance is underpinned by theoretical understanding. That understanding is not a separate embellishment that a person possesses over and above a marked practical expertise: it is the kind of conceptualising capacity that issues in intelligent action and feeds into and sustains reflective practice.

Secondly, professional activity involves an obligation to clarify and to justify the aims and purposes towards which that activity is directed. When professional activity is concerned to bring about changes in others or to engage others in experiences that are judged to be in their interests, there is an overwhelming moral obligation first to make the nature of the changes and experiences absolutely explicit and secondly to provide a rational justification for whatever changes are sought or experiences are provided. That dual obligation must be met if a proper professional relationship is to be established with pupils or with clients and if the confidence of the community, upon which all professional activity ultimately depends, is to be guaranteed.

Thirdly, professional activity in teaching, in community education and in social work takes place against a background of widely differing philosophies of the aims that should be sought and the means by which they might be realised. These differences are encountered because professional activity in these areas is not as exact and precisely calculable as, say, mathematical or scientific activity; because the different contexts in which they are conducted and the different problems they involve make variety of approach and methodology inevitable; and, finally, because these professions, concerned as they ultimately are with human values, cannot escape the pluralism of values which characterises the modern world. While the existence of philosophical and other differences does not rule out the possibility of areas of professional consensus, it clearly entails that professional activity will call for an openness to change, a commitment to experiment and innovation, and to the testing of new approaches. Where lines of action are contested, provisional or uncertain, the most appropriate professional response is not to adhere stubbornly to traditional practice but to explore alternative approaches and to test their effectiveness or appropriateness in one's own professional situation. Professional activity therefore entails a clear commitment to the testing of new approaches to the solution of professional problems.

Finally, and following directly from the commitment to innovation, professional activity entails an inescapable commitment to self-monitoring and evaluation. Whichever new approaches are developed have to be monitored and evaluated so that judgements can be made about their effectiveness and whether or not a new approach can be added to the repertoire that every professional ought to possess. It is through this process of continuous self-appraisal and the subjection of professional action to systematic scrutiny that teachers, community educators and social workers extend their skills and enhance their professional development. Indeed, that commitment to self-criticism is probably *the* hallmark of professional activity.

That analysis of professional activity and of the values presupposed by it provided the college with a framework within which its own central tasks could be evaluated and developed. While these are subject to detailed and separate analysis in subsequent chapters it is worth highlighting here the main features of the institution's appraisal of its central functions.

The first of these functions concerns initial professional preparation for teaching, for community education and for social work. The commitment to the qualitative improvement of this work was taken to require an extension of degree opportunities; closer partnership with the professions in the training process, in recognition of the fact that substantial amounts of training actually take place in professional settings outside the college; the increased coherence of training in the sense that college-based and placement-based activities should be

clearly, closely and continuously co-ordinated; and the closer integration of theory and practice and their development, in mutually
reinforcing ways, across training locations. These developments were
all indicative of a move towards more thoroughly professional
programmes of initial training. Such developments are sometimes
criticised on the grounds that they represent a narrowing of the training
process, an unacceptably restricted concentration on practical skills at
the expense of broader educational objectives. Criticisms of this kind
are based on a misunderstanding of what a proper professional
preparation entails. Of course, there must be a preoccupation with
competent professional performance and that certainly implies that
proper attention is devoted to the cultivation of the wide range of skills
that professional action now involves. However, competent professional performance is not reducible to a range of practical capabilities. Its various skills are embedded in a repertoire of understandings.
It is manifestly the case that professional activity requires a grasp of a
whole range of conceptual understandings; it calls for the capacity to
decide what is valuable, for judgement and reflection, for the analysis of
action, for self-criticism, and for the kind of cognitive perspective that
illuminates a person's professional circumstances and enables one to
locate these in a human and a social context. In all of these ways the
pursuit of professional competence is surely educative.

The college's second major task involves the provision of professional support for teachers, community educators and social workers
in post. It is universally acknowledged now that initial training, no
matter how thorough and well conceived, can never equip the
members of these professions with the full range of skills and
understandings they will require throughout their careers. Developments in professional practice are inevitable; new approaches to
familiar professional problems continue to be made available; social,
technological and other changes are likely to bring about major
transformation in the lives of pupils, clients and citizens and in the
professional circumstances of teachers, community educators and social
workers. It is unquestionable that the members of these professions will
require continued support in coming to terms with changes in their
professional work and in the revitalisation of the practice of their craft.
It is a pre-eminent function of colleges of education to provide that
support.

Thirdly, colleges of education have a commitment to research and
development. It has already been acknowledged that changes in
professional practice are inevitable and that the best current practice
must be regarded as provisional. These changes are brought about by

research and development work that is intended to deepen and extend our understanding of how teaching, community education and social work may be more effectively practised and of the context in which they are conducted. Arguably, the quality of a college's initial training and in-service work depends on the maintenance of a culture in which research and development activities can thrive. Indeed, such activities may be regarded as the life-blood of colleges of education. And without such a commitment a college's credibility and professional authority simply cannot be sustained.

The endorsement of these tasks as the central and authentic preoccupations of the college and the commitment to the values underpinning professional activity transformed the role of the college lecturer. The traditional conception of that role was restricted: it was almost exclusively concerned with working with students on courses of initial training and with the supervision of students' placement experience. The modern role certainly incorporates both of these activities but extends well beyond them. It encompasses work with experienced professionals on in-service courses in the college; collaboration with teachers, community educators and social workers in their own professional settings; participation in research and development activities of one kind or another; membership of local and national working parties and committees; consultancy; and, finally, a commitment to intensive curriculum development and evaluation in connection with the college's own courses and activities. These extensions of role provide staff with a more diverse range of undertakings and create a new and demanding challenge to their professional resourcefulness. Indeed, the whole credibility of colleges required that these role extensions were officially sanctioned: in a period in which recruitment of new staff had been practically discontinued it was vital to ensure that college staff continued to develop professionally and to revitalise their work by maintaining close contact with professional practice and through involvement in development work.

The strengthening of links between the college and its professions

While colleges of education have been regarded as the 'training arm' of the professions they serve, and while these professions have always had a recognised involvement in the training process, the relationship between college and professions was traditionally informal and opportunistic rather than based on clearly agreed principles and formal procedures for collaboration. Two developments strengthened the case for a reinterpretation of that traditional relationship. In the first place, it became acknowledged that placement experience was not simply an adjunct to the college course but was an absolutely central and integral component of the total programme. Moreover, the effectiveness of placement experience was seen to depend on the extent to which it was deliberately planned for and was consistent with the principles underlying the whole period of professional preparation. That is, the activities and tasks expected of students on placement should be properly sequenced and structured in relation to college-based studies to provide students with a coherent and progressively demanding initiation into professional activity. Clearly, therefore, if that level of coherence was to be achieved, there was a need for the closest possible collaboration between colleges of education and the professionals in schools and other agencies whose task was to supervise students' placement. The centrality of placement experience in the training process made professional partnership between college staff and professionals in the field absolutely imperative.

The second impetus to increased professional collaboration was the realisation that the experiences and insights of established professionals constituted a legitimate knowledge base for those aspiring to teaching, to community education or to social work. It became acknowledged that the 'craft' knowledge or the 'clinical' knowledge of the experienced practitioner was a valuable source of professional understanding, one that complemented the theoretical perspectives that might be gleaned from reading or from study in college. If that 'craft' knowledge had an important contribution to make it was essential to plan for it to be made available in a structured way. That, too, called for closer partnership between college staff and professionals in placement agencies.

At Moray House the principle of partnership was reflected in a variety of different initiatives. First, the college decided that on every course committee — these are the groups now responsible for the detailed planning, management and evaluation of college courses — relevant professions would be represented. The involvement of professional representatives on these committees was a way of ensuring that their experience and insights would feed directly into the planning and operation of courses. In some instances, the extent of professional involvement has been very considerable. For example, with regard to the college's new Primary BEd, more than twenty teachers, headteachers and advisers joined with college staff in perhaps the most ambitious planning enterprise the college has ever undertaken. That level of professional collaboration has been gratifying and the quality of the degree programme is a striking illustration of what professional collaboration can achieve.

Secondly, partnership between college staff and field professionals has extended beyond the planning of courses to their implementation. It is now acknowledged that colleagues in schools and other agencies who will be supervising students on placement require to share basic assumptions underlying a training programme and must be fully aware of the skills and understandings students are expected to practise and develop during placement. All college programmes have taken decisive steps to ensure that that level of partnership understanding is realised. The most striking example of this kind of partnership is to be found in the procedures adopted in relation to the new four-year degree for primary teachers. With the approval of the Directors of Education in the four regions adjacent to the college there was established an agency known as College/Regional Organisation of School Experience (CROSE). Consisting of senior representatives of the college and primary advisers from each of the four regions, CROSE plans and supervises the detailed arrangements for collaboration between college tutors and teachers in placement schools. Through CROSE the college proposes to build an extensive collaborative network with schools and teachers. There is no doubt, however, that every one of the college's training programmes will require to adopt arrangements of the kind currently being pioneered by CROSE. While these arrangements certainly require significant adjustments on the part of college staff, they also call for a change of attitude on the part of the professions, for they demand that the supervision of students should be an acknowledged aspect of the role of the teacher, the community educator and the social worker.

A third means of implementing the partnership principle lies in the selection of students. The drastic reduction in intake to colleges of education, with no corresponding diminution in the number of applicants for places, has forced colleges to devise more rational and principled selection procedures. While over the years the college has involved the professions indirectly in the selection process, by using the reports on applicants provided by the schools, there were no formally established procedures for involving members of the professions directly in the process. The college now considers that that direct involvement is essential: the views of experienced professionals have an important contribution to make in the development of rigorous and fair selection procedures.

A further area where partnership is developing strongly is agency-based in-service work. Traditionally, in-service activities for teachers and others took the form of attendance at courses and conferences held in the college. While that is continuing, the major thrust of in-service activities is now based in schools, in community education centres and social work agencies. It is now acknowledged that professional difficulties are perhaps best approached in the context in which they arise — in working with pupils and with clients in their own situation. Consequently, there has been a dramatic increase in the type of in-service which takes members of staff out of the college and into close and direct relationship with professionals in a field setting. This development has been of inestimable value, for it has obliged college staff to develop a sharper professional focus to their work. Professionals in the field, for their part, have benefited also from this development as is evidenced by the continued demand for support and collaboration from outwith the college. In the years ahead this form of professional collaboration is likely to be intensified. In the process, college staff can be expected to shake themselves free from the traditional role in which they were expected to act as authorities and as the dispensers of professional wisdom. Instead, they will increasingly assume and welcome the role of the consultant, working on professional problems with their professional equals.

Finally, partnership between the college and the professions is developing through the exchange of staff. It has proved possible to enable members of staff to have extended experience of work in primary and secondary schools for the purpose of refreshing and extending their skills and for keeping their professional practice completely abreast of current developments. In addition, staff from schools have been seconded for varying periods to work in the college. For example, when colleges of education received additional funds to enable them to recruit 'new blood', it was decided that two such posts should be on a secondment basis; two members of staff will serve for a period of three years before returning to their former or an equivalent post. Three other members of staff have been seconded, each for one year, to undertake, in association with college staff, development work in areas of current professional concern. These secondment arrangements will certainly be of benefit to the college, for they allow the recruitment of staff with recent successful and substantial professional experience and in that way help to enliven and enrich the college's work. At the same time, their experience of college of education work will enable seconded staff to return to their work with fresh insights and approaches as well as enhanced capabilities.

It would be wrong to claim that all of these ventures in professional collaboration are as far advanced as they might ideally be. The college is committed to partnership and has moved some way towards the realisation of the ideals which partnership implies. The boundaries between the college and the professions have been shown to be more permeable than previously recognised. The quality of the college's work and of the work of the professions themselves will depend on even closer and more extensive collaboration.

External validation of courses

The college's commitment to improving the quality of its work was bound to involve a review of its existing courses and the preparation of new courses in response to changing professional needs. The analysis of professional activity required that courses should have a clear professional orientation, that theory and practice should be explicitly interrelated, that college-based studies should point forward to and build on placement activities, and that every programme should constitute a coherent educational experience initiating students progressively into the skills and understandings that make up professional action. Of course, a college might be able to satisfy itself that its courses met clear qualitative criteria of that kind, but accountability demands that the quality of courses should be publicly attested. That pointed to the need for courses to be externally validated. Accordingly, the college embarked on a programme of course revision and development for validation by the Council for National Academic Awards (CNAA).

CNAA validation imposes extremely challenging demands on an institution. It is based on the assumption that course proposals should survive the rigorous scrutiny of an independent group of academic and professional peers. It requires institutions to provide detailed and comprehensive documentation on all aspects of a course — its aims and objectives, syllabus content and reading, modes of teaching and learning, assessment and evaluation strategies, principles of course design, as well as operational information relating to course logistics. All of these aspects of the course must then be defended in discussion with a validating party drawn from universities, polytechnics, colleges of education, as well as the professions themselves. Members of such validating panels are not only familiar with the professional problems involved, with course design and evaluation, but they also have experience of the course validation process. Moreover, outsiders with no axe to grind are able to speak with absolute impunity on a course proposal, thus ensuring that the whole process is not only professionally credible and authentic but is also impartial and objective.

While members of staff sometimes begrudge the time spent in

course planning, in the compilation of documentation and in validation meetings, there is no doubt that the allocation of time to such activities represents a sound investment. It means that staff involved have to be asbolutely clear and explicit about the principles underlying a course; they have to have satisfied themselves that the course's various components cohere; they must demonstrate precisely how the detailed practical arrangements and logistics are fully compatible with course principles; and they must elaborate on the strategies that will be deployed to monitor and evaluate the course's operation. In all of these ways external validation places an obligation on an institution to adopt a principled and systematic approach to course planning, management and evaluation. What is more, the subjection of a course proposal to independent scrutiny by peers enables a college to key into a national network of expertise. A course proposal can be improved by incorporating the comments and suggestions by a group of knowledgeable and distinguished commentators.

A further advantage of CNAA course validation is that it is accompanied by an institutional review, an examination of an institution's whole mode of operation by a group of experienced educationists drawn from other institutions. No course can be validated unless CNAA is satisfied that the institutional context is one which will ensure that the quality and standards of the proposed course can be maintained. Accordingly, an institutional review involves an appraisal of an institution's academic structure, its decision-making machinery, its procedures for assessment, for monitoring and evaluation, for the admission and counselling of students, its deployment of staff and their involvement in research and related activities, its exploitation of learning resources and its physical accommodation and amenities. All of these matters are clearly vital to the health and development of a course: good courses, no matter how immaculately designed and documented, cannot thrive unless the institutional context in which they are embedded is appropriately supportive.

While external validation by CNAA constitutes a powerful lever for staff and institutional development, and while it is recognised to be a most rigorous and penetrating form of course appraisal, it nevertheless attracts criticism. It is maintained, for example, that CNAA validation fails to acknowledge the wide diversity of views on course design and on professional activity: institutions, it is argued, are under pressure to conform to CNAA orthodoxy and are discouraged from developing distinctive and divergent course proposals. In reply, it has to be emphasised that CNAA does not express allegiance to any particular course model: the onus is entirely on institutions to explain and justify whatever model of course design they consider to be appropriate. It is true that CNAA insists on certain principles — for example, that professionals should be involved in the detailed planning of courses and that students on courses of teacher education should be required to demonstrate competent classroom performance before obtaining awards, and so on — but principles of that kind are part of a widespread consensus on professional training and to come up with a course proposal that was manifestly at variance with that professional consensus is to abandon a commitment to the maintenance of standards. Besides, the existence of such basic principles does not point ineluctably to any single course design. Indeed, CNAA has over the years encouraged institutions to be adventurous and innovative in developing course proposals. It has also been prepared to modify its general guidelines governing courses in response to changes in the professional consensus. It is therefore a misunderstanding to claim that CNAA imposes a procrustean inflexibility on institutions.

A second criticism relates particularly to the Scottish context. There are those who feel that CNAA, as a London-based body, is ill-placed to validate courses in Scotland, which has a distinctive educational tradition. The prevalence of this view led in 1983 to the establishment of the Scottish Council for the Validation of Courses for Teachers (SCOVACT), a consortium of Scottish universities and colleges of education. The emergence of the new body means that colleges will have a choice of validating body — CNAA or SCOVACT. However, the establishment of SCOVACT should not be interpreted as evidence that the criticism of CNAA was justified. CNAA is a UK body with a UK remit. Besides, a large and growing number of members of CNAA are drawn from Scottish institutions and all members of visiting parties to Scottish institutions receive a briefing paper on Education in Scotland, prepared by SED. While CNAA therefore recognises the importance of the Scottish dimension, there is a corresponding responsibility on the Scottish colleges to describe the professional circumstances for which a particular course constitutes a preparation and to demonstrate precisely how the course will effectively equip students with the appropriate skills. What is certain is that the criteria of an effective course are neither English nor Scottish: they are professional. It is by invoking professional rather than national criteria that the quality of courses is to be judged. Finally, it has to be said that a system of regional as opposed to national external validation may threaten the objectivity of the process.

For its part, Moray House embarked on a programme of validation by CNAA and to date all eight submissions, including three degree proposals, have been successful. That programme continues and further submissions are in preparation. The college's aim is that all of its courses carry the stamp of public and professional acceptability which rigorous external validation confers.

The introduction of external validation now means that all courses offered by Scottish colleges of education must survive three phases of critical scrutiny before a single student can be enrolled. First, courses must be approved by the SED. Secondly, they must be scrutinised by the appropriate professional accrediting agency — teacher education courses by the General Teaching Council for Scotland (GTC), social work courses by the Central Council for Education and Training in Social Work (CCETSW), and, very probably in future, community education courses by the Scottish Community Education Council. The third stage involves external validation. While this three-fold scrutiny may appear excessive, it may well strengthen public confidence in the quality of professional training.

Academic restructuring

The connection between the quality of college courses and activities and the institutional context in which they are set has already been noted: high standards of academic and professional activity can only be maintained in an appropriately structured academic environment. In 1981 the college therefore embarked on an extensive restructuring of its academic organisation and its machinery for academic decision-making. There were four principles underlying that restructuring.

First, it was acknowledged that an effective academic structure had to be based on the maximum participation of staff. The problems facing a college of education, some of which are deeply intractable, are more likely to be resolved by the pooling of expertise and perspectives than by the application of one person's analysis, however penetrating and profound.

The second principle concerns the decentralisation of decision-making. That principle may be defended on the grounds that it requires the kind of participation already discussed. A further argument in its defence is severely practical: it is simply inefficient to locate all decision-making 'at the top' or 'at the centre' of an academic organisation. There is a need for a strong infrastructure of sub-groups operating below the level of a college's board of studies or academic board, with responsibility for carrying out functions on behalf of that board and in line with its policies.

The third principle is accountability. As the college's accountability to outside agencies intensifies — to SED, to the GTC, to CCETSW, to CNAA and to the professions themselves — it is essential that strong lines of accountability should be established within its own walls. Unless the principle of accountability is built into the fabric of institutional life, unless, that is, the principle of decentralisation is appropriately circumscribed, a college's academic activities are conducted incoherently by a variety of self-programming groups and individuals that are answerable to no one. It is imperative, therefore, that clearly defined principles and procedures should be agreed to provide the framework within which academic activities will be conducted and to establish the nature of accountability relationships. Procedures will be necessary in relation to 'legislative' and to 'executive' accountability. The first of these concerns the relationship between the Board of Studies and the committee infrastructure and involves the Board of Studies in defining the procedures according to which its sub-committees and sub-groups will operate. Executive accountability refers to the designation of duties to be undertaken by individuals and the structure of supervisory relationships.

The final principle concerns interdepartmental collaboration. Moray House has inherited a strong departmental organisation reflecting the traditional academic subject divisions. While that organisation attracted strong support from staff, it was conceded that an institution with as many as thirty separate departments was bound to encounter problems with regard to co-ordination and coherence. Besides, the departmental organisation was out of step with developments in course structure and design. In a college in which no single department had responsibility for all the teaching on any course it was reasonable to locate course planning, supervision and evaluation in an interdepartmental context and to create machinery for bringing staff from different areas of the college into close professional collaboration.

The first step in the academic restructuring was to endorse the college's system of sub-boards, one for each of the major areas of college work — Primary Studies, Secondary Studies, Community Studies, Education Overseas, and In-service. These sub-boards, consisting of staff drawn from different college departments, were made directly responsible to the Board of Studies for ensuring that the courses under their jurisdiction were planned, implemented and evaluated in accordance with the procedures stipulated by the Board of Studies. Each sub-board was to be chaired by a director, a senior member of staff responsible directly to the Principal for the efficient conduct of all matters relating to the courses and developments within the designated area of college work. Each sub-board was empowered to set up course committees, one for each major course, or group of cognate minor courses, within the jurisdiction of the sub-board. These course committees were to be composed of staff involved in teaching the course, representatives from the appropriate professional area, and students. Each course committee would be directly accountable to the sub-board for the detailed planning, supervision and evaluation of its course. It would be chaired by a course leader, a designated member of staff appointed by college management and directly responsible to the appropriate director for the day-to-day management of the course and for ensuring that all functions of the course committee were efficiently discharged in accordance with college procedures.

Three observations might be made in connection with the revised academic structure. In the first place it created a rational context for course planning, development and evaluation, one that brought together college staff, students and members of the relevant profession. Moreover, by switching the locus of course supervision from the department to the course committee it effectively challenged the conventional wisdom on departmental autonomy and made departments accountable to course committees. Secondly, the course supervision matrix, in which the activities of departmental staff are co-ordinated through a structure of committees which are course-specific, constitutes a highly flexible apparatus for course planning and evaluation. It overcomes the rigidity frequently encountered in faculty structures, for it enables most departments to contribute to several of the major areas of college work, and it offers maximum scope for interdepartmental groupings, for interdisciplinary activities, and for the most intensive professional collaboration. Finally, the revised structure established and reinforced clear lines of accountability. Legislative accountability was established by making course committees answerable for the supervision of courses to the appropriate sub-board, which in turn is responsible to the Board of Studies, the body that delineates the procedures governing the supervision of courses. Executive accountability was established by making course leaders, as conveners of course committees, responsible to the appropriate director, and directors, in turn, are responsible to the Principal, who is responsible for 'the whole organisation and discipline of the college'.

The sub-boards and course committees that have been described form only part of the infrastructure of the Board of Studies — the part that is concerned with the academic supervision of courses. In addition to the sub-boards and course committees there are three major standing committees with functions that do not relate to any specific course but are concerned with the maintenance of the general academic environment. These are the Research and Development Committee, the Learning Resources Committee, and the Policy and Resources Committee.

The Research and Development Committee exists to promote and support research and development in the college, to identify key problems and priority areas for research, and to maintain and extend the quality of the college's research and development effort. The Learning Resources Committee replaced a number of separate committees that were each responsible for a major learning resource in the college. It was considered that a single committee that was concerned with the Library, the Computer service, the Educational Television service, and the Audio-Visual Resource Centre would enable a coherent and comprehensive policy on learning resources to be developed. The new committee has brought together two sets of staff: those responsible for the provision and management of specialist services and those staff who use these services to enliven their teaching and to facilitate students' learning. The Board of Studies is responsible for the quality of courses and has to satisfy itself that conditions exist for effective teaching and learning. The Board is able to discharge this responsibility through the work of the Learning Resources Committee and its monitoring and evaluation of the disposition and exploitation of the college's learning resources.

The Policy and Resources Committee has the task of advising the Board of Studies on the educational priorities that should be established and the implications of these for resource provision. It is essential that a college of education has a clear understanding of institutional purpose and direction; that institutional priorities are set; and that, particularly in conditions of fiscal stringency, the resource implications of academic policy decisions are noted and that academic policy decisions take due account of resource constraints. In advising the Board of Studies on such questions the Policy and Resources Committee has a critical co-ordinating function to perform. It seeks to collate, on an annual basis, all the various developments proposed in the different areas of the college and to consider how far the available resources will be able to support what is proposed. The work of this key committee has helped to move the college away from *ad hoc* changes and to move forward on the basis of a rational and realistic scheme of priorities.

Institutional policies and procedures

These structural changes in the college academic organisation and decision-making machinery could not, by themselves, create an effective academic environment for the pursuit of professional activity. They require to be complemented by academic policies and by principles of procedure which govern the whole institution and the relationship between its constituent parts. That is, the college had to ensure that the structure it had created genuinely facilitated the decision-making process, the academic supervision of courses, and the maintenance of academic and professional standards. Accordingly, between 1981 and 1984 the Board of Studies approved an extensive number of policy and procedural documents covering all aspects of the life of the institution. For example, college-wide procedures were agreed for the monitoring and evaluation of all courses and for the compilation for each course of an annual evaluation report which incorporates evidence on the operation of the course and recommendations for its improvement. Similarly, the Board of Studies stipulated procedures for the internal validation of courses, the process by which every course proposal is carefully scrutinised within the institution before being submitted for external validation. Other policies agreed related to in-service work, staff development, research, the organisation and development of learning resources, student counselling, assessment and accountability. Many of those policies are considered in subsequent chapters of this volume but their significance is worth highlighting here: they formulate the ground rules according to which college activities must be pursued and developed.

Conclusion

This chapter has sought to describe how during a period of contraction and retrenchment, and despite the impossibility of diversification into new areas of activity, the college nevertheless undertook an extensive programme of institutional development. Starting from an analysis of professional activity the college sought to exemplify in all its work the standards and values entailed by professional activity. In addition, it sought to transform its whole mode of operation and to create a kind of academic environment in which professional activity could be effectively pursued and in which the college's role as a major centre for innovation and development in relation to teaching, community education and social work might be further enhanced.

3

Teacher education

Edmund A. Ewan

Introduction

Over the last decade or so undoubtedly the major feature of teacher education in Scotland has been massive contraction. One of the prime effects has been to give both impetus and opportunity to a thorough-going review of teacher education in Scotland. This review has been concerned not only with the externals of the structure of the college of education system but also much more fundamentally with the rationale of teacher education against the background of the upheaval in the school system resulting from contraction and other powerful influences. Amongst these influences have been the demands on the profession stemming from radical changes in curriculum and assessment patterns, society's ever-expanding expectations of the teacher and in some repects confusion about the role of the teacher in the 1980s. This chapter is concerned with some key ideas and issues involved in such a review of teacher education, Moray House College's response to these, and its contribution to the continuing developments in teacher education.

Of the myriad of issues in teacher training exercising the minds of educationists at all levels in the system from central government to local institution, school or college, a number can be seen as arising more or less directly from the effects of contraction, while several others may be regarded rather as having been thrust into sharper focus and given greater urgency by it. Yet others are the subject of ongoing study and debate and derive their significance from larger aspects of the state of current society and views of the proper role of education therein. Broadly, these three groups of issues in the order mentioned above represent a progression from the contingent and less fundamental to the essential and more profound; and they are considered here in that order.

Contraction

Among the direct effects of contraction the following issues loom large:

Much greater rigour in the selection of students

Rationalisation of secondary training courses

Generalised methods training across specialist subject boundaries

Modular course structures

Questions of student-contact time in college

Development of in-service training, particularly agency/school-based with increasingly close links with the field

Staff development to offset the ossifying effects of an ageing staff.

When there is a shortage of teachers the problem of selecting students has low priority. As job opportunities reduce, however, and restrictions are placed on numbers of students to be admitted to particular courses in the college, sometimes resulting in quite small numbers in secondary subject courses, it is important that the most suitable students are admitted and that drop-out is kept to an absolute minimum. Selection of students, therefore, becomes very critical. Until comparatively recently in Scotland most selection was done on the basis of academic qualifications and school reports with the addition of a short interview, often unstructured and with few, if any, developed criteria, where considered necessary. In 1976, however, the college began to look at considerably more sophisticated methods of selection involving a variety of techniques on the lines of practice in several other areas such as the Civil Service, the Armed Forces and multi-national corporations. These investigations led to the establishment in 1982 of a nationally-funded research project led by Dr. J. D. Wilson, Head of Moray House College's Department of Education under the title 'Criteria of Teacher Selection' (CATS).[1]

The CATS project addresses three sets of questions concerned with the use made of evidence currently collected, improving the quality of the background evidence, and improving the quality of evidence obtained in face-to-face situations. In view of the nature of teaching, selecting 'out' at the entry stage is critically important: at present the correlation between pre-entry measures and college grades on the one hand and subsequent career performance on the other is not high. It is difficult, therefore, to predict which student will perform well in later years (CATS Newsletters Nos. 1 and 2). Reliability and validity are not the only problems in selection: logistics and cost are also important. Until a clearer picture is available of the actual nature of the task of teaching as a basis on which to build a satisfactory profile of the

characteristics required to perform effectively, the principle of economy of effort would dictate continuing emphasis on a screening for
negative indicators. Other studies referred to later in this and other
chapters indicate that work is going ahead to clarify the issues involved.

For the 1984 entry to the new Four-Year BEd Degree a quite
elaborate selection system was piloted as part of the CATS project.
Criteria developed included oral communication, written communication, commitment to teaching, practical teaching ability, range and
quality of interpersonal skills, and depth of character. Each candidate
was assessed in a range of situations over a whole day by panels of
assessors drawn from both college staff and the field. One interesting
issue in the procedure is how valid it is to try to assess practical teaching
ability as a basis for entry to a course designed to develop just that
ability. Is it not a prejudging of the very competence the college is in
business to develop, and a concession that the course does not so much
train to teach as put a veneer of professional acceptability on an already
present competence?

For many years the repercussions of the transfer of training debate,
and its failure to produce any positive evidence of effective transfer
from one subject to another, had provided the backcloth to a developing tradition that each subject in the secondary school teacher
training programme required its own separate methods content. Even
the three sciences and mathematics maintained their methodological
isolation as did the modern languages. Now it has to be conceded that
physics teaching requires markedly different methodologies from say,
mathematics or chemistry in respect of apparatus and safety aspects;
that, however, is not the issue. If teaching is in any meaningful sense
a profession, it must be supported by certain common principles
regardless of the subject area in which these principles are to be applied.
To deny this is to put teaching on the level of a series of specific crafts
related to the material worked with, and to reduce teacher education to
a straight apprenticeship model.

One reason for the long continuance of this separatist tradition was
the fact that, in spite of years of work by psychologists and educationa-
lists on learning theory, little effective analysis had been done of the
actual teaching process. The developed theoretical base for a sound,
generalised methods course simply had not been available. Recent
studies have begun to remedy this fundamental deficiency. Further
consideration will be given to the implications of these developments
under the topic of the theory and practice of teaching; for the moment
the point is to stress the impetus contraction has given to this
movement. As secondary student intakes have dropped, it has become

not uncommon to find as few as two or three students in a subject specialism. Clearly, demands of efficient staff utilisation and the absolute requirement to keep up school/agency-based in-service work put enormous pressures on departments and college administration to seek alternatives to an ostensibly repetitious and wasteful system whereby each subject department has its own full programme of methods training.

At the most basic level, groupings of subjects are being sought where a substantial amount of common methods work can be studied with provision for extension to cover the special features of individual subjects such as chemistry with its problems of safety, storage and handling of chemicals, or business studies with its special equipment. The pressures here are, of course, not only exigencies of resources, but also reflect curricular and organisational changes in the schools. Where emphasis in schools is moving away from rigid subject boundaries to a broader interdisciplinary approach and to the introduction of new areas of study not readily identifiable with any of the traditional subject fields, it is entirely reasonable that patterns of teacher education should be modified accordingly. Contraction undoubtedly brings major problems for the management of institutions of teacher education. In a sense it can be said that the severest challenge to any management arises out of contraction: but it also offers opportunities for management to carry through important and sometimes long-needed reviews which would have been very strongly resisted in more halcyon times. Moray House College is seeking to capitalise on these opportunities by fostering broader inter-departmental links in methods training and, as was explained in Chapter 2, by operating a strategy for course supervision which brings staff from different areas of the college into close professional collaboration.

For a number of years concern has been expressed at the very high level of class contact time for students. In some cases this has been as high as 27 hours per week. Even taking into account the fact that this figure incorporates a variety of different types of contact — by no means all lecture/tutorial situations — it is still far too high to allow a reasonable level of student-directed activity and provide a satisfactory basis for the continuing self-education which must be the mark of any true professional. Until very recently, while most staff would agree that the courses were over-timetabled, few, if any, were able to see any possible changes other than a reduction in some other part of the students' timetable to give them the additional time they needed to cover the ever-increasing demands of their own subject discipline. Contraction produces two main effects in this issue: first, since contact

hours tend to translate into staff accreditation, departments are under-
standably extremely reluctant to see their own timetable commitments
reduced and somehow this reluctance seems to carry over even into
resistance to any proposal to cut contact hours on a pro-rata basis across
departments; and second, since staff accreditation is linked not only to
contact hours but also to size of group taught, and any contact hours
with small groups must be compensated for by other staff-accrediting
activities such as school/agency-based in-service, staff can see an
ineluctable need to reduce contact hours with small groups. Again,
therefore, contraction has positive educational benefits as well as costs.

Provision of more self-directed study time and a re-orientation of
teaching methods to inculcate more effective learning strategies are not
the only reasons for reducing student contact time. As the complexity
of the task of the teacher in school grows, so do the demands on teacher
education. College staff need more and more time for activities other
than direct teaching. Course development in the context indicated
above is no longer the job of a head of department alone: a great
investment of staff time is required to ensure the necessary consultations, contributions and understandings to facilitate effective implementation. Participative college management also impinges heavily on
staff time in attendance at Boards of Studies, committees, working
parties and other consultative meetings. In the sort of rapidly changing
environment in which teacher education is currently conducted staff
development becomes a major priority. While much of the course
development work is a most valuable form of staff development in
itself, direct approaches are also called for in areas such as assessment,
profiling and course evaluation. Moves towards external validation also
have enormous implications for staff time.

One of the gravest of all the problems arising out of general
contraction in the system both at school and college level, is the
inexorable rise in the average age of staff as the recruitment of new
young staff dries up. On top of all the other reasons why staff
development is increasingly necessary, an ageing staff demands an
otherwise disproportionally high investment of time and energy. If,
then, as was noted in Chapter 2 time for these and many other activities
not detailed here is to be found, student contact hours simply must be
brought down.

An obvious national response to limited markets is some form of
rationalisation of provision among the colleges of education. Before the
severe cutback in teacher training such a policy already operated in the
establishment of specialist units in specific institutions. Examples
include the concentration of further education and men's physical

education at Jordanhill College, Glasgow, the dispersal of the National Curriculum Development Centres and the establishment of the national centres for Education Overseas, the Education of the Deaf, and Studies in School Administration at Moray House. With the drastic reduction in numbers of students in training in the specialist subjects in the secondary school, the Scottish Education Department issued a consultative document in March 1982 (SED,[2] March 1982) raising the possibility of the allocation of particular subjects to colleges on a national basis. To a certain degree the process had already begun as colleges lost minority subjects where sole lecturers retired or took voluntary redundancy. In this way Moray House lost its classics department in 1980. To date no national decisions have been announced, but a great deal of anxiety has been expressed in the colleges where specific departments might be under threat. While it is easy to appreciate the logic of such a plan in a static situation from a purely pre-service training point of view, the strong opposition it has encountered cannot be attributed solely to hysterical self-interest on the part of the colleges and departments. There is a clear need to distinguish between the provision of pre-service courses in a particular subject in any given year or years in a college and the continuation of the existence of the department in that subject. Apart from the expected upturn in the demand for secondary teachers in the 1990s there is the very pressing present need for extensive support to the schools in the throes of the implementation of the massive reforms of the Munn and Dunning programmes and the 16-18 Action Plan affecting all subjects — a service that can be provided satisfactorily only on a local basis. This is the sort of decision where longer as well as short-term factors must be clearly articulated if the proposals are to command any confidence among the profession. And these factors are not limited to the demographic; curricular issues are also critical.

Accountability in teacher education

Besides these more or less direct effects of contraction, two other classes of issues remain to be considered. The first of these, while their roots lie deeper, have been to a greater or lesser degree sharpened by the pressures of the contraction process. They include such matters as accountability, in general, and among its particular contingent manifestations increasing centralisation of government control, and external validation.

Over the last decade or so the public accountability movement has exerted increasing influence on education in a variety of ways. School

Councils have provided the main vehicle as far as parents and the public are concerned and, even now, proposals to strengthen their impact are under review (SED,[3] 1984). In the case of teacher education, the main pressures have been from professional colleagues and the Scottish Education Department representing central government. As far back as 1977 the, until then, quite remarkable autonomy of the colleges was severely curtailed by legislation giving the Secretary of State for Scotland a large measure of control over the courses to be offered in the colleges of education. Session 1983-84 was the first in which the colleges were subject to inspection by HMIs and reports on the system (but not, as yet, individual colleges) are to be published shortly. Thus control is being exerted on both curriculum and actual teaching. Probably more significant at present is the elaborate course approval procedure through which all new college courses now have to be put. Two dimensions of the process are important. First, there is the general procedure for college initiated courses of any kind. Here the first formal step is the presentation to the SED of a 'Stage A' submission — a brief outline of the proposed course, including details of the demand for it, its rationale and likely resource implications. After Stage A approval has been granted, a further very detailed 'Stage B' submission must be presented with detailed information about course content, methodologies, assessment procedures, staffing and other resources. No proposals may be submitted to external validating bodies without this SED approval. A very close control is therefore possible, both on the nature of courses offered by the college and also, at a rationalisation of provision level, on which colleges may offer which courses.

On top of this, a new development has been increasing control by means of published national guidelines for certain courses of major significance. Examples include the original Diploma in Learning Difficulties Courses (now Diploma in Special Educational Needs (Non-recorded Secondary or Primary Pupils)), and the new four-year primary degree course which replaced the three-year diploma from session 1984-85. While these guidelines do allow colleges enough freedom to make possible individualistic features of the course in each college, they do place very considerable constraints on course planning to a degree that has at times caused concern in outside validating bodies. Yet another illustration of this trend to greater national control is the three tiered structure of in-service qualifying coures now imposed on the colleges. Fortunately, the colleges have reasonable opportunity to influence these guidelines and structures at present. For example, the original proposal in the in-service field was to require all post-qualifying degree courses to be of two years' duration. When vigorous protests were made that this requirement disadvantaged Scottish teachers as against their colleagues elsewhere in Britain who could obtain such a qualification in one academic or calendar year, some flexibility of interpretation was allowed. Clearly, however, the spectre of direct central control looms large and a framework exists for the imposition of political control of course content, should such be the will of government. Great vigilance is required on the part of the colleges to preserve the necessary responsiveness to the market and a degree of academic autonomy. To some extent, this has already happened in the inclusion of multicultural education in such guidelines.

The crucial feature of guidelines is how they are drawn up and by whom. So long as working parties truly representative of the relevant interests are given the responsibility, with no undue influence from any one quarter, balance should be preserved. In an applied field like teacher education there is a clear case for allowing employing authorities, practising teachers and the SED a voice in their compilation. A more difficult question is how far and by what means the views of parents and the public should be represented. Recent moves by the Minister in England to extend the powers of governing bodies in the schools sector and increase the influence of parents therein (Green Paper: *Parental Influence at School*,[4] 1984) reflect a growing desire for greater effective accountability that the teacher education sector cannot expect to escape. The Open University, for example, now provides a course on Contemporary Issues in Education intended for parents and others outwith the profession (OU[5] Course E200). And apart from ideals of democratic participation, the ever-diminishing predictability of future conditions even a generation ahead has largely divested the professional of any unique authority he may have been able to claim in such matters in the past. Here, expertise is being delimited to the 'how' as opposed to the 'what' of education. This is not to argue that the professional should have no say in the 'what', bur rather that, in the realm of the 'what' his contribution is simply one among other legitimate interests and, unless he can carry the others with him, he will have to accept the view of the majority. Incidentally, such a view of curriculum control has certain interesting implications for teacher education in that it is not enough for the teacher to be well trained to teach pupils: he must also be helped to develop the ability to think through and present effectively his case to adults and fellow professionals.

One of the most effective ways of convincing staff of the need for this kind of expertise is external validation, the advantages of which were discussed in Chapter 2. There is no doubt that external validation has been one of the most profoundly significant developments in teacher education in Scotland in the last few years. Apart altogether from questions of accountability, the process of submitting courses of teacher education to external validation has afforded enormous advantages. It has stimulated rigorous self-analysis by the colleges, both of their courses and of their resources, it has afforded opportunities to involve in a meaningful partnership in course development representatives of the teaching profession and of the employing authorities, and it has encouraged productive links with Her Majesty's Inspectorate. Within the institutions themselves it has been a most powerful force in bringing together hitherto separate, if not separatist, departments and sections in a new atmosphere of joint endeavour. In times of low morale and disillusionment induced by the trauma of ill-prepared system-wide contraction, it has provided unrivalled opportunities for effective institutional and staff development.

The new Scottish Council for the Validation of Courses for Teachers, which was established in 1983, ought to offer a route to external validation able to take particular cognizance of the peculiar needs of the Scottish educational system, although it has obviously not had time to establish any tradition. This very advantage could become a liability, however, should it be tempted to seek to establish over-prescriptive norms. Fortunately, experience with CNAA suggests strongly that any such fears are likely to prove unfounded. The very rationale of external validation could, in any case, be used to argue powerfully for a choice of validating body to be available. It is therefore the more heartening that colleges have the option of going to either CNAA or SCOVACT as they wish.

Changing perspectives on the structure and content of courses

In addition to these concerns stimulated or given further impetus by outside pressures, there has been for years continuing professional debate over a number of crucial aspects of teacher education. While the move to external validation gave urgency and thrust to fundamental thinking about both primary and secondary teacher education courses, the college had been engaged in reviewing both for some time. Chief among the issues under consideration were basic models of training — objectives or process models; the theory/practice nexus; professional studies, professionality, reflective analysis and action research; collaboration with the schools; and assessment and profiling. Strong reaction against the over-formalism of an excessive Mager-type approach to objectives (Mager, 1970,[6] 1975[7]) issued in a passionate advocacy of process and input models of curriculum best typified in the work of

Stenhouse (1975,[8] 1983[9]). As so often in such cases the reaction was really against the abuses of objectives models rather than against these models themselves. Stenhouse himself admitted as much when he wrote 'Now it might be thought that this is to designate procedures, concepts and criteria as objectives. . . . This strategy could, of course, be followed, but it would, I believe, distort the curriculum' (Stenhouse, 1975). But with that rather unconvincing aside he dismissed the objectives approach altogether.

Objectives models accord with the view that effective management in almost any conceivable situation demands some form of objectives towards the achievement of which planning can be aimed, and effort directed, and by which success or failure can be assessed. In teacher education such objectives would include knowledge and understanding of both children and their learning, and subject matter, skills of many diverse kinds, and attitudes. With total commitment to fully professional development Moray House has adopted such a model for all its teacher education courses with the addition of a further element stressing the context or contexts of all the other facets of the model. The four constituents of the model are Planning — selecting appropriate aims, selecting and sequencing suitable content and resources; Implementing — motivating and managing; Evaluating — checking results against intentions, appraising effectiveness and appropriateness of aims; and Contextualising — studying the various contexts within which the activities concerned occur and the effects of such contextual factors, and exploiting these as appropriate. This model is seen as applying both to the task of teaching in the schools and to teacher education as preparation for that task. It also makes meaningful accountability possible, but, more importantly still, facilitates, indeed positively requires, that self-critical reflection that is the mark of true professionality.

Application of the model to teacher education leads directly to a rigorous analysis of the teaching task from a whole range of points of view — an analysis which demands the synthesising of theory and practice, the apparent divorce between which has for so long been the Achilles heel of teacher education. Accordingly, the college has developed a policy of integrating the contributions of the professional studies departments — education, psychology and sociology — with those of the methods departments into a single, major component under the heading of Theory and Practice of Teaching. This involves not only a thematic approach, but a professionally stimulating co-operative experience as members of different departments work together on themes such as learning, child development and socialisation, curriculum planning, evaluation, and resourcing, and contextual factors such as family, school, community, the educational system and professionalism and professionality. In the four-year degree programme the Theory and Practice of Teaching component runs through the whole course with increasing emphasis in the latter years. Staff cooperation is extended to include school experience as well as college-based time. The student is thus constantly encouraged to see and reflect on his or her experience from a variety of standpoints.

Again, this approach is not simply a methodological device: it is intended to promote a mature professionality on the part of both staff and students and particularly to foster that vision of teacher professionality enshrined by Stenhouse in the phrase 'teacher as researcher' (Stenhouse, 1975) and developed in depth in a number of recent and current action research projects (e.g. Adelman and Elliott,[10] 1973; Cameron-Jones,[11] 1982; CARN,[12] 1982; and Elliott, 1980[13]). Initial teacher education is therefore no longer viewed as merely a basic grounding to be built on later by stages in appropriately planned in-service courses. Rather, the concept includes the goal of helping students to develop both the means and the motivation for continuing professional growth. The earlier mentioned resource pressures to reduce contact time on initial teacher education courses therefore coincide with important professional needs to ensure that students have adequate time for informed and critical self-reflection.

But such a philosophy of teacher education has an impact beyond the college: any effective action research activities demand close co-operation from the schools in which the students will be placed for school experience periods and in which they will ultimately take up post. In 1978 the Sneddon Report (SED[14], 1978) proposed an ambitious programme of school–college collaboration in teacher education. Among its many recommendations perhaps the most radical was the designation of a senior member of staff (at assistant headteacher level at least) as 'regent' responsible for the proper conduct of students' school experience. These responsibilities included briefing and induction to the work of the school as a whole, ensuring they had appropriately balanced timetables, general supervision and contributing to their assessment. A similar recommendation was made that colleges should designate a senior member of staff to be responsible for all placement arrangements, including selection of suitable schools.

Other important recommendations were concerned with the participation of practising teachers in college course planning teams and the promotion of collaborative research efforts. While it could not be claimed that all of the Sneddon recommendations have been fully implemented in every course, very considerable progress has been made to secure college–school partnership, and all Moray House teacher education course planning teams have teacher and education authority representatives. Other important recommendations such as the provision of a lighter timetable for probationer teachers and for those teachers involved in supporting students and probationers in school have, to date, been largely frustrated by other pressures on school staffing.

While most of the following aspects of the increasing professionalisation of teaching are developed in other chapters, it would be inexcusable not to make some brief reference to them here in terms of their impact on teacher education. Such extended, indeed life-long, development of the professional teacher is increasingly seen to be necessary as the view of the tasks and responsibilities of teaching is enlarged. No longer are the professional competences of the mature teacher perceived as limited to a sound practical knowledge of subject matter, the way children learn and pedagogical methodology. Curriculum alone has become a major study in its own right, a discipline with its own distinctive methodology and vocabulary. Under the umbrella of Curriculum Studies are included the major sub-areas of curriculum development and curriculum evaluation. These are dynamic concepts: any idea of study of a static entity has been superseded by the realisation that the curriculum must be an ever-changing, ever-evolving response to a whole range of factors including the needs of the individual child and involving an extensive, planned articulation of the whole spectrum of school experience.

Assessment, likewise, both formative and summative, has been the subject of intensive and ongoing study. New techniques such as criterion-referencing and profiling make unprecedented demands on the teacher, for more than a simple change of philosophy from norm- to criterion-referenced assessment is involved. New skills of observation and analysis are called for as well as the ability to interpret both to one's own professional judgement and to others, colleagues as well as parents. The whole area of diagnostic assessment leading in to the effective handling of learning difficulties at all levels of ability is yet another added dimension to the professional role of the teacher.

Whereas formerly the concern of the mainstream teacher was with 'normal' children, others considered in need of 'special education' being provided for by other staff specially trained for the purpose, the current view of children with special educational needs has further profound implications for the extended professional demands on all teachers. Rigid and simplistic divisions of children into easily identifiable groups have given way to expectations that the teacher will command a greatly enhanced competence not only to identify learning difficulties and special educational needs in routine class situations, but be capable of making the necessary adjustments to the curriculum, the child's learning situation and his or her own teaching strategies and methodologies to deal effectively with a far wider range of such problems than would hitherto have been considered feasible.

In attempting to discharge these varied and complex responsibilities the professional teacher is expected to be able to make appropriate use of a wide range of resources. A quick tour of any well-equipped college or school resource centre will show just how formidable educational technology has become. Sophisticated reprographic machinery, sound and video recorders, computers with a bewildering variety of software of all degrees of complexity from games and teaching programmes through testing to records and reporting systems await his competent bidding; and he has also the challenge of keeping up with his ever alert pupils in coping with some of these. Educational technology, however, is not just the hardware: the sort of highly developed techniques of curriculum generation and management, assessment and evaluation of both courses and one's own professional practice are all part of the vastly expanded technological world of teaching. The management of all of these greatly extends the range of competences truly professional teachers must command.

Beyond all questions of organisation, strategies, and methodology lie the fundamental issues of aims and values. Amid all the exigencies of contraction and contingent pressures attention has also been directed to such basic matters as the elucidation of appropriate aims for school education, and consequently for teacher education, in an age of changing circumstances and even values. Value relativism, large-scale and probably continuing unemployment, the increasing multicultural nature of society and the purposes and nature of assessment are among the most critical problems of the 1980s.

Whereas in a reasonably static social context the general aim of 'preparation for life' could offer some rational base on which to structure a framework of education for the rising generation, no real consensus exists among futurologists as to the world of the first half of the twenty-first century, for which educationists today are trying to prepare young people. If the prevalent view of the future is one of the constant change, and not even evolutionary but often probably revolutionary change, any kind of coherence in education is exceedingly difficult to achieve. And where the view is taken that values are equally fluid with circumstances and life-styles, the task of the educator becomes so vague as virtually to render any meaningful preparation for it impracticable. This is the great danger of uncritical relativism in values. Even a virtue like tolerance must have its limits — there are lines of criminality, for example, that any cohesive society must define. Guidance staff in schools have particularly important responsibilities in this respect. Any school must evolve some kind of coherent ethos and, as an educational community, take its stand firmly on certain shared values among the staff if its pupils are not to be subjected to a highly disintegrative experience. Sometimes proponents of relativism, in opposing explicit value stances, forget that relativism is itself an explicit value stance. One way in which the college tries to face this problem is to ensure that each course of pre-service teacher education incorporates elements of religious and moral education.

Probably the most urgent overt manifestation of the current societal flux is the cultural and ethnic diversity so prevalent in many areas of Britain. With its large School of Education Overseas and the presence among its staff of a member with national responsibility for multicultural education in Scotland, Moray House has, for many years, been deeply involved in this area. In June 1983 the college adopted an explicit policy on multicultural education to inform all courses, including teacher education. This policy predicates a pervasive approach whereby the multicultural dimension provides a backcloth to the conduct of each course. Ways are also sought of capitalising on the presence in the college of large numbers of students from overseas both in organised shared curricular experiences and informal student international activities. The goals here must be limited — attitudes rather than in-depth understandings are the appropriate focus. But again values are inescapable; understanding must not be confused with endorsement or approval where practices may conflict with moral and humanitarian values. Examples here might range from halal killings to equal rights for women.

It is here that the wheel comes full circle: ironically the one area of current contention in which the college has recently taken an unequivocal value stance is in the context of pluralism. Its multicultural policy embodies unqualified advocacy of 'rejection of a policy of cultural and linguistic assimilation along with the assumption of its desirability and inevitability.' (Checklist appended to College Policy on Multicultural Education, 1984.) There are other important areas in teacher education in respect of which it is time to heed the word, 'If the trumpet give an uncertain sound, who shall prepare himself to the battle?'

References

1. CATS (1983, 1984)   *Criteria of Teacher Selection Project Newsletter* Nos. 1 and 2. Moray House College of Education, Edinburgh.

2. Scottish Education Department (1982)   Consultative Paper: *Rationalisation of Secondary Teacher Training in Colleges of Education.*

3. Scottish Education Department (1984)   Consultative Paper: *The Future of School Councils in Scotland.*

4. Department of Education and Science (1984)   *Parental Influence at School.* HMSO.

5. OU (1981)   Course E 200 'Contemporary Issues in Education'. Open University, Milton Keynes.

6. Mager, R. F. and Pipe P. (1970)   *Analysing Performance Problems.* Fearon.

7. Mager, R. F. (1975) 2nd edition   *Preparing Instructional Objectives.* Fearon.

8. Stenhouse, L. (1975)   *An Introduction to Curriculum Research and Development.* London, Heinemann.

9. Stenhouse, L. (1983)   *Authority, Education and Emancipation.* London, Heinemann.

10. Adelman, C. and Elliott, J. (1973)   'Reflecting where the action is: the design of the Ford Teaching Project.' *Education for Teaching.* 92.

11. Cameron-Jones, M. (1982)   *The Primary Teaching Practice Project.* Final Report. Moray House College of Education, Edinburgh.

12. CARN (1982)   Classroom Action Research Network Bulletin No. 5. *Action Research for Professional Development and Improvement of Schooling.*' Cambridge Institute of Education.

13. Elliott, J. (1980)   'The Implications of Classroom Research for Professional Development' in Hoyle, E. & Megarry, J. (1980 ed), *Professional Development of Teachers — World Yearbook of Education.* London, Kogan Page.

14. Scottish Education Department (1978)   *Learning to Teach.* HMSO.

4

Community studies

J. Callan Anderson

Origins and developments

It was a former Principal of Moray House, Dr. W. B. Inglis, who laid the foundation of what became the School of Community Studies. He was Principal from 1951 to 1966 and came to the college from a background which today would have been described as community education. He was a member of the National Council of the YMCA, a lecturer in the Department of Education at Glasgow University with a particular remit for developing adult education in Clydebank, and, immediately prior to his appointment to Moray House, served as youth officer for Renfrewshire. In 1941 he became a founder member of the Scottish Youth Leadership Training Association, the body which instituted training at national level for youth leaders.

By 1944 that Association had established the first professional course of training for youth leaders to be held in Scotland. Fifty applications were received and 26 candidates admitted to the course. All instruction was given by the staff of Moray House Training College and the syllabus included Social Environment, The Psychology of Childhood and Adolescence, Club Organisation and Management, Principles of Education and Aims of the Youth Service.

By 1945 Youth Service appeared to be well established. Not only was the first professional course in operation, but the Association was involved in regional training ventures, particularly related to the training of part-time tutors. The 1945 Education (Scotland) Act, with its conception of a planned system of primary, secondary and further education, brought this service more completely within the general educational orbit. The annual report of the Scottish Education Department for that year put the matter succinctly in these terms:

> In the field of what has hitherto been known as Youth Service
> the first steps were taken to give effect to those provisions of the

act which, by requiring Education Authorities to provide adequate facilities for recreation and social and physical training for all persons resident in their areas, have expanded the scope of the Youth Service to that of a Social and Recreational Service covering the adult population as well.

In line with these developments the Association repeated its emergency course in 1945, extending its student group to include community centre workers. The joint training of youth and community workers thus commenced within Scotland at Moray House.

The significance of this five-year period for the future was that teachers, youth leaders and community centre workers were trained not only within the one institution, but in mixed groups and by college staff. Additionally, students were involved in social service in different parts of Edinburgh and under the supervision of youth workers then employed by the local authority. The foundations of a shared training including teachers, youth leaders and community workers was thus laid in the college and responsibility for the assessment of practical work equally shared by field workers and tutorial staff.

Four years later, under national economic stress, the educational services were subjected to financial cuts. The vagueness of the 1945 Education (Scotland) Act in relation to youth and community work made it inevitable that training for that sector should suffer and the professional course come to an end.

Towards the end of 1956, Dr. Inglis proposed that a national conference be held to examine the state of youth service and to consider the problems that would follow when the bulge of the population entered further education around 1960. That conference was held at Bridge of Allan in May 1957 and was attended by representatives of the Scottish Education Department, 24 education authorities, 11 voluntary organisations, the Scottish Standing Conference of Voluntary Youth Organisations and the Scottish Leadership Training Association. At the final session Dr. Inglis presented for discussion a draft statement that might be addressed from the conference, expressing the desire that encouragement be given to youth service and community centre work through the sympathetic and active interest of the Secretary of State. This requested that financial provision be made, both for the training of voluntary workers and for professional workers in that field. That statement was unanimously approved and despatched to the Scottish Education Department. In December 1959 the Secretary of State established the Standing Consultative Council on Youth Service in Scotland and the following year professional training for youth leaders in the form of a one-year course was established at Moray House.

By 1963 these courses had extended to two years' duration in Moray House, and Jordanhill College of Education instituted a similar course commencing in September 1964. Writing in that year Dr. Inglis had this to say:

> The courses at Moray House are intrinsically valuable, but it should be observed that they are having desirable concomitants in the training of teachers. The governors have established a Social Study Department under Mr. B. J. Ashley, designed not only to train leaders but to promote among student-teachers a better understanding of the social background of the children and young people whom they will teach. The college is thus committed to the policy of associating teachers with others who are also concerned with the welfare of the young. In October 1965 it is intended to commence courses for Health and Welfare workers and for those engaged in Child Care. These developments are under the guidance of a Consultative Committee appointed by the governors of Moray House.

In that same year a course of professional training for the Certificate in Social Work was offered within the department, under the auspices of the Council for Training in Social Work. The years immediately following witnessed a period of growth for social work and youth and community work in Scotland and Moray House responded to the demand for qualified staff by rapidly increasing its intake to both courses, which led to the college becoming the centre for the largest number of students in training for these professions in Scotland.

One unfortunate consequence of this development was that the Department of Social Study, later to be termed the Department of Sociological Studies, outgrew the premises made available within the college and had to move to an annexe, first in Portobello, almost three miles from the main college, then to Regent Road, still a mile distant from the campus. In effect this meant that, while it remained possible for training to be offered on a generic basis to those preparing for youth and community service and social work, teachers were excluded from this approach to training. The goal which Dr. Inglis had set himself, to bring about an integrated training for teachers and youth leaders, and one which in the early days he almost achieved, thus receded not as a result of educational or philosophical debate, but because of lack of space.

In 1968 a three-year course leading to the Diploma in Social Work was instituted as a result of representations made to the Central Council for Education and Training in Social Work. This was based on the experience of the college that young, well-qualified applicants were available for direct recruitment to a professional course of training for that field and that such applicants were often lost to the profession either because they had to delay their entry until they were older and had gained experience in employment, or had to undertake university training followed by a post-graduate course. In the beginning the Diploma in Social Work was offered with the possibility of some students deciding to choose to qualify for youth and community work within it. Subsequently, the Scottish Consultative Council on Youth and Community Service decided to institute a similar diploma in youth and community work.

The generic principle

Since the college regarded these two courses as closely related, students followed a common curriculum throughout the first year. This joint training continued into year two, with specialism beginning in the third term and in the final year also certain course components were shared by those training for both professions. The commitment was to the philosophy which values integration as distinct from separation, focuses upon skill development as distinct from the setting in which that skill will be practised, and to a blurring of professional differences in the interests of meeting client needs. While this did not, for reasons of geography, involve those training for the teaching profession, that philosophy continued to underpin the training offered to social workers and to those training for youth and community work.

This approach was supported in 1968 by the passing of an Act and the publication of a report. The Social Work (Scotland) Act of that year brought together into a single organisation a number of services previously separate and give this unified organisation wider responsibilities than any of its components ever had. The services thus conjoined included the Probation Service, the Child Care Service, the Welfare Services and the Mental Health Service. Previously, those operating within any one of these undertook a training specific to that field of work. The weaknesses inherent in that system have been described as follows:

   (i)   The needs of individuals are closely related to family and community; but the existence of separate services has led to a fragmentation of the help given, so that family members receive help from a variety of workers, employed by different authorities, each attempting different forms of treatment for needs which are in fact interrelated.

  (ii) Training and research in social work have increasingly emphasised the unity and interdependence of the separate forms of social work, and their growing reliance on a common body of knowledge. But the existence of separate organisations had hitherto inhibited the growth of a common body of practice.

(iii) Unevenness in provision, discontinuity in care and duplication of services have been among the outstanding weaknesses of the old structure. At the same time it has been difficult for services to respond to new or to changing needs, and policy has been inflexible in the face of change. Divided responsibility has led to lack of accountability, and has prevented the most economical use of existing resources.[1]

The Social Work Departments established by this Act placed upon local authorities the responsibility for bringing together those from previously distinctive professional backgrounds and encouraged the creation of a generically based service.

The report was entitled 'Community of Interests',[2] published by the Scottish Education Department on the advice of the Standing Consultative Council on Youth and Community Service. This examined the relationship between schools, youth service, community service, further education colleges, evening classes and sports organis- ations in the provision of social education. It recommended a lowering of professional barriers and the development of a co-operative appro- ach in order to address the needs of individuals and communities more effectively.

These developments within the professions for which training was provided not only endorsed established practice, but further en- couraged the development of generic training. By 1971, the year in which the Department of Sociological Studies became the School of Community Studies, 249 students were involved in courses leading to professional qualifications in social work or youth and community work. Staff, recruited from a wide variety of professional and academic backgrounds, numbered 14 in that year and were recruited on the basis of their willingness to operate within a shared training structure. Thus, within itself, the School had the opportunity to provide the basis of co- operative understanding between the two professions. The courses were organised on the assumption that many of the principles and objectives of the two professions are the same. The challenge to people from different professional backgrounds working together in this integrated way provided opportunities to learn from each other and reflected the reality of work in the fields for which the School trained. The creation of Social Work Departments had brought together professionals trained in one area of work only and required of them that they operate according to the needs of the changing service and thus from a generic base. Within youth and community work also the need to extend from a centre-based service into one which accommodated the needs of issue-based groups and developing communities placed upon that service the need to restructure and operate according to extended criteria.

A professional service which is based upon generic principles, like a training process which operates from a generic base, requires to have a clarity as to its professional uniqueness, if its professional nature is not to be called into question. Throughout the 1970s questions surrounding the professional nature of social work and of youth and community work were prevalent. Not only had the former incorporated within it a number of areas of responsibility quite new to that profession, but the latter had been forced to re-examine the nature and content of its professional responsibility.

There were those within both fields who voiced a preference for training which would more effectively separate preparation for the two professions. By some it was felt that the emphasis placed upon genericism under-emphasised significant elements within the training for social work: by others it was felt there was a greater need for specialist training particularly related to the field of youth and community work. The fact that neither staff nor students in the School of Community Studies shared this view is amply evidenced in a report published in the mid-1970s as a result of a joint staff/student committee established to make recommendations to the Board of Governors as to the future of the School of Community Studies. In that report the staff view was recorded as follows:

> It would certainly be a retrograde step if Moray House, which
> pioneered within training institutions the close relationship
> between these related areas of work and epitomised it within the
> School of Community Studies, should now revert to a pattern of
> training which would lead to a less effective service in the field.
> There is no doubt that students going out into the field will have,
> as a result of their courses and of the relationships formal and
> informal which exist within the School, an ability to understand
> on a broader base than would otherwise be possible the needs of
> the individuals and the groups with whom they will come into
> contact in their work.

The student view was no less positive:

> It is our definite and considered opinion as students of the School
> of Community Studies that whatever plans and developments

are brought into being for the School, the principle of the joint training of Social Workers and Youth and Community Workers within the School must be maintained. It would, in our view, be an extremely retrogressive move to seek to alter this situation, particularly at this time when the value of such a training situation is being increasingly recognised, and particularly in an institution which pioneered this approach.

The current scene

The fact that Moray House College accommodates the largest social work course leading to the CQSW in Scotland and the only three-year course leading to that qualification in Britain, is indicative of confidence in the pattern of training employed within the School of Community Studies by the social work profession. With regard to community education the college is the second largest teaching unit within Scotland and since 1978, in addition to offering the three-year course, the two-year course and the one-year post-graduate course, is the one college to offer the post-graduate qualification on a sandwich basis to unqualified graduates employed in the field of community education. While, then, programmes in social work and community education are firmly established in the college, there are three key issues which will influence further involvement in this field.

Firstly, there is the matter of autonomy. While it has always been the case that the professional validating body for social work courses has held power to determine course structure and approve content, these powers have been greatly increased over the past few years. While Moray House may offer a Diploma in Social Work, CCETSW awards the professional qualification and does so on the recommendation of accredited external examiners. The balance between college-based study and field-work practice is determined by that body, and the ratio of students to qualified social work staff is also subject to the approval of the Council. In community education, developments initiated by the Scottish Community Education Council over the past two years point in the direction of a similar relationship between that profession and the college of education. Thus, the autonomy of the training institution is weakened in certain respects and the powers of the professional bodies increased.

These changes are taking place at the same time as the college seeks academic validation for its courses from CNAA, the granting of which can be seen to weaken further the autonomy of the college and to challenge the powers traditionally vested in the trainer.

There can be no question of the appropriateness of such moves on the part of professional bodies to influence and determine the training offered to those aspiring to professional membership. Similarly, the submission of courses for approval by CNAA is a logical development which will serve the interests of both professional fields. However appropriate such an accountability structure is on the part of the trainers to the professions for which they prepare staff and to national academic bodies such as CNAA, the attendant loss of traditional freedoms and the very real curtailment of autonomy call for readjustments which can be difficult both for individual trainers and for training agencies. The ivory tower is under attack; trainers from within and trainers from without have equal say in the selection, curriculum and assessment of those preparing for professional status. Failure on the part of the college to respond positively to these changing demands can only result in the college's ceasing to have a continued involvement in training for community education and social work.

How is Moray House coping with these changing demands? The development of the course committee structure, which brings together staff from the college, students in training and representatives from the professions for which that training is planned, is one significant step towards a co-ordinated training pattern. These committees have responsibility for planning the structure and content of courses and are directly responsible to the higher courts of the college. Secondly, changes introduced to policies relating to the visiting of Social Work students on placement stress the changing relationship between the college tutor and the field work teacher, placing increased emphasis on the role of the latter in the preparation of workers for the field. Thirdly, the involvement of external examiners in the detailed scrutiny of course content and in the prior approval of student projects further emphasises the growing accountability of the college to the profession. With regard to Community Education, recommendations now before the Secretary of State for Scotland on the future of training have been developed following a lengthy review on the part of the Scottish Community Education Council's Training Committee, representatives of regional authorities, voluntary organisations, trainers and workers involved in this professional field.[3] If these recommendations are accepted, modifications similar to those called for in social work training will be required and the voice of professional interests more loudly heard.

The second issue facing the college relates to the need for the further professional development of already qualified workers in social work and community education. As new needs emerge in both fields, post-professional training must become a priority and the degree to which training agencies respond to these needs will increasingly become an indicator of their survival-potential. Can Moray House make a relevant contribution to developments of this nature? Can the college which, for over twenty years, has been required to focus upon the pre-service training of workers for both fields, rise to the challenge of providing courses of post-professional training for these fields? Even faced with a positive response to both of these questions, how can the college make an effective contribution to these needs at a time when it is increasingly difficult for employing agencies to second staff to college-based courses?

The college already houses the first post-qualifying course approved by CCETSW in Scotland and the only remaining post-qualifying course for social workers with the deaf. This course, of one academic session's duration, is in its sixth year and is open to qualified social workers and workers from related fields whose professional practice involves a major element of work with the hearing impaired. Additionally, the college offers a post-professional course 'Training and Support of Part-time Workers in Community Education' which is of one year's duration. The evidence of need for such a course was provided by employing bodies, many of whom were unable to second staff for college-based training of this nature. Accordingly, the course is based upon distance-learning methods and is therefore readily accessible. Entering its fourth intake, this programme has recruited professional workers from Scottish regions and from England, Wales and from Youth Service staff employed by British Forces on the European mainland. It is professionally validated by the In-service Training and Education Panel of the Department of Education and Science and, combining work-based study with tutorial support at a distance, a short residential component and work-related research, effectively addresses the need for training and the difficulties which surround staff secondment.

The college is currently planning two further courses which will rely mainly on distance-learning methods — 'Decision Making in Social Work' and an advanced diploma on work with adolescents. The latter aims to address certain of the needs experienced by teachers, social workers, workers in community education and staff of adolescent units and will combine studies in psychology, sociology with skill development in work with this age group. It aims also to respond to the needs articulated by CCETSW, formal education as well as community education agencies in relation to this age group, and thus rests upon a generic framework, bringing together into course planning representatives of each of these professions.

The third issue relates to the emphasis now being placed upon collaborative work involving college of education staff with practising professionals within the community. Such developments complement the national emphasis of the college of education and call for a commitment to locally based work.

The college has now an active commitment to the Certificate in Social Service, an alternative training to the CQSW, for those involved in social work, approved by, CCETSW and designed to facilitate training on a sandwich basis for unqualified workers employed in that field. Moray House played a significant part in establishing the Forth Scheme covering Lothian, Borders, Central and Fife regions and continues to play an active part in the servicing of this training in conjunction with professional and training agencies from the four regions. An in-service course in social care of one year's duration is also offered and attracts an annual recruitment of 50 part-time students predominantly involved in residential and day-care settings.

Within the field of community education the college co-ordinates the work of the South East Scotland Training Association (SESTA), a regional training body representative of the statutory and voluntary agencies within Lothian and Borders regions involved in the field of community education. This body offers a modular training structure for part-time workers engaged in that field and recruits about six hundred trainees in any one academic session. SESTA also offers in-service courses to professionally qualified workers and has developed a range of courses which it offers by distance-learning for both voluntary and paid workers in the field. Among recent initiatives taken by this association is the Certificate in Neighbourhood Work, developed by SESTA and the college in partnership. This pattern of training is designed to enable part-time workers to reach a professional qualification in community education, and a structure developed to accommodate that routing has been reflected in the recently published national report relating to training for these fields.

Developments in the world of children's play also feature in the college's activities and the National Centre for Play is housed within the college. College staff are involved in the training of play workers within the locality and plans are afoot to develop this area of work which will hopefully lead to the first award-bearing course in play to be offered in Scotland.

In conclusion, the part which the School of Community Studies has played in the 'Pathways to the Professions' project, which is discussed more fully in Chapter 7, merits reference. Dr. Inglis in the 1940s envisaged a generic form of training embracing youth workers, community centre wardens and teachers. The physical separation of the School of Community Studies from the main college prevented the realisation of that ideal throughout the late sixties and seventies. Its return to the main campus, coinciding with the start of the above project, provided the basis for the development of a generic focus involving trainee social workers, community education workers and teachers in a common programme of study and in elements of shared learning. One of the significant features of this project is that it has brought staff from different departments into close collaboration, in keeping with the project's commitment to inter-professionalism. Over the years community education and social work students have benefited from the existence on the campus of a wide range of academic and professional expertise outside their field and, indeed, that was the justification for locating training for these professions in a large multi-purpose college. In the same way, specialists in community education and social work have been able to contribute to teacher training courses. More significantly, this project achieved the bringing together of students in training for the three professions and actively encouraged the sharing of views on school-based education, work experience and the contributions which each professional group make to society. Such interaction should clearly belong to a college of education and this project comes some way to addressing that need and to illustrating some of the steps towards its realisation.

References

1. University of Edinburgh (1969)   Social Work in Scotland: Report of Working Party on the Social Work (Scotland) Act 1968.
2. Scottish Education Department (1968)   *Community of Interests*. HMSO.
3. Scottish Community Education Council (1984)   *Training for Change*. Scottish Education Department.

5

Education overseas

Alexander McLellan

The background

The first cohort of overseas students entered Moray House College in October 1955, at the beginning of the 1955-56 session. Prior to this, Scottish courses conducted in the college had witnessed from time to time the inclusion of overseas students: those who held educational qualifications equivalent to the normal Scottish entry qualifications joined the established courses along with home-based students, while special courses adapted to their individual needs, and bearing certificate awards, had been provided for 'those whose academic attainments did not reach the standards required in Scotland'.

Nineteen fifty-five, it seems, marked a new departure and a new emphasis; at the instigation of the then Colonial Office, the previous somewhat casual arrangements were formalised and broadened into a special one-year course in Education for Tropical Areas, for teachers from Nigeria, who after training would return to their own country; the course was to be similar to that for long conducted at the London Institute of Education and was to include English for foreign students, Tropical Hygiene and Social Anthropology. This development was the first identifiable step in the evolution of the Scottish Centre for Education Overseas as we know it today. In 1958 a further course in the Teaching of English as a Second Language was introduced for some twenty students who were funded by the British Council; the revenue accruing from this permitted the appointment of qualified and experienced staff from the field and the purchase of specialist books for the college library. The establishment of an Overseas Department dates from this particular time, and during the 1960s, in common with the rest of the education sector, the department expanded its activities, diversified its interests and increased its complement of courses and students, in recognition of which in 1973 it adopted the style and title

of the Scottish Centre for Education Overseas and the acronym of
SCEO.

The constituents

Save for the occasional wobble, the vagaries of which are attributable to
fluctuations in the expenditure patterns of governments at home and
abroad and to socio-economic factors of an international nature, the
trend consistently since has been towards diversification and expansion;
so much so that in any one academic session we are looking for
enrolment figures in excess of 200 course members, from something
like forty or fifty overseas countries in the Third World. To a large
extent the reason for this diverse representation from the developing
world is their colonial inheritance; by far the greatest proportion come
from Anglophone countries with Commonwealth affiliations of different degrees of intensity, from Africa and Asia, Caribbean and Oceania,
and they are cast in two broad moulds, one producing educators of one
sort or another, and the other English language specialists.

Those in the category of educator, a broad band, tend to be
products of British-type education systems, and the management
structures and administrative procedures of the institutions they once
attended, and now administer, carry this imprint. In the colonial days,
frequently recalled by students and staff alike, the main functions of the
government school, or for that matter, the Church or Mission School,
were the production of a primary school teaching force and a literate
bureaucracy intended to occupy posts at humble levels of the administration, thus releasing the expatriate masters to pursue higher levels of
policy activity. For this purpose the student beneficiaries were nurtured
on Cambridge Certificates and literature syllabuses that would have
graced the bursary competitions of the Scottish Universities.

In the early years of independence those privileged enough to have
enjoyed this indoctrination shot to the top, in some cases as politicians,
in others as senior administrative personnel in the education ministries,
for the education service still contains a vast proportion of the educated
manpower in many developing countries. Thus now, some twenty or
thirty years on, there is a massive British inheritance at levels where
important policy decisions have to be taken and a deep well of goodwill
towards UK-based institutions. Extended periods of study in the UK
are of course a further source of bonding.

For the teacher and the educational administrator the pragmatic
way to reform or improve an education system is by transfusion rather
than by transplant, by borrowing on a gradualist basis. In any event the

lag effect of changes introduced is enormous, and for the new cultural imperialists — to name them, the USA and the USSR — this represents a formidable obstacle unless the objective is a straightforward demolition of the inheritance; it would take some fifteen or twenty years for an intrusive aid programme to make any impact on an existing system, and this is a task not to be entered upon lightly. This is the area where lies the residual appeal of being trained in Britain; it is not simply a desire to share the artifacts and spoils of the British Aid Programmes and the incidental access to the high street stores, though these in themselves can be persuasive enough factors; thus a modern-day educational imperialism lives on and SCEO serves as its handmaiden.

The place of English

For the English language specialist the deep-seated reasons, as well as the peripheral attractions, are very similar with further national and compelling reasons adding to the pull towards Britain. There was a time when a dearth of English language skills represented a handicap in diplomatic or in commercial circles; more recently this was clearly disadvantageous in the pursuit of higher skills and degree qualifications in science and medicine since for the most part these had to be studied abroad and the language of available textbooks was English; more recently still the advent of modern technological developments and computerised software, again in the English medium, even in Japan, have emphasised that English language is a key activity in development programmes, which governments and politicians can ignore only at their peril.

Under such compulsions we are now witnessing a drive towards greater proficiency in English, among the oil barons from Saudi Arabia and other countries around the Gulf, and from Malaysia, where for over twenty years following independence English enjoyed an unenviable national opprobrium as the language of the colonial oppressor. Again in the countries of West and Central Africa, with a proud Francophone tradition as their inheritance, we now observe the same compelling trend, in Cameroon and Mauretania, in Senegal and the Ivory Coast, in Guinea and the Congo, and in the Central African Republic and Chad. Visits from high-ranking officials and dignitaries from these countries precede the arrival of their English language specialists and pleas for linking arrangements between Moray House and their institutions proliferate. At present levels of interest the future for English language teaching is bright and assured.

The courses

SCEO is now a broad church, providing a rich variety of courses in the following main areas:

    Education/Educational Management and Administration
    English Language Teaching
    Special Educational Needs
    Home Economics and General Science
    Country-specific courses, each designed to suit particular
       national requirements.

The locus may be in SCEO but increasingly the focus is across the whole range of college provision, with access openly available to any of the thirty or so departments that can meet the identifiable needs of our overseas clients. With few exceptions our courses are designed for those already in middle-level posts overseas; the typical course member — course member is a designation preferable to that of student, which carries other connotations — will be within the age range of thirty to forty, be well qualified academically from an overseas university and with his basic professional training completed some years beforehand. As a rule he will have been earmarked for promotion and now carries the promise of high office in his home country; he may even be from the ranks of those senior personnel too valuable to release for more than a single term. At any rate this prospect of advancement they bring with them, together with the opportunity for personal development afforded by the courses, constitutes a strong source of motivation among the participants. A few find their way here at their own expense; others from countries rich in oil revenue have come with the assistance of their governments — Saudi Arabia, Brunei, Libya, and Nigeria, to name only some; increasingly countries seeking fulfilment of their development aspirations do so with help from the World Bank, the Asian Development Bank, the European Economic Commission and other donor agencies; but characteristically in the past we have depended heavily for our clientele on holders of official awards under the British Aid Programmes, administered and funded through the British Council and the Overseas Development Administration (ODA).

Methodology and content

Members of our management courses are invariably holders of responsible posts in educational administration at regional or ministry level, members of the inspectorate or heads of educational institutions;

alternatively these are the next posts they will occupy on the promotion ladder. Course content lays heavy emphasis on relevance — on aspects of educational planning, institutional evaluation and curriculum development, techniques of inspection and supervision, on the management of personnel, and on the application of management and administrative techniques, all directed to the situations found in developing countries. With help from the subject departments in the college provision can also be made to update content and methodology in specific subject areas whether in the primary or secondary sector. The methodology of our courses is diverse and matched to the diagnosed needs of the adult learner; different techniques abound, including group discussion, seminars, workshops, roleplaying, simulation exercises, syndicate work, self-directed study, case studies and the analysis of critical incidents; thus the basic approach is learner-centred rather than teacher-centred.

An integral part of every administrative course is its programme of visits and attachments to schools and related institutions. With SCEO as the only main overseas centre north of the border, course members have the whole of Scotland as their oyster. Regularly they are to be found in the schools examining curricular programmes and organisational structures in the central belt, in the Lothians, Fife and the Borders; more selectively, a trainee administrator may be encountered in the education offices of Dumfries and Galloway, or the Highland Region, while students of the rural scene, its schools and communities, find their way to the remoter parts of Grampian, or the Orkneys or the Western Isles — all of this in adaptation of the principle 'to each according to his needs'. Where identified specialist needs demand and where practice in Scotland leads the field, they will be there — in the regional offices, in the advisory services, in the curriculum development units, in the outlying offices of Her Majesty's Inspectorate — in a word, in our centres of excellence.

Such attachments are not undertaken lightly, each having its own period of prior study and rigorous preparation. It is perhaps fitting that despite the wide range of teaching techniques that go with course methodologies, the processes of evaluation consistently establish the attachments as the most prized elements of any course component. Whether this in some measure is due to the friendly reception accorded overseas visitors, the personal contacts they enjoy during the visits period, or the observation of new practice, is difficult to identify, but as a learning process the attachments enjoy the highest standing.

The activities of our English language courses are directed at many diverse groups and at several different levels. These include practising teachers of English as a second or foreign language, graduates and non-graduates; for these categories the core elements of courses consist of the methodology of language teaching at various levels of the primary and secondary sectors, language skills and language studies, and the phonology and pronunciation of spoken English. For those who are experienced, trained or graduate teachers, who aspire to occupy the policy-making position of departmental head, examiner, syllabus designer, textbook writer or teacher trainer, the main thrust of the courses, which are organised on a modular basis, includes linguistics, the methodology of language teaching and an analysis of the inter-play between these two areas.

In the main, the courses described here are at diploma level and of one academic year's duration. As elsewhere, shorter courses, usually lasting one term, are provided to meet identified needs of senior personnel; practical methods work is done by micro-teaching techniques and a variety of optional subjects is available in specialist areas such as the teaching of literature or educational management. These activities are reinforced by programmes of visits and attachments to schools and other relevant institutions.

Other activities programmed in this sphere of SCEO's activities include provision for those aspiring to take external examinations conducted by the Royal Society of Arts, for example the diploma qualifications in the Teaching of English, as a Foreign Language to Adults, as a Second Language to children from ethnic minority groups, and in multi-cultural education. The Centre also provides components for Scottish students on post-graduate training courses in the teaching of English as a Foreign Language and in current trends and developments in education in developing countries. Intrinsically interesting as these components are, there seems little doubt that the compelling reason for their continuing appeal is that they are seen as an insurance policy for home-based Scottish teachers who may have to follow their fortunes overseas, faced as they are with declining job prospects in a diminishing home situation.

The relentless march towards degree provision for senior personnel operating in overseas contexts is also confirmed in the field of English language teaching; here under CNAA auspices the college has introduced an MA Degree Course in Teaching English for Speakers of Other Languages (TESOL). The target group includes experienced personnel in mid-career who are involved in the training, supervision or inspection of other TESOL personnel. It is thus aimed at TESOL specialists who are currently employed (or see themselves as likely to be employed) in teacher training institutions, the inspectorate, government advisory services, or in some kind of supervisory capacity in a school or college.

Special educational needs

The growth of Universal Primary Education (UPE) in our client countries, already well advanced in Nigeria and Tanzania, has revealed increasingly a need for courses in special education. From a beginning with courses for teachers of the blind and visually impaired, conjointly provided by SCEO and the college's Department of Special Educational Needs, the range of facilities now available includes provision for diploma courses for teachers dealing with retarded and disadvantaged children, and with the deaf and hearing impaired, this last-named in collaboration with the Scottish Centre for Education of the Deaf. Here as elsewhere in our overseas courses the prescription is not simply 'do as we do', but a special emphasis is laid on matching technical advice realistically to conditions prevailing in overseas countries, where the hardware and technical bric-a-brac of the developed world are not readily available. As the move towards the implementation of UPE programmes gathers momentum it is anticipated that the demand for training in these areas of teacher education will grow, even though much of it in time will have to be implemented in the context of the home country itself. This likelihood posits the provision of a more complex programme and greater degree of sophistication in the needs of those overseas personnel who will be the trainers of the trainers: it is considerations of this kind that have given rise to an inter-institutional degree programme leading to the award of the MEd, Special Educational Needs, and involving the Departments of Special Education Needs in Moray House and Jordanhill College of Education in association with the University of Stirling.

Country-specific courses

As new needs are identified in overseas systems and as their economies develop, increased resources are being allocated to the improvement of certain specific problem areas. These programmes not infrequently are underpinned by the international banks or bilateral donor agencies. Tied as they are to limited objectives, they demand a precise match of what we provide in relation to the specified needs. Experience in recent years identifies these 'country-specific courses' as a growth sector. The training of educational administrators for Tanzania or for the Pakistan Primary Education Project; the upgrading of science and home economics teachers from the Gambia; management training for the community head teachers from the Maldives; techniques for the massive multi-class teaching project in Malaysia; training methodologies for the staff trainers of the Institute for the Development of Educational Administrators (IDEA) in Thailand — all of these confirm this trend.

Activities overseas

SCEO's Edinburgh-centred programmes emphasise college-based teaching-learning strategies and provide opportunities for comparative study exemplified in the practice of Scottish institutions. In all of these our constituents forsake their warmer climes for a sojourn in Scotland. A series of complementary and related tasks are undertaken overseas by college staff at various times during the session or in their vacation periods. It is on these that the staff top-up their previous overseas experience conducting seminars, fulfilling consultancy roles, advising overseas governments on a wide range of projects, and assisting with in-country training and development. Locally-based programmes of this kind, making impact on a wider audience, considerably enhance the multiplier-effect, but in addition they enable SCEO staff to stay in fine tune and at first hand with developments and problems overseas. Such assignments are undertaken at the behest of international bodies, overseas governments or UK organisations and they can include advisory services, project planning and evaluation, and the conduct of workshops and courses. Many of these activities take place in countries from which our students come, and in recent years college staff have discharged their duties in South America, the Caribbean, East and Central Europe, in most corners of Africa and extensively throughout the Arab world and the Far East. It is a rare occurrence for the whole complement of overseas staff to be found in Edinburgh at the same time; indeed a typical year's tally of these activities will be between 20 and 30 man months. Put another way, this is the equivalent of having two members of staff engaged in overseas projects for the whole of one year.

The paymasters

Normally SCEO operates within the Scottish college of education system and so comes within the fief of the Scottish Education Department. Unlike other holdings in this curtilage, its activities must be self-sufficient, making no claim on the public purse. In fact, its interests and its services have their origins outside of Scotland, and hydra-headed it looks in many other directions, to the British Council offices throughout the world, to the Overseas Development Administration implementing UK Government Aid Policies to international agencies like the World Bank, the Asian Development Bank and to the education policies of overseas governments who can afford to pay their way. Thus, SCEO is not simply a teaching department in a Scottish college of education; its practice, its performance and its aspirations are more in line with the concept of the key resource centres, UK-based, as identified by ODA; broad in its interests, diverse in its personnel, and flexible in its resources and in its capacity to meet the wide-ranging and rapidly changing demands of the overseas market.

With these issues in mind, ODA and the British Council in recent years determined on a policy of increased concentration on a small number of major centres, five in all, of which SCEO is one; it is the only one which is not located in a university, and the only one in Scotland, the other members of the 'big five' being based in the Universities of Bristol, Leeds, London and Newcastle. In terms of size SCEO comes second only to the Department of Education in Developing Countries in the University of London Institute of Education.

Accordingly, for the time being some 60 per cent of awards made under the auspices of ODA and the British Council are offered to the main centres in the first instance. If for one reason or another institutions in this category are unable to accept the students, the award is offered elsewhere to one that can. There is nothing sempiternal about this arrangement; it has a short life expectancy and as the pattern of demand in the training needs of overseas governments diversifies, so institutions must be prepared to adapt accordingly; if they fail, it is a short step to diminution and barely a slightly longer one to closure. ODA and the Council will match the need to the service and place the students in the institution that can provide it.

The constraints

The pattern of public expenditure in the UK in recent years has constituted a serious threat to the traditional activities of the universities and institutions operating in the Higher Education sector. Departments in all these institutions, in the face of financial constraints, borne of reductions in government expenditure, have found it not only difficult to expand but also to maintain their activities at previously accepted levels. As personnel reach retiring age or transfer to other jobs — not that there has been much activity in the latter category recently — they tend not to be replaced, so that the seed corn, as the argument goes, is in short supply. The identification of the main centres is an attempt to redress this trend; while it is not possible to maintain all the centres previously operating in the overseas market, against a declining number of awards, it is imperative to retain a few that retain some measure of capacity for regeneration.

It is difficult to identify precisely the number of awards available from one year to the next; the years 1981 and 1982 appear to have been the nadir, with perceptible increases in 1983 and again in 1984, but the reviews of the British Aid programmes carried out by the Foreign and Commonwealth Office on an annual basis make predictions for the short-term hazardous, never mind the longer term; indeed, for long-range planning purposes tomorrow is a long way off.

Until the late 1970s under the Commonwealth Education Fellow-ship Scheme the quota of awards going to education was protected; these were specifically earmarked for education and could not be re-allocated to other ministries. This arrangement put education ministries in a very favoured position *vis-à-vis* others, including those of transport, sewage, agriculture, industry and similar areas short of skilled man-power but vitally important in terms of social infrastructure or for socio-economic development. With the removal of the ringed fence, education ministries have tended to fare badly in the subsequent allocations of awards, and are now winning a much smaller proportion; the size of the cake to be shared among UK education institutions perforce must be less, and competition that much keener.

This trend is made worse by the drop in the number of students in the home market with its implicit threat for jobs traditionally secure. Increasingly the universities and institutions in the Higher Education sector are seeking to fill their vacant places from abroad and we find ourselves in competition with the peripatetic sales forces of units once complacent in their ivory towers. Competition for the overseas student is now consistently fierce and at times even frenetic.

For the time being, it has been reassuring to know that against this background Moray House can still attract a substantial share of the overseas market, as is confirmed in the following table.

Session	Enrolments	FTEs	Countries
1982–83	145	132	40
1983–84	176	161	47
1984–85*	230	190	42

[*Estimated as at November 1984]

These figures are testimony to the continuing quality of the courses provided and the college's ability and willingness to match its provision to the identifiable needs of its overseas clients. Another factor under-pinning this, of course, is the very considerable amount of low-key sales activity undertaken by a large number of college staff, both in their duties at home and in their visits abroad, activities which must continue to have high priority.

New demands

At the social end of the market SCEO's college-base was a distinct advantage in the 1960s and the 1970s, when the needs of many overseas countries were adequately met by the provision of certificate and diploma courses. In those days the identified needs were relatively straightforward, namely the basic skills required by teachers in specialist areas of the curriculum, primary and secondary, and to a lesser extent the relatively simple techniques necessary for the discharge of duties in inspection, supervision and administration. But now, some twenty years on, these overseas systems are undertaking such tasks themselves and we contemplate the needs of their teacher trainers, their curriculum developers, their education planners and their senior administrators and managers. The complexity of our provision must keep step with these developments and respond to the increasing pressure both from individual students and their governments to upgrade our courses to degree standard. There is clamant demand for this in a number of areas of identified need including Educational Management and Administration, Home Economics, English Lan-guage Teaching and throughout the Primary Education sector. Further progress in these areas is essential if Moray House is to continue to enjoy its present share of the market.

Conclusion

SCEO therefore lies at the confluence of two great tributaries, one involving the theory, practice and traditions of education in the Western World, joining with the needs of the under-resourced Third World in the other; it attempts to use the sophisticated techniques of developed societies to improve the fortunes and practice of less favoured institutions and this is a noble and rewarding calling. SCEO's overseas role is right and proper; its location in Scotland and in Edinburgh fitting; it is in accord with a long line of distinguished contributions made by Scots abroad, from eminences like David Livingstone, Mungo Park and Mary Slessor and a host of other luminaries who at various levels in education ministries and institutions overseas, 'in the colonial times', established a pattern of dedicated service to improve the quality of life in the communities and systems they served.

SCEO's presence in Scotland's capital gives its clientele access to a wide range of attractions and amenities throughout Scotland. For the college the privilege of having within its walls a large and diverse overseas population is a source of enrichment that brings its incumbents, staff and students alike, face to face with the practical applications of living in a multi-cultural society; thus the activities and interests of the parent institution are prodded to remain catholic and outward-looking. For all of these reasons SCEO and its overseas activities deserve to have a long and continuing presence in the annals of Moray House.

6

Professional development of teachers

Hugh Perfect

Introduction

Scottish education is witnessing change on an unprecedented scale. At every level from nursery school to institutions of higher education traditional practices are being examined and new approaches are being applied to familiar problems. Within early education professional roles are being redefined in the search for closer relationships between schools, their local communities and parents. In primary schools there are major national initiatives in expressive arts and environmental studies, and ways are being sought of managing progression and continuity between the primary and secondary phases of education. For the 14-16 age range the Standard Grade national development programme is effecting a fundamental transformation in every area of the curriculum and of the ways in which pupils' learning is to be assessed and their achievements recorded. At 16+ the Action Plan has raised further questions about the nature of progression and choice in the context of a modular curriculum and the relationship between secondary schools and further education establishments.

Across these broad sectional concerns, common themes can also be discerned: the importance of recognising and managing individual learning needs; the implications of micro-technology both in respect of teaching and learning, and in supporting institutional management; and the development of a curriculum which is appropriate to a pluralistic and multicultural society.

In every section of education, then, new approaches are being attempted and in every sector the perennial problem of managing change is being encountered: how can teachers be familiarised with new strategies and helped to incorporate these into their ongoing professional work in classrooms?

The Scottish context

The National Committee for the In-service Training of Teachers (NCITT) was established in 1967 and reconstituted as a standing advisory body in 1976 with the following remit:

> To simulate and keep under review the provision of in-service training for teachers on a national level . . . to advise the Secretary of State for Scotland and to consult and advise colleges of education and other agencies on matters relating to in-service training.

In October 1979 a Report, 'The Future of In-Service Training in Scotland'[1] (the Green Report), was submitted to the Secretary of State. Its principal recommendations included the creation of a realistic national policy for staff development, the recognition of the need for a more formal and open planning process for in-service training, and the development of a more systematic range of award-bearing courses with a central role being played by the National Committee itself.

The Secretary of State responded favourably to some of these recommendations:[2] the Committee's suggestion that there should be a national policy for staff development was endorsed and the need for a structure of award-bearing courses was accepted. Working parties of NCITT undertook an in-depth study of the nature of staff development for teachers and of the provision of a coherent system of award-bearing courses. Subsequently, two Reports, 'Arrangements for the Staff Development of Teachers'[3] and 'The Development of the Three Tier Structure of Award-Bearing Courses',[4] were forwarded in June 1984 to the Secretary of State for his consideration.

The Staff Development Report, following a review of current practice, identified general principles according to which any model of professional development might be judged. These principles fall into three categories:

> (i) the professional dimension: staff development should be viewed as an important element of the normal role of a teacher or manager in educational agencies and as a continuous process through which the professional competence of staff is maintained and enhanced throughout their careers.
>
> (ii) the organisational dimension: staff development needs to be seen as a planned and co-ordinated process supported by explicit institutional policies. However, staff should be consulted about, and have the opportunity of participating

in, all the stages involved in the planning and organisation of staff development activities.

(iii) the process of programme management: activities have to be carefully selected and designed so that they are clearly matched to the needs of the institution as a whole and of the individual members of staff.

Following the approach advocated by a number of authors,[5, 6] the National Committee supported the concept of staff development as:

... the planned process whereby the effectiveness of staff, collectively and individually, is enhanced in response to new knowledge, new ideas and changing circumstances in order to improve, directly or indirectly, the quality of (students') education.[3]

A model of staff development, based upon the above principles, was elaborated, with an emphasis on the following interrelated processes:[3]

(i) identification of needs

(ii) matching of appropriate activities

(iii) monitoring and evaluation

The first of these processes is without doubt the most complex. The staff development needs of any educational institution will be as varied as the individuals comprising its staff. Moreover, at a time when recruitment is relatively restricted and when opportunities for career advancement are curtailed, staff development has a critically important role to play in ensuring that morale and commitment are maintained.

An important issue concerns how such a variety of individual needs can be organised within an agreed institutional policy. A process of planned needs identification might well raise expectations in staff which could not be met by an institution from any resources available to it at the time. Consequently, a staff development policy should involve the collaborative drawing up of priorities in respect of individual, group and institutional needs.

The importance of such collaborative planning has been highlighted by a number of research projects, including the Rand Change Agent Study.[7] Findings have indicated that where staff development programmes are planned and implemented in a 'top-down' model, involving little consultation with individual members of staff, they are more likely to fail to meet their objectives. Similarly, individual staff-initiated work, lacking any broad-based institutional support, is also more likely to be unsuccessful. The inherent tension which can exist in the process of staff development has been recognised by a number of workers in this field. The need to view staff development as a co-operative initiative has been aptly summarised by Elliott:

> The professional development of teachers is a self-determining process bounded in collegial discussion, through which shared understandings of both professional tasks and the means of accomplishing them are progressively generated.[8]

The second feature of the model involves the provision of appropriate activities to meet identified needs. A wide range of in-service activities is available to educational staff in Scotland. The majority of these are school- or agency-based, and are planned and implemented by individual schools for the benefit of their own staffs, often in collaboration with outside consultants such as education authority or college of education staff. Recently, some education authorities have developed programmes of day closures in their secondary schools, authorised by the SED, in order to support the staff development necessary for the introduction of the Scottish Standard Grade. A variety of short courses is also available to teachers with the main providers being education authorities and the colleges of education. The NCITT itself sponsors an annual programme of such courses, following a process of consultation which involves all the principal interested parties of Scottish education with regard to priorities. National courses attempt to examine in depth the implications of the most significant and important recent educational developments and course reports are published with the intention of extending the national discussions in the fields concerned.

Research has also shown that where major professional development is required, involving substantial changes in the skills of staff, the necessary support has to be sustained and appropriately resourced over an extended period of time.[9] Where necessary, such support has to be provided at the classroom level for the individual teacher, in recognition of the fact that teacher-learning is a long-term process. Thus, whilst day closure programmes and short courses are appropriate in-service activities in which the development of teacher awareness and knowledge is the identified purpose, other strategies have to be employed in which the implementation of new, and substantially different, pedagogic skills is involved. Consequently, the NCITT has recommended that a coherent and systematic programme of post-qualifying award-bearing courses for teachers should be developed, based upon three levels of award[4] as follows:

Level 1: Certificate courses of one term full-time study or part-time equivalent

Level 2: Diploma/In-Service BEd degree courses of one year/four terms full-time study or part-time equivalent

Level 3   Master's degrees of four terms full-time study or part-time equivalent

The provision of such courses is the responsibility of the colleges of education, the universities, including the Open University, and the Scottish central institutions. The National Committee has also emphasised the importance of external validation for these courses through CNAA or SCOVACT.

It is hoped that over the next decade a planned system of award-bearing courses for teachers will evolve under the aegis of the National Committee. Such a scheme would provide opportunities for teachers to enter at an appropriate level, whether Certificate or Diploma, and to progress to the level of award consistent with their own professional needs. The development of courses based on a 30-hour module of curriculum construction would also enhance opportunities for credit accumulation and credit transfer. There is also a noticeable trend for institutions to offer courses in a variety of modes — full-time, block-release, day-release, sandwich, part-time or open-learning — partly in response to the increasing difficulties which education authorities are experiencing in supporting full-time secondment.

The final process of the model emphasises the importance of monitoring and evaluation. Such a process should enable an institution to examine whether its intentions, as specified in policy and procedures, are reflected in actual outcomes. The complexity of the process of needs identification, the drawing up of individual and institutional priorities, the matching of appropriate in-service activities to such priorities, and the effectiveness of the programme in bringing about the professional development expected — all of these require careful and continuing evaluation.

Implications for the college

During recent years there has been a major change in the conventional role of college staff: from being mainly involved in initial training work, staff now undertake a wide variety of school/agency-based consultancy work and contribute to an increasing programme of post-qualifying award-bearing courses. Indeed, the agency-based and college-based in-service activities of the college now make up a significant element of the total work of the institution. Since 1977 these types of in-service activities have been recognised and supported by the SED through a specific staff allowance. At Moray House this allowance amounted to nearly 25 per cent of the college's total staffing entitlement in session 1983/84.

The principal purposes of the agency-based aspect of the college's in-service work include support for agencies in curriculum planning, development and management; the development of teaching resources; consultation on matters such as teaching, assessment and evaluation strategies; and work in agencies specifically sponsored by regional and other authorities. The overall aim of such activities is essentially one of assisting the staff development of professionals in the field, whether teachers, community workers or social workers. The scale of college involvement can be judged from the 1983-84 statistics: nearly one thousand such activities were planned and implemented, involving a total of over ten thousand field professionals.

However, it would be all too easy to allow such work to develop in an *ad hoc* manner. The college has to ensure that its resources are committed to meeting the priorities of education authorities, agencies and, where appropriate, professionals in the field. It is essential, in this matching process, that procedures be established to enable the college to liaise with education authorities and schools so that staff are deployed in ways which acknowledge established priorities.

The college believes that the agency-based work of staff should benefit not only individual schools but also professionals in the wider context and consequently supports the dissemination of reports, resource packs and software. In recent years the college's Environmental Studies Development Unit, under the directorship of Tom Masterton, has been involved in the production of over forty publications through the Resources for Environmental Studies Teaching initiative. These resources have been based on close collaboration between college staff and teachers in primary schools. A similar programme is planned by the newly established Multicultural Resource and Development Unit. Other agency-based activities which have led to major reports that have been widely used in schools include the work by Cecile McLachlan and Elizabeth Mackenzie on aesthetic subjects in Special Education and Tony Van der Kuyl's software pack to support Modern Studies. In addition, several resource packs relating to subjects in the Standard Grade development programme have also been prepared and disseminated.

With regard to post-qualifying award-bearing courses, the college's strategic intention is to be able to offer as wide a variety of such courses as is feasible within the resources available. Because of the necessity of ensuring that these courses are related to the professional needs of the teachers and other staff enrolled on them and thereby credible in their eyes, the college planning procedures involve certain key elements. All such courses are designed to fall within one of the award categories comprising the national three-tier structure. The policy of the Board of Studies is that all its award-bearing courses should be subject to external validation, either through CNAA or SCOVACT. Where appropriate, course planning is undertaken in relation to existing national guidelines. The college is also committed to the collaborative planning of such courses with practising professionals from the field.

For some groups of teachers the college already has an extensive and varied programme of award-bearing courses. For primary teachers the opportunities available include the In-Service BEd (Primary) degree and honours degree, the DPSE in Early Education and the Associate-ship in Upper Primary Education. Courses available for teachers interested in aspects of special educational needs include the DPSE in Special Educational Needs (Recorded Pupils), the Diploma course for Teachers of Deaf and Partially Deaf Children, the Diploma course for Teachers of Visually Impaired Children, the DPSE in Special Educational Needs (Learning Difficulties Primary) and the DPSE in Special Educational Needs (Learning Difficulties Secondary). The college also collaborates with the University of Stirling and Jordanhill College of Education in offering an MEd in Special Educational Needs. While the college offers a number of courses — for example, in management, guidance, and computing — it has not as yet developed such a comprehensive range of award-bearing courses for secondary teachers. With the support of education authorities and other interested agencies, and the agreement of the SED, the college's intention is that a modular Certificate/Diploma system of courses should be collaboratively planned to meet the needs of this group of professionals.

College staff development policy and procedures

An institution which is committed to providing professional support for teachers and others needs to ensure that its own staff also have the opportunity to continue their professional development. The college recognises that the staff development process ought to be based on an articulation of needs and that this is a collaborative exercise between the college as a whole and individual members of staff. Whilst individual members of staff are best fitted to identify their own staff development needs, this process should be undertaken within the context of the established needs of the college. The process of needs analysis consequently should be systematic, continuous, participatory, and carried out within the framework of agreed college procedures.

The necessity to obtain the commitment of staff to their own personal professional development and the need to retain an institutional perspective is managed through two related processes. All staff are offered the opportunity to discuss their individual staff development needs, with this process taking place against a framework of institutional priorities as recorded in the College Development Plan. However, this institutional statement is itself a summary of the views of all the areas of college life obtained through a process of consultation.

Each year the Board of Studies identifies those major staff development needs which are regarded as priorities in relation to its ongoing programme of work. Such institutional needs are matched to the strategic view of college developments recorded in the College Development Plan. Thus for the academic session 1984-85 the College Development Plan identified a number of priority areas. These included the need to create opportunities for staff to undertake sustained experience in schools in preparation for work on primary courses or for work relating to Standard Grade; the necessity for offering appropriate retraining for those staff wishing to make more extensive contributions to the ELT courses of the Scottish Centre for Education Overseas; and the organisation of a programme of courses to enable staff to develop the competence to handle micro-computers in relation to their own work.

The staff development needs of the college are met in a variety of ways including full-time or part-time secondment for recognised retraining purposes including the obtaining of further qualifications, and by attendance at short courses and conferences. In addition, the college's staff development programme includes an annual series of staff conferences. Topics are chosen which relate to the whole range of college work rather than to any specific area. Recent issues have included profiling, institutional and course evaluation, the maintenance of academic and professional standards, college teaching and learning strategies, and academic counselling. In the field of international education the staff of the college's Scottish Centre for Education Overseas are extensively involved in British Council and Overseas Development Agency work and negotiate with a large number of individual overseas governments and their agencies. Major consultancy activities are undertaken in many countries, with work in the current session involving staff in Senegal, India, Bangladesh, and Tanzania. The staff development policy also recognises that whilst a substantial component of its programme of supported activities can be achieved through a formal programme of activities, staff development also takes place in less formal ways and is fostered whenever staff meet to plan or evaluate a course, engage in research or development activities, or collaborate with colleagues in the field.

Conclusion

At a time of substantial social and educational change it is necessary to ensure that staff are provided with the necessary resources to develop those new understandings and skills which developments in professional practice require. Staff development has to be seen as an integral part of the professional activities of all staff whether in schools or in institutions of higher education. The climate of institutions should be supportive and should provide opportunities for self-evaluation and counselling. Successful innovation can be accomplished only if it is facilitated through a comprehensive and sensitively organised programme of staff development. No matter how competently new knowledge and skills have been developed, their application and implementation into the actual professional work of individual members of staff require a positive and conscious commitment on the part of those staff. Such a commitment is more likely to be achieved through a supportive institutional climate.

References

1. National Committee for the In-Service Training of Teachers (1979) — 'The Future of In-Service Training in Scotland.' A report submitted by NCITT to the Secretary of State for Scotland.

2. Kirk, G. and Fairlie, T. (eds) (1982) — 'Perspectives in In-Service Training for Teachers.' Report of conference promoted by NCITT in association with the SED and Moray House College of Education.

3. National Committee for the In-Service Training of Teachers (1984) — 'Arrangements for the Staff Development of Teachers.' A report submitted to the Secretary of State for Scotland.

4. National Committee for the In-Service Training of Teachers (1984) — 'The Development of the Three-Tier Structure of Award-Bearing Courses.' A report submitted to the Secretary of State for Scotland.

5. Bailey, P. (1975) — *Educational Administration*, 4 (1), 11.

6. Billing, G. E. (1977) — 'The Nature and Scope of Staff Development in Institutions of Higher Education', in Elton, L. and Simmonds, K. (eds), *Staff Development in Higher Education*. SRHE.

7. McLaughlin, M. L. and Marsh, D. D. (1978) — 'Staff Development and School Change', *Teachers College Record*, Volume 80, No. 1.

8. Elliott, J. (1983)   'School-Focussed INSET and Research into Teacher Education', in *Cambridge Journal of Education*, Volume 13, p. 23.

9. Joyce, B. R. and   'Improving In-Service Training: The Message of Re-
   Showers, B. (1980)   search', in *Educational Leadership*, pp. 379-85.

7

Research

John Wilson and Hugh Perfect

Historical perspectives

Stephen Wiseman[1] remarked that 'research must be seen by the student to be an essential and inevitable strand in the professional education of the teacher, and one of the most powerful weapons in the battle to improve the competence, the expertise, the status and the prestige of the teaching profession'. There is no doubt that quality research which leads to major publications and to practical implementation ensures the visibility of an institution and of the individuals who conduct it. Moray House's international reputation as a teacher training college is probably as much a reflection of the prestige of the Moray House Verbal Reasoning tests as of the quality of its courses. The tests were developed in the 1930s and 1940s under the direction of the psychometrist Principal, Godfrey Thomson, who combined that role with the Professorship of Education at the University of Edinburgh. Subsequently, when the posts of Principal of the College and Professor of Education were separated, the Moray House tests continued to be produced in the University, which used the proceeds from their sale to fund the Godfrey Thomson Unit for Academic Assessment.

Under Thomson's successor, W. B. Inglis, research on aspects of intelligence testing was undertaken by John Sutherland, principal lecturer in education, and by James Maxwell, principal lecturer in psychology. Maxwell[2] eventually took secondment at the end of his career to conduct a major study of standards of reading in Scotland. Meanwhile another psychologist, Jack Duthie,[3] had made an important contribution to the development of the new field of research on classroom observation. The case for the introduction of auxiliaries into Scottish primary classrooms was largely based on the evidence reported in the 1971 *Primary School Survey*,[3] a work also important for its theoretical contribution. Duthie went on to a chair in the education department at Stirling University, and it is interesting to note that two other key staff in that department, Donald McIntyre and Arnold Morrison, were formerly members of staff in Moray House in the mid-1960s. Although the Principal at the time, Douglas McIntosh, was a noted champion of research — he chaired the Scottish Council for Research in Education for a lengthy period, and played an important role in the creation of the National Inter-College Committee for Educational Research (NICCER) in 1974 — little in the way of sustained research was supported by the college, and indeed the very notion that the college might set up a research committee to promote research was rejected out of hand. In the 1960s and 1970s, although a few members of staff, like Bert McCann, were initially appointed to undertake research, for the most part research was very much a matter of individuals 'working away in the corners', with most staff too exhausted by the daily round of teaching and teaching practice supervision to get involved. One of the very few people able to devote a substantial amount of time to research was Fergus McBride of the Primary Education Department, who developed, with the assistance of the Vice-Principal, Peter McNaught, Stage 3 of the Edinburgh Reading Test (ages 10:0 to 12:6), the other stages (i.e. 1, 2 and 4) being prepared by a research team at the Godfrey Thomson Unit. The test was subsequently published by Hodder & Stoughton Educational, and has been widely used, for example by HMI in the 1978 survey reported in *Learning and Teaching in Primary 4 and Primary 7*.[4] Such has been the success of the test that the publishers readily agreed to a proposal from Ron McKenzie and colleagues for the development of a parallel version to Stage 3. This was published in 1982. A shorter transfer stage reading achievement test has also been commissioned.

The setting up of NICCER in 1974 provided a national college forum for discussion about research, and brought the Scottish Education Department's newly established Research and Intelligence Unit sharply into focus in the stimulus and direction of college research. It was not until 1979, however, that the Moray House College Research and Development (R and D) Committee was set up. The college's resort to the Council for National Academic Awards (CNAA) for validation of its courses has further stimulated research since strong research relating to teaching is a prerequisite for institutional recognition. SED meanwhile recognised that 8 per cent of college staffing should be for activities under the heading of research, development and retraining, and half of this was agreed informally for research. The publication in 1979 of the Green Report[5] on the three-tier structure of in-service training envisaged colleges offering MSc and PhD level awards, validated either through a neighbouring university, or CNAA or another validating body, but this aspect is something for the future.

In the past it would be probably true to say that Moray House has produced more researchers than research. But the climate has changed in recent years, and the scale of activity has increased as the projects described below illustrate. The notion of research, too, has changed in important ways. How far students have been aware of research activity in the college is a moot point, although in a number of courses some effort has been consistently made to introduce them to techniques and current research preoccupations and findings.

College policy

In 1979 the Board of Studies set up a standing committee on Research and Development. The committee is chaired by an Assistant Principal. Its membership is drawn from different areas of the college; it also includes individuals from outwith college with a professional interest in the subject. Research is defined broadly as including the acquisition, dissemination and application of knowledge, skills and techniques, which can be promoted by means of fundamental or applied research, consultancy, scholarship and professional practice. It is an expectation of college management that all members of academic staff will participate in research as part of their normal professional responsibilities, and research is now regarded as equal in importance to such other activities as teaching and consultancy. Resources for research, in the form of time and money, have been made available, although they are still less than ideal. SED, for example, recognises staff time for research as a specific component of the college's staffing entitlement, while the college competes for funds provided annually by SED to NICCER, and may also obtain support from other agencies such as the Economic and Social Research Council (ESRC), the Overseas Development Agency (ODA) and various national trusts. SED also provides colleges with an annual discretionary grant (currently £2,500 for Moray House) which enables support to be offered to a number of small scale and/or feasibility studies. In session 1983-84 the college housed 18 nationally-funded and 18 college-funded projects involving contributions from 30 per cent of the college's academic staff. Researchers inevitably make substantial and often urgent demands upon general college resources including accommodation, library, computer and reprographic services. In meeting these the college fulfils its responsibilities for housing projects and encouraging the 'development of an ethos of research'.[6]

The Research and Development Committee is often faced with more research proposals than can be supported from the resources available. The Committee seeks to evaluate research submissions by means of a number of criteria, spelled out in a policy document, which stipulates a *proactive* role for the college in identifying priority areas for research. These criteria include that 'research should have potential for yielding findings which are pertinent and relevant to the framework of the priorities identified either within the College Development Plan, or in the national context, (and) could have a positive impact on the professional activities of college staff or professionals in the field'. A further criterion is that research proposals should be clearly defined and the chosen methods of study relevant. The aim is to ensure that work. undertaken by college staff should be of such a value and standard that it positively contributes to the college's role as a recognised centre for education, research and development, and that it complements and illuminates other major aspects of the college's work, assisting college policy making and problem solving in areas such as evaluation. On occasions the Research and Development Committee will commission studies to guide staff on possible issues for research in areas where no proposals have been forthcoming. In short, the committee takes the view that certain areas of research have greater value than others, 'value' being defined in terms, for example, of the presence of characteristics such as applicability, practicability and professional relevance. While seeking to identify priorities in this way, the Research and Development Committee also recognises the importance of supporting proposals which exhibit an intrinsic excellence, and yet do not fall within the priorities identified.

In 1984-85 priority areas included multicultural education (from an institutional perspective and in terms of national needs), micro-computers, special educational needs, and curriculum development at national level, and the programme which was funded broadly reflected these priorities.

Recent research projects

There are a number of ways to categorise research projects. College Research Bulletins classify in terms of sources of funding, but this tends to underestimate the significance of some small-scale research. The approach adopted here is more target-centred, although the distinctions are by no means clear cut, in terms of (a) research related to college teaching, (b) research linked to policy issues within the wider education system and (c) research in support of national developments in the curriculum of primary and secondary schools. A further category is research undertaken out of personal interest, or for personal gain (such as PhD projects), but this aspect is not considered here. Moreover, it is not possible to do more than exemplify some of the work that has been undertaken since the R and D Committee was set up: complete listings are available in the three Bulletins of the R and D Committee published in 1981, 1982 and 1984.

Undertaking research today is not a one-man effort: it involves co-operation from colleagues in college and in the field, and access to a range of essential support services, as the following account makes clear.

Research related to college teaching

The curriculum of college courses in teacher education and community studies has evolved markedly over the past 15 years, partly through the influence of new technology such as educational television, partly through the development of new courses, and partly through the development of educational and social research and its influence on our conceptions of learning and teaching.

One of the neglected areas of educational research is special educational needs. The British Sign Language (BSL) project was set up in 1979 under the direction of Mary Brennan (English department) and Martin Colville (School of Community Studies/Scottish Centre for the Education of the Deaf) to examine the nature of the communication system used by profoundly deaf people in Britain. The impetus for the research included the recognition that BSL was virtually unstudied and unanalysed, the increasing use of some form of sign communication in schools for the deaf, and the realisation that many of the difficulties faced by hearing people trying to learn BSL were caused by a lack of information concerning BSL structure. The primary aim of the project was to provide a detailed description of the key areas of BSL and to examine the implications of such a description in relation to general linguistic issues. The project was the first in a college of education in Scotland to receive Social Science Research Council (SSRC) funding on the termination of three years of SED funding: it has produced its own publications and videotapes.

College researchers have been stimulated by the need to develop materials to assist them in teaching, and by an awareness of the ways in which students react to and cope with the demands of their courses. One of the principal researchers has been Margot Cameron-Jones of the college's Education department. She has worked on two interrelated projects in the period since 1977. In the first — the Pedagogics Project

(1977-80) — a foundation course on primary teaching was produced. This linked the kind of study of teaching students would meet in theory classes with that they would meet in college classes preparing them directly for teaching practice. A key role was played by staff in the ETV department in filming serving teachers at work in the 'naturalistic' situation of their own classroom. Staff from the college's department of Primary Education were also involved. The products of the project were a student's workbook, and a series of related videotapes. Part I of the workbook focused on aspects of classroom life; Part II raised questions of classroom structuring in a number of standard teaching situations. Each section included observation points, topics for discussion, and a brief background note on related literature on classroom research. The materials have had a wide sale within the UK and overseas. They have now been fully incorporated into the programme for the college's new CNAA validated BEd degree, which commenced in 1984-85. Margot Cameron-Jones followed this up with the Primary Teaching Practice Project (1980-82) in which she and her team attempted to implement some of the teaching practice recommendations of the joint SED/General Teaching Council for Scotland's Sneddon Committee.[7] The project developed a Teaching Practice Manual, which described training roles and procedures. It also offered training in supervisory skills for most of the co-operating teachers and tutors involved, and sought to change tutors' activities during their visits to students in project schools by including three-way meetings of supervising teacher, student and tutor. Over two hundred teachers, students and tutors participated in the project.

Another project with major implications for college teaching is Pathways to the Professions (1980-84) under the direction of Paquita McMichael, of the Psychology department. This project was developed to find the origins of the widely reported hostility between social workers and community workers and between both these professions and teachers. Pilot and main inquiry questionnaires and interviews confirmed suspicions that even amongst students there are significant differences in attitudes. Whether they are mature or post-graduate students or younger three-year students, the social and community workers are more socially and educationally radical in outlook than primary teachers. Their views on education derive partly from their school experiences, which in general were negatively perceived. Many ascribe their critical attitudes to teachers to these experiences and to student teachers' political conservatism and apathy over issues such as educational cuts. Student teachers' attitudes to social and community workers were largely positive though uninformed.

In order to prevent the hardening of hostile attitudes detected amongst the entering social and community work students a series of intervention projects was begun. First-year student teachers were amalgamated with first-year social and community workers for a course in social psychology in which they shared lectures, discussion groups and experimental procedures. The course was favourably received overall leading to some intergroup association out of the classroom. However, though the student teachers (initially more positively disposed) became yet more positive in their response to the social and community work student group, the students of the latter group remained neutral in their attitude. A number of voluntary placements in social and community work settings which were enjoyed and considered valuable were arranged for student teachers.

Members of staff in the Scottish Centre for Education Overseas have been researching ways of enhancing the language teaching skills of their students, with implications for classroom teaching. For example, Michael Wallace's project on 'Applications of Microteaching to the Teaching of English as a Second or Foreign Language in Teacher Training Situations' (1978-81) developed skill-based modules aimed at the teacher training needs of developing countries where hardware is unlikely to be available. Each module consisted of three sections: a rationale which describes the skill, an observation schedule which helps the trainee to interpret some classroom data chosen to relate to the skill, and a microteaching section which specifies the microteaching tasks and makes further suggestions for self-observation. Leslie Dickinson, William Cousin and David Carver focused on aspects of self-assessment in English language teaching (1981-82), an issue which emerged as salient in the ongoing programme in self-directed learning of English offered to overseas students. A further project involving the use of cloze procedures (finding an appropriate word to fit a context from which a key word is missing) suggested that the computer programmes devised could function better for self-instructional rather than assessment purposes.

Research related to policy issues

The present interest in the United Kingdom in the relationship between research and policy making stems from the publication of the Rothschild Reports[8] on research funding. Research and policy making is also the subject of the 1985 *World Yearbook of Education*.[9] Research may be funded specifically to clarify policy issues, or its findings may have implications for policy which only become clear subsequently.

There is general consensus that research rarely has a direct 'impact' on action. Its role is often defined as being to illuminate issues by clarification and by developing a vocabulary for structuring interpretations of a particular field, so that an agenda for action can be defined.

One uniquely Scottish development in the field of policy oriented research with which the college has been associated is the Scottish Educational Data Archive (SEDA) held within the Centre for Educational Sociology in the University of Edinburgh. The data comprise questionnaire responses from a series of surveys of Scottish school leavers conducted since 1962: one purpose of the archive is to enable researchers to construct an alternative version of Scottish secondary education to that presented in official reports. The data bank — which includes information on the characteristics of college entrants — has been offered to users in the education system on a collaborative model, both in terms of access to the data, and in the contribution of questions for data sweeps to be conducted in subsequent years. A number of college staff have voluntarily trained as data users, and Winifred Keeves of the School of Community Studies and Andy Hocking of Geography took advantage of one-term secondments to SEDA in 1980-81 and 1981-82.

One perennial issue in Scottish education is corporal punishment. For long there has been a consensus that it would be desirable to phase it out, but how? A research report by Chris Cumming of the Education department — *Making the Change*[10] — provided a constructive answer to that question, and would appear to have had a major influence in shaping government statements on abolition. The project illustrates something of the demands suddenly placed on members of college staff, and the complex nature of staff involvement in educational research. Chris Cumming was called on at short notice to analyse data collected by a researcher at SCRE who had resigned for domestic reasons. With the co-operation of the Convention of Scottish Local Authorities (COSLA) he was able to recruit a small team of teachers, educational psychologists and others who assisted him in writing up the evidence already collected and in further adding to it by visits to schools and discussions with headteachers and teaching staff. The report demonstrated that some Scottish secondary schools had been able to develop strategies for handling difficult and disruptive pupils without recourse to the 'last resort' of corporal punishment.

One of the principal policy issues of the 1980s — in England and Wales, and the USA as well as in Scotland — is teaching quality. SED has funded three projects in the Education department on this theme.

Two of these are staff development projects, viz. Focus on Teaching related to primary education and under the direction of Margot Cameron-Jones, and the Secondary Schools Staff Development Project directed by Chris Cumming. The third project — the Criteria of Teacher Selection (CATS) — is directed by John Wilson. Several members of staff are associated with each project as part of an SED concern to develop an apprenticeship research model whereby inexperienced researchers would learn by working alongside those with greater experience.

The two staff development projects have moved in different directions: Margot Cameron-Jones has focused on action research and the reflective primary teacher, the objective being to increase teachers' critical awareness, use and modification of pedagogic concepts in the course of their own day-to-day work in classrooms. To this end materials are being developed which will support teachers in analysis of their own practice. Chris Cumming's project has been concerned to build up a descriptive account of how staff at different levels in secondary schools attempt to identify staff development needs and to realise these. This project, too, has adopted an interventionist strategy in monitoring in-service activities planned on the basis of meeting staff's expressed needs.

The CATS project has surveyed current practice on selection for initial teacher training in the colleges of education in Scotland[11] and also developed, in response to an invitation from the college, a model of selection for the BEd degree in 1984-85 radically different from any in current use. This involves candidates attending at college for one day and providing evidence to teams of assessors in a variety of situations. Besides providing written evidence and having a half-hour interview the candidates are observed undertaking a practical teaching task, in a one-to-one situation. The college has decided to repeat the selection process for BEd in 1985-86 and to extend it to post-graduate primary applicants.

Research and development work linked to national developments in the school curriculum

The 1970s and 1980s have witnessed major developments within the school curriculum. Much of this has stemmed from the curriculum development machinery created around the Consultative Committee on the Curriculum (CCC) and its sub-committees on primary education (COPE) and secondary education (COSE). At secondary level the development programme set in train following upon the adoption of the recommendations of the Munn and Dunning Reports has been specially significant.

With regard to the primary curriculum, Sinclair Macleod's Primary Science Development Project (1981-84) has worked with staff from over 150 schools to establish the forms of support staff thought they required to overcome the practical problems of teaching science and to assist in the development of a policy for science in schools. The project, which is directed by a member of the Biology department, has also concerned itself with the place of science in the early years of primary school, and links between science, health education and practical mathematics. It has established clusters of schools throughout the country and has produced booklets and video materials on these themes. Another worker in the field of primary science has been Arthur Gibbons of the Physics department who has been involved in revising teachers' resource materials, while in the field of environmental studies Tom Masterton, in Geography, and colleagues have brought out a wide range of materials in the series 'Resources for Environmental Study Teaching'. One of these, on the environmental study of woodland, was produced by Livingston Russell of the Biology department.

Some projects are undertaking work relevant for both primary and secondary sectors. These include the Scottish Resources in Schools Project initiated by the CCC, and directed by Eric Simpson of the History department. This project aims to assist teachers to enrich courses in the fields of language and literature, social and environmental studies, and the creative and aesthetic arts, by reference to the Scottish dimension and cultural traditions, and thereby foster a greater degree of awareness of the indigenous cultures of Scotland. Another is the project on Resources on the Third World for Teachers in Primary and Secondary Schools by Andy Hocking. This aims to produce visual and other resources for primary schools on the theme of African environments with studies of peoples and their ways of living in country and town. This project will also produce materials for secondary teachers on minerals and energy in West Africa.

At secondary level some of the major work has been in regard to the development of item banks of test materials. Jean Fergusson (Mathematics) directed a project which constructed an item bank of over 1,000 short response questions in mathematics, suitable for use in the assessment of pupils in the lower ability range of S3 and S4, and explored how teachers use the bank (and construct their own tests from its items). Peter Barker (Computing) has contributed to the development of a computer-assisted system for producing tests, marking pupils' responses and producing reports for pupils and teachers, both for the test currently being taken and on a curriculum basis. An application of a computer-assisted item banking and reporting system in science has also been developed and piloted.

A further project in a subject area of the school curriculum where research has only infrequently been undertaken, is the Assessment in Home Economics project directed by Allison Long (Home Economics). This has involved the development of case studies of teachers working in schools and explaining the nature and the meaning of assessments undertaken. Additionally, Pat Mowat (Modern Studies) has developed modules for modern studies as part of the Standard Grade Development Programme.

In the field of special educational needs, a good example of an integrated project is that undertaken by Cecile McLachlan (Visual Arts) with mildly mentally and physically handicapped children. This involved college staff from Physical Education (Liz Mackenzie) and English (Gordon Liddell) as well as Art. The project is preparing a film (and an accompanying handbook) to illustrate the ways in which the specially devised course contributed to the children's development.

Finally, three projects show the response of college staff to individually perceived problems which led them to undertake research and pursue funding. Eileen Francis, of the Speech Unit, was concerned with reticence among college students, and this interest extended into her exploring ways of developing discussion skills amongst pupils at secondary school, especially in regard to aspects of the curriculum where discussion is a principal teaching mode. SED funded the 'Discussion Skills Project' in 1981-82, with the aim of developing awareness and insight into discussion group processes and of developing skills in discussion group management among teachers in local secondary schools. Subsequently in 1982-83 the college funded the establishment of a 'Discussion Development Group' to provide in-service training courses and a resource base for secondary school teachers. The project is receiving further SED funding over 1984-86.

Lionel Jackson (English) found little work had been undertaken on non-fiction reading in secondary certificate courses and so surveyed teachers on attitudes and usage. He also obtained reactions to selected passages of prose which he had compiled. In addition to a publication and several articles on work to date, a further collection of passages for use in the lower stages of the secondary school is in course of preparation.

Mike Hildred (Art) was concerned to develop the curriculum in art appreciation. He devised a programme which made use of the wealth of collections available in Edinburgh galleries by focusing on the postcard reproductions of the works of art themselves, both in terms of their creation and their relationship to the original paintings. This idea has been piloted and incorporated as a module within the Standard Grade programme.

Dissemination of research

It is one thing to do research; it is another to communicate its findings to others. Educational research is rarely seen by the media as important to report, and even within the educational world there are many conflicting priorities which may distract the target audience's attention. In fact there is a variety of ways in which researchers may seek to ensure that their work becomes more widely known.

First, of course, there is the process of the research itself, which may involve co-operation with many colleagues in schools and college. Second, for major projects, there is the role of the advisory committee which invariably includes senior education authority personnel, teachers, HMI and other professionals. An Advisory Committee serves as a watchdog on a project and proffers advice to researchers, but its involvement in project thinking can also serve to affect the attitudes of the members themselves. Third, researchers explore ideas by means of seminars and conferences, and the findings of research are often featured strongly in in-service courses. Researchers, too, contribute to conferences organised by bodies such as the Scottish Educational Research Association (SERA) and specialist groups, and several college staff have presented papers to international conferences such as those organised by the Association for Teacher Education in Europe (ATEE). Many projects produce newsletters and bulletins which are ideally short, eye appealing and easy to read and which provide ready access to current thinking. More sustained articles may appear in *Times Educational Supplement Scotland*, *Scottish Educational Review* and other journals, and in bulletins of the Scottish Curriculum Development Service. Within the college a programme of informal research seminars is held from time to time, and the college publishes periodically a Bulletin of its research and development activities. Major SED funded projects are also listed in SED's annual Register of Research.

Conclusion

Inevitably a chapter such as this must end by raising questions about the quality of the research so far undertaken by the institution, and the conditions under which the quality of that research may be maintained and enhanced. Research depends on individuals with ideas, skills and determination to undertake the hard and detailed work involved; it also depends on a context in which management is committed to supporting research and translates that commitment into positive support in terms of time, money, accommodation and other resources which demonstrate understanding of the nature of the research process.

Looking back to the 1930s and 1940s there is no doubt that someone of vision was at the helm, although many today would question the direction in which energies were channelled. In the 1950s, 1960s and 1970s while the evidence of talent amongst the staff is undeniable, the context for research was largely unresponsive; research was principally done by universities. Today things seem to be different. First, there is evidence of widespread involvement of many staff in research and development work; second, a number of staff have directed work of national and even international significance, helped in many cases, it should be noted, by the services of often outstanding research workers on short-term contracts, and paid poorly for their efforts; third, the institutional context, as this chapter indicates, is more responsive than at any previous time, although constant reappraisal of what can be afforded (in time and money) is also a feature. But does all this add up to evidence of a sea-change in attitudes to research, reflected in staff membership of research associations, in subscriptions to research journals, and in the reading and discussion of research publications? Stephen Wiseman would have been heartened by the improvement in the status of research in Moray House over the past 20 years, as he would have been impressed by the range of activity which is now undertaken in its name; at the same time he would probably have seen scope for further enquiry into how far research had become part of the woodwork of the institution.

References

1. Wiseman, S. (1967)   'The Role of Research in Colleges of Education', in *Educational Research in Colleges of Education*. SRHE, mimeo.

2. Maxwell, J. (1977)   *Reading Progress from 8 to 15*. NFER.

3. Duthie, J. (1970)   *Primary School Survey: A Study of the Teacher's Day*. HMSO.

4. SED (1980)   *Learning and Teaching in Primary 4 and Primary 7*. HMSO.

5. National Committee for the In-Service Training of Teachers (1981)   'The Future of In-Service Training in Scotland' (The Green Report), mimeo.

6. CNAA (1984) *Research and Related Activities: Policy Statement*, mimeo.
7. SED/GTC (1978) *Learning to Teach* (the Sneddon Report). HMSO.
8. Rothschild, Lord (1971 and 1972) *The Organisation and Management of Government Research and Development* (Cmnd 4814). *A Framework for Government Research and Development* (Cmnd 5046). HMSO, London.
9. Nisbet, J. D., Nisbet, S. and Megarry, J. (eds) (1985) *Research, Policy and Practice: World Yearbook of Education 1985.* Kogan Page.
10. Cumming, C. E. *et al.* (1981) *Making the Change.* Hodder & Stoughton.
11. Wilson, J. D. *et al.* (1984) 'Selecting "the best": entry to initial teacher training in the Colleges of Education in Scotland.' *Scottish Educational Review*, 16 (2), 88–103.

8

Placement and reform

M. Cameron-Jones

Introduction

This paper is about placement — the means by which students preparing for the professions have some of their training off-campus, in appropriate professional settings, in association with practitioners and in interaction with real clients. Because the point of placement is to help students to develop high standards of professional thought and practice in situations which correspond as closely as possible to those in which the students eventually will operate in-service, placement is a crucial means of training for every profession including medicine, social work, law and health visiting. This paper, however, while discussing principles and trends common to all such professions, will concentrate in particular on the example of primary pre-service teacher training. There, very significant reforms indeed are being made. Placement is at the heart of these reforms not only in Scotland but elsewhere in Britain and also overseas. It is mainly through it, I believe, that we shall achieve the new age at last in primary teacher training.

There are many ways in which change here will be obvious already, even to someone who is only slightly familiar with the past. It is immediately signalled, for example, in the term which is used, since 'placement' includes profession-wide, community and whole-school experience as well as, crucially, the carefully structured and systematic learning of teaching in the classroom. It denotes therefore important changes in the scope and demand of the off-campus curriculum as compared with the 'Teaching Practice' of the past. Other differences are equally visible. Thus, more than twenty years ago Conant's classic work described placement as the most important element in teacher education. Since then, the emphasis given to it has increased even more, which can be seen in the proportion of programme time devoted to it and in the quality and amount of research, development work and literature now sustaining it (Kluender, 1984; McIntyre, 1983). In the sections which follow, I shall deal with five such developments. They are all international trends to which work done at Moray House has in some way contributed, and the first of them is a conceptual shift which has had the greatest possible consequence for our present practice.

Placement redefined

The handling of placement was often a kind of satrapy of the teachers' colleges in the past, since they made placement a separate province from the rest of the students' training administratively and, much more damaging, conceptually. So much was this the case that it is astonishing now to look back and remember how separate placement was from the rest of the course, not only locationally but in many other ways.

In Scotland, for example, even the GTC paper (1978) which prefaced the change-over to the new primary degree, although it thought that Teaching Practice should be externally validated, felt it 'unlikely that the validating body for degree subjects could appropriately be involved in the validation of teaching practice'. Only more recently did the idea of placement as an integral part of the total course come to be accepted. In his recent meta-analysis, McIntyre (1983) doubts that this conception is accepted widely enough in the States even yet, but in Britain we learned a great deal from the pioneering work of Cope (1971) and Gibson (1977), so when the CNAA research (1980) came along it quickly brought the new conception into currency. That research firmly defined students' school-based training as part of the total course, and accordingly was a strong pressure on the training institutions to take it more seriously and negotiate it with teachers more carefully than had been common in the past.

The importance of this redefinition can scarcely be over-emphasised. From a situation in which its administrative complexity had often legitimated its definition and restriction by the training institutions as a separate entity, thought out, assessed and run quite separately from the in-college course, placement was brought together mercifully at last with the whole of the on-campus curriculum to strengthen, illuminate and invigorate it. This has been a most fertile development for contemporary teacher training. Until it came about, only very limited innovation had been possible. In our own college, for example, we had been able, with external funding from the Scottish Education Department, to produce training materials which linked up, though only within the college, student classes on pedagogy (Cameron-Jones, 1980); but, without the major conceptual shift described above, more fundamental reforms of primary teacher training, which depended upon the training institutions wanting and making new kinds of college/field relationships, were not able to go forward.

That there has been a crucial shift in thinking about this can be seen in the criteria now used in our own college and everywhere else for evaluating the quality of teacher training curricula and the role of the placements in them. These criteria insist on the integrity of the course in its entirety and demand (in the case of the Scottish guidelines mandatorily) that the on-campus and the off-campus parts of it are designed together, run together and adhere together to the intentions, principles and forward thrust of the course as a whole. In fact, it is an interesting aspect of teacher training today that, although such authoritative criteria derive from vastly different sources — as different as independent research studies and the 'official' pronouncements which you might expect to be less pure (!) — they all insist on the need for a unified training curriculum which, as it moves in a progressive way forward, threads back and forth to develop strongly and continuously across the different training sites (e.g., Butts, 1983; CNAA, 1982; CNAA, 1983; HMI, 1979; HMI, 1982; HMI, 1983; HMSO, 1983; McNamara and Ross, 1982; SED, 1983; UCET, 1982). This is what we tried to achieve in our college's new primary degree (Moray House, 1983).

The new placements

Not until a training institution understands the idea of the unified curriculum (a massive change from its seeing 'the course' as one thing, and 'Teaching Practice' as quite another) can it accept the need to make careful proposals about the role, timing, spacing and length of the placements across the whole of a course and with field staff to negotiate properly for each placement within a course its objectives, content, teaching/learning strategies and assessment methods. The immediate effect of all this is that much more about placement comes to be explicitly designed, much less to be unstated, done according to previous custom or simply left to chance. A common result is that placements tend to occur earlier in the course, to move more closely in rhythm with the rest of the course (thus, in 'shallow-ended' programmes like our new primary degree, the first placements give students limited learning tasks on a weekly series of single days but these grow later into block placements of several weeks which finally approximate through their increasing length and level of professional demand to a load not far off from probationership), to be more systematically related to the on-campus curriculum (either to its entire span or, quite commonly, to its largest generic element, with provision for the interface of specifics) and, in terms of the total course experience of the individual student over time, to provide a more representative selection of prototypic learning opportunities which match the character of professional practice in the field as it is prescribed by the curriculum for training. It is noticeable that once the design task is seen as a whole in this way, debates about placement change quite dramatically. Some time back, for example, an evaluation by Whalley (1980) had a final chapter called enticingly 'Teacher Education in the Eighties. Some Conclusions', but the first thing it said about Teaching Practice was to report a detail from a questionnaire, that 'the majority view was that teaching practice should be arranged in several periods of two to three weeks each or perhaps in periods of half a term'. There are many similar examples in the earlier literature where details of administration or procedure overshadowed principle (e.g. Elliott and Draba, 1978) but they are less common now that there is a wider and better understanding of the principles in this field and its major issues.

Two of these major issues will be dealt with briefly as examples now. They are, first, the increased scope of placement and, second, the increased importance of analysis. First, scope. The scope of placement has changed in two main ways. Mention was made earlier of the first of these changes — the widening of its overall aims, a widening entailed by the more demanding conceptions of professionalism (Hirst, 1980; McMichael and Gilloran, 1984) and endorsed by the quality controls (SED, 1983) which require new courses of primary training in Scotland to help students to learn interprofessional and intra-professional understanding and collaboration. Our placements have accordingly widened in their scope so that students have not only carefully structured opportunities to learn the skills of teaching and to gain school-wide experience, but also have means of learning personally and directly from parents, from the community, from the other professionals who care for and serve the children, from the children's pre-school provision and from the professional thought and practice of the secondary school.

As well, the students' classroom-based training now is changed in scope, being more serious in acknowledging the need (Gleissman, 1984) not only for students to learn the observable features of effective teaching but also to learn their underlying concepts and rationale in context. This is because, in our new degree, for example, the basic definition of competence in teaching includes not only the observable features of teaching but also the theoretical understandings from which they come. Among British writers, Stones (1983) has been the most prolific in advancing such views of competence and the most insistently critical of Teaching Practice in the past for trying to divorce student learning of what is observable of the skills of teaching in the classroom, from their supporting base of theory and of principle. The implications of such views are enormous. They enlarge the scope of placement to include the theory as well as the practice of teaching, and erase completely the idea that theory can be guarded as the unique province of the college and its staff, and that, in contrast, practice is the only permissible territory of the professionals in the field. The first consequence of this, so far as students' learning of teaching is concerned, is the enhanced importance, during placement, of pedagogical analysis by students and their discussion of teaching in its classroom context with the teachers as well as with the college tutors.

Analysis, then, because it is essential to students for exteriorising, examining, reflecting upon and adjusting their teaching, is the hallmark of the new placements. Without it, students could not learn to think and act professionally in the ways that we now seek and they would have no basis for the continuing reflection on practice on which self-monitoring, self-evaluation and development in professional life depend. During placement, accordingly, analysis comes to the fore in helping the student to learn more effectively, more thoughtfully and more critically — including self-critically — with greater understanding, and with a better knowledge of alternatives (Beyer, 1984; Biott, 1983; Copeland, 1981; Hobar and Sullivan, 1984; Zeichner and Teitelbaum, 1982). There is a great difference between these approaches and the idea that the student role on placement is imitative or replicative, even of the most successful current practice of practitioners. In contrast to the latter view, the new approach sets out to ensure a potential for growth, development and change in the individual student and hence, eventually, in the education system as a whole. (This new approach, of course, depends on our minds being able to absorb the astonishing idea that our students, being the teachers of the future, must be better than, not just as good as, we all are!)

To effect this approach, the new styles of student supervision emphasise analysis as a teaching/learning tool. This can be seen in the swing away from supervisors giving global grades and general comment to the student on her teaching, and towards them providing students with much more analytical discussion of teaching in its context. To provide this for the student, of course, supervisors need to have more highly developed analytical skills themselves than were previously expected of them, and the trend now is to develop these skills by means of supervisory training, both of on-campus and of off-campus staff (Cogan, 1973; Nagley and Evans, 1980; Stones, 1984; Yates, 1980). With Scottish Education Department funding we piloted this kind of activity collaboratively with primary teachers (Cameron-Jones, 1982), with whom we developed, and then in one-day work-shops used, various methods for improving student supervision in the primary classroom. These included principles of training, filmed skill models of supervisory practice and other guidelines to the effective supervision and improvement of students' practice teaching. This kind of work, however, is not at all widespread in Britain yet. At the time of writing this paper, for example, it has not begun for the new degree, though we have produced (Moray House *et al.*, 1984) some of the documentation to support it in relation to student supervision and also, importantly, assessment.

Advances in placement-based assessment

Placement-based assessment cannot be claimed as one of the glories of the past (Stones and Morris, 1972; Wragg, 1982) and some people doubt that things are better now! For example, in their recent paper on one-year primary teacher training courses in England and Wales, Gilbert and Blyth (1984) remark gloomily that 'the assessment of practical teaching appears to have experienced little change, apart from efforts to abolish five-point ratings of teacher competence' and a paper on the subject from the States (Peterson, 1984) sadly notes a 'dichotomy between what is discussed and what is done'. In our college, however, we may be doing a bit better than that in some ways.

First, which is obvious enough once one has thought of it, we are extending our methods of placement-based assessment so that they do span the full range of the aims of the placement. It is important to remember that these aims include learning to observe teaching and to conceptualise it as well as to carry it out effectively. Thus, in our new degree, students on placement are formally assessed on placement-based analytical, observational and interpretative tasks (shadow studies, interaction analyses, curriculum analyses, resource evaluations, etc.). But of course, and supremely importantly, students must be assessed, too, on their competence in teaching on the placement and it is concern about how this assessment is done which lies behind current pressure on teacher trainers to improve their practice. The pressure for this improvement is international (McIntyre, 1983), it is at the bottom of many of the Teaching Quality issues (HMSO, 1983; Joseph, 1982) and it is in contemporary advisory reports. For example, the UCET report states that 'the assessment of practical teaching is recognised as unequivocally the most important part of the total assessment of students' (UCET, 1982).

To improve what we do about it in our new degree, we have designed and piloted a profile for criterion-referenced assessment (Moray House, 1983; Popham, 1978). It specifies in terms of 18 criteria the main competences which the new course seeks to develop in students (these having first been derived from the model of teaching which underlies the whole degree, and then tested for exhaustiveness against the descriptions of the different components of the degree) and also specifies gradations of performance of those competences. Our intention is that, with increasingly large and detailed subsets of the criteria coming into play in the successive years of the course, the same profile will be used throughout the four years of the degree as an aid for self-assessment by the students themselves (students' self-assessment being supported in the Scottish guidelines as well as being intrinsically desirable) and as a means for the various kinds of assessment (formative, summative, informal, formal) of students on placement by teachers and by tutors. Our hope is that both of these groups (an explicit role in the assessment process for teachers and tutors being proposed) will use the profile as a guide to observing teaching, as a framework for discussing teaching with the student (without such frameworks this kind of discussion can be extraordinarily difficult to conceptualise in a fruitful way — Gitlin, 1984), and as a guide to the kind of written comment which is likely to be effective, appropriate and helpful. Our hope, therefore, is that the profile will be used as an assessment aid in the fullest positive meaning of the term. Accordingly, the profile, it can be seen, has high aspirations which go far beyond those of the traditional assessments of Teaching Practice in the past. It intends to be clear and helpful to all parties involved in its use (students, teachers and tutors); to increase their understandings of what is being assessed; to be principled in operation by ensuring that the evidential bases of any judgement made are explicit and that the decision rules which apply to them are rational and clear; and to encourage open, critical review by all parties and audiences not only of our assessment procedures in themselves but also of our entire degree curriculum, since that, of course, is precisely what the content of the profile communicates to the world at large.

Scotland at the moment is a particularly helpful country in which to do this work because of the consciousness here of its potential on account of current changes in the schools themselves. Thus, in anticipation of such trends and as advised in the various guidelines for teacher training (SED, 1983; UCET, 1982), we are also working for the Scottish college system as a whole on a method of profiling which will, at the end of a course, report in a standard way a student's placement achievements to prospective employers and thus act as a guide to the student's best deployment and development in the first year of probation (McGettrick, 1984).

Both of these examples, clearly, have broken new ground for Scottish teacher training. But they need much more work put into them yet. With respect to our new degree profile, we have, for example, only scant preliminary evidence about its validity, reliability, utility and, importantly, feasibility. The very fact, however, that the profile exists at all signals a serious intention to take much more seriously now at last an aspect of teacher training which, in my view, has been inexplicably neglected in the past. This aspect recognises the crucial role of the placements' teachers. Accordingly, it can be seen that here, as in every other theme outlined in this paper up to now, the key to quality in teacher training lies in the growth of partnership.

Partnerships

Placement is the seed-bed for partnerships in training and the concept and practice of partnership, like that of the unified curriculum discussed earlier in this paper, is the subject of universal advocacy. The concept itself is a complex one, however (Butts, 1983; Proctor, 1984), and the spirit of it will not necessarily be realised in action merely by increasing the amount of contact between on-campus and off-campus personnel or just by increasing the amount of time that students and college staff spend working in or visiting the field (Wiles and Branch, 1979). Gordon (1980) has recently defined the three logical possibilities for college/field relationships in respect of student training as those of conflict, duplication (in my view the least fertile possibility of all) and co-operation. The last contains the spirit of what we seek.

Clearly, full co-operation requires enabling conditions for achieving it. In Scotland we have had these nationally since they were created long ago by the acceptance throughout the system of the Sneddon Report (SED/GTC, 1978) and we have also had facilitating statements from the Regions (e.g. Lothian Regional Council, 1984) but, as is clear in the literature on change and innovation, and as we confirmed in the follow-up to Sneddon at Moray House, developments in partnership for a particular course of training require the individual college's own culture to support them and also need the appropriate machinery to sustain them over groups (college/local authority, college staff/school staff, individual tutor/individual teacher) and over time. In Moray House we now seem to have the paradigm machinery for this in CROSE (the College/Region Organisation of School Experience group) which was set up to negotiate the placement procedures for the new primary degree and to facilitate their continuing development and progress (Moray House et al., 1984).

There is a gigantic literature to inform such progress once you have support for it. At the bottom of it all is the simple but powerful fact that, standing in various different relationships to the first clients of the primary education service (namely, children aged 3 to 12), there are very different parties indeed in the placement enterprise. In the case of school-based placements, there are three principal parties involved — schoolteachers, students and college tutors. It is their roles, responsibilities and relationships which most concern the various literatures. One CNAA checklist, for example, asks this all-encompassing question about them all: 'What are the roles of (a) tutor, (b) teacher in school and (c) student in (i) the planning, (ii) the implementation and (iii) the assessment of school-based and school-related activities?' (CNAA, 1983). Much of the literature defines these roles, especially for teachers and tutors, in a very strong way, emphasising the importance of teacher understanding and involvement (and thus de-emphasising tutor authority) and accordingly showing very clearly how the balance of affairs on placement is changing. Examples are numerous. They include the UCET recommendation that 'schools should be full partners' in training (UCET, 1982), the Teaching Quality paper which requires that initial training should involve 'the active participation of experienced, practising school teachers' (HMSO, 1983) and the Scottish guidelines which state that new primary teacher training courses will include 'a role in the assessment process for practising teachers, particularly in the teaching experience element of the course' (SED, 1983).

Three things are at stake in all of this. First, the improvement of student training. Second, the improvement of student assessment. And third, ways of making the idea of professional development — 'to cover the teacher's professional life from the time he enters college until his retirement' (SED/GTC, 1978) — a reality. I shall concentrate now on the first two of these, the third being discussed at the end of this paper. In both of these areas, recent work has focused on the schoolteachers who supervise students' placement teaching much more than on the tutors. This selective focus could be explained by the assumption, according to Stones (1984) an unwarranted one, that college staff already are trained in student supervision, but it is due more, I think, to various studies which suggest that the teachers who supervise students on placement are the most powerful influences of all on student teaching (Barnes and Defino, 1983; Karmos and Jacko, 1977; McIntyre, 1984) and therefore to the belief that teachers will be the most effective users of any training in supervision which can be made available. (A logical extension of such beliefs, of course, is the current DES experimentation in England with predominantly school-based one-year postgraduate courses which maximise the training influence of practising teachers.) Whether of teachers alone, however, or of teachers and campus staff together, we now have a basis on which to proceed with such developments (Butts, 1983; Cameron-Jones, 1982; Gitlin, 1984; Morris, 1980; Stout, 1982; Thies-Sprinthall, 1984; Turney, 1982; Yates, 1980). Typically, these give a 'training in training', which includes principles, skills and analytic procedures, often of an iterative kind and often derived from clinical supervision. Whatever the specifics of the various programmes, however, two things are necessary — that what's done should increase shared understandings among the groups involved; and that those understandings must be developed personally with the individuals at the sharpest end of the training business, namely the class teachers. Thus, on the first point, and this has threaded itself throughout this paper, all parties to any particular placement do need to understand its role in the total course, its general purposes and the point of every aspect of it, including its training and assessment procedures.

This means that the agenda for partnerships now should not just include straightforward administrative matters such as how many students will be arriving on the placement and when, but should also include serious discussion of fundamental issues such as the conceptualisation of teaching, the nature of performance assessment and the cultivation of professional excellence. The danger that class teachers may not be included in such discussions is well known and was put vividly some time ago in an HMI report on school experience: 'Where the system most frequently broke down, however, was at class teacher level and particularly in relation to the forms of experience which had specific rather than general aims. The evidence of the survey suggests that without regular personal contact between tutors and teachers directly concerned, written communication is likely to have little effect in removing misunderstanding' (HMI, 1979). Class teachers are key contributors to student training because of the nature of their clinical knowledge and because they are the group of practitioners whose pedagogic skills and knowledge are subjected daily to the sharpest tests.

Practitioner knowledge

Practitioner knowledge is the fundamental issue for our conceptions of placement today and in the future. Interest in it has revived in the past decade and has not been confined to the teaching profession. Thus Schön, for example (Schön, 1983), has recently taken his thinking further, but long ago (Argyris and Schön, 1974) he tried to explain the nature of practitioner knowledge in a way that would hold true for any profession. This work was among the first to attack the idea that theory and practice could be learned by trainees separately in college and field respectively, and among the first to propose that the way for students to learn professional skills was through discussion with, as well as observation of, thoughtful practitioners. Rather similarly, Benne (1973) has defined as a mere misfortune of Western epistemology that practitioners' 'actionist' knowledge is not more highly regarded, since students need to learn it and, importantly, to learn the ways in which it is tested and validated by practitioners in action in the field quite as much as they need to learn other kinds of knowledge and their associated tests within the training institutions. Similar views have been explored by numerous other writers (Carr, 1983; Hirst, 1983; McNamara and Desforges, 1978; Shulman, 1984). They differ in their detail but share a recognition of professional (i.e. placement) settings not as places,·which was often implied in the past, where teachers practise in some supposedly theory-free way, nor as places where teachers merely apply the theories and principles generated for them elsewhere by other people, but as places in which theories and principles are actually generated, formulated and tested by teachers in the very process of their use. For some writers these views have meant a shift of ground and an enhanced respect for teachers' distinctive contributions to educational theory: 'It is not so much that what I wrote in 1966 was mistaken as that what I omitted led to a distorting emphasis. Educational theory I still see concerned with rationally defensible principles for educational practice. *The adequate formulation and defence of these principles I now see as resting not simply on an appeal to the disciplines but on a complex pragmatic process that uses its own practical discourse*' (Hirst, 1983).

As you would expect, this kind of rethinking has had a dramatic impact on current conceptions of teacher training (Copeland, 1981; McIntyre, 1980; Rowell and Dawson, 1981; Smith, 1980; Smith, 1982). Its first effect was to enhance the importance of placement as the means by which students learn to think as well as act in real professional settings. Thus, Copeland's assertion that 'clinical settings are much more important than simply the arenas in which these behaviours are practised. Their systematic use is central to teacher education.' Its second effect was to honour teachers' knowledge and to give an explicit place to it in placement programmes. This has been for the reasons given by McNamara and Ross (1982): 'Moreover "knowing" about contemporary classrooms on the basis of working in them day by day is of a different quality from "knowing" about them by visiting schools or reading the literature'; and it has also been for specific reasons related to intentionality — i.e. that logically only the teacher can know the reason why (i.e. can know the theory on which) she acts as she does and therefore only she can make available that theory to the student. Its third effect has been to spotlight the generative contribution which practitioners could make to the advancement of new knowledge about teaching. This foresees teachers contributing to future research on teaching in what McIntyre calls 'new and I believe more fundamental ways' (McIntyre, 1980).

Clearly then ideas about the nature of teachers' knowledge are at the roots of the different approaches to placement which a training institution can adopt. By the most traditional approach, teachers were given little recognition for what they could contribute to student placement as thinkers as well as actors. By the newer approach, in contrast, teachers' explanations of their rationales were valued and it was recognised that students could learn from them. However, without structured arrangements for discussion with teachers and for reflection with them on alternatives, even this newer approach could create self-sealing placements and ultimately a self-reproducing profession with little prospect of development or change. Now, however, by the current approaches, with their development of analytic bases for understanding, discussion and reflection and with the active involvement of teachers as well as tutors in these activities with students, a new kind of training will come. Clearly it depends on changes being brought about not only in initial training courses but also in the primary schools themselves. Some of these changes are under way already, exploratorily in connection with initial training (for example, the IT/INSET project, Ashton, 1983), or purely with in-service teachers, in connection with discovering what is needed to make possible in schools the kind of continuous reflection on practice which is important for development throughout professional life. These latter studies are concerned, through the teacher-as-researcher and similar approaches (Cameron-Jones, 1983), with defining, creating and re-sourcing the ethos of 'The Thinking School' — the kind of school which is systematically and intentionally educative, developmental and stimulating for its staff as well as for its pupils. Realistically, this is a task for the future, of course — hence Nisbet (1984): 'One of the tasks of in-service training in the future is to weave a research approach into the expertise of teachers' — but at least it is beginning now and its implications are enormous. They raise the possibility of placement not just transmitting existing practitioner knowledge, but of it actually releasing new styles of teacher thinking which, some writers believe, could revitalise and redirect pedagogic theory in itself, and hence radically redefine the whole of professional training in the future.

Conclusion

This paper has described some current placement developments and has put them at the heart of reform in teacher training at the present time. Five main ones were described. These were, first, the definition of placement as an integral part of the training course and therefore deserving the care and respect of the training institutions; second, the effect of this on placement design; third, the advances this brought about in placement-based assessment; and fourth, developments in partnership. The fifth development discussed was of a different kind, which some scholars expect so radically to change our very conceptions of teaching itself as to have almost unimaginable consequences for the ways in which we shall think about placement and the whole of teacher training by the next decade. In all of these areas, work based at Moray House has contributed substantively beyond our own locality. When it was done, some of this work was highly marginal to the culture of the college, and it could not have survived at all without external funding and external teacher support. Now, however, with great change in Moray House itself and with the influence of CNAA, the spirit of such work is all but quite indigenised within the college too. I believe that it is important to persevere with work of this kind even if it is not welcome in the institution at the time. Without such work there would be no new thinking, no change and ultimately no future worth having. Without it in the field of placement, for example, Teaching Practice would still be done in the traditional fashion and the developments in partnership we now seek would still be unenvisaged.

I am grateful to the Scottish Education Department for funding the Pedagogics Project, the Primary Teaching Practice Project and the Focus on Teaching Project, and to Professor W. J. Popham, UCLA, who with the help of SCRE generously came to discuss the profiling work on the new degree at Moray House. The views in this paper are my own, however.

References

Argyris, C. and Schön, D. A. (1974). *Theory in Practice: Increasing Professional Effectiveness*. Jossey-Bass, San Francisco.

Ashton, M. E. (1983). *Teacher Education in the Classroom. Initial and In-service*. Croom Helm, London.

Barnes, S. and Defino, M. (1983). *The Contexts of Student Teaching*, AERA Report No. 9040, AERA. AGM, Montreal.

Benne, K. D. (1973). 'Educational Field Experiences as the Negotiation of Different Cognitive Worlds', in Bennis, W. *et al.*, *The Planning of Change*. Holt, Rinehart & Winston, New York.

Beyer, L. E. (1984). 'Field Experience, Ideology and the Development of Critical Reflexivity', *Journal of Teacher Education*, 35, 3, pp. 36-41.

Biott, C. (1983). 'The Foundation of Classroom Action Research in Initial Teacher Training', *Journal of Education for Teaching*, 9, 2, pp. 152-160.

Butts, D. C. (1983). 'A Concept of Partnership', University of Stirling/Central Region Education Authority, mimeo.

Cameron-Jones, M. (1980). 'Cast Your Bread. The Final Report of the Pedagogics Project', Moray House College of Education, mimeo.

Cameron-Jones, M. (1982). 'The Primary Teaching Practice Project. Final Report', a follow-up to the Sneddon Report. Education Department, Moray House College of Education, mimeo.

Cameron-Jones, M. (1983). 'Focus on Teaching. Staff Development in Primary Schools.' Project synopsis in *Educational Research 1983 — A Register of Current Educational Research Projects funded by the Scottish Education Department*. SED, Edinburgh.

Carr, W. (1983). 'Can Educational Research be Scientific?', *Journal of Philosophy of Education*, 17, 1, pp. 35-43.

Cogan, M. L. (1973). *Clinical Supervision*. Houghton Mifflin, Boston.

Conant, J. (1963). *The Education of American Teachers*. McGraw-Hill, New York.

Cope, E. (1971). 'A Study of a School-supervised Practice', University of Bristol School of Education, mimeo.

Copeland, W. D. (1981). 'Clinical Experiences in the Education of Teachers', *Journal of Education for Teaching*, 7, 1, pp. 3-16.

Council for National Academic Awards (1980). 'School Experience in Initial BEd/BEdHonours Degrees validated by the CNAA.' A Research Report by Myra McCullough. CNAA, London.

Council for National Academic Awards (1982). 'Perspectives on Postgraduate Initial Training.' A Report of the Working Party on One-Year Courses. CNAA, London.

Council for National Academic Awards (1983). 'Initial BEd Courses for the Early and Middle Years.' A Discussion Document from the Committee for Education, Undergraduate Initial Training Board. CNAA, London.

Elliott, P. G. and Draba, R. E. (1978). 'A Placement Procedure that Prevents Problems', *Clearing House*, 52, 4, pp. 157-160.

General Teaching Council (1978). 'Recommendations of the Committee Studying the Implications of Replacing the Diploma Courses for Primary Teachers by Degree Courses.' General Teaching Council, Edinburgh.

Gibson, R. (1977). 'The Value of Teaching Practice', *Education in the North*, pp. 25-30.

Gilbert, J. E. and Blyth, W. A. L. (1984). 'Recent Development of PGCE

Primary/Middle Courses in England and Wales', *Journal of Education for Teaching*, 10, 1, pp. 39-51.

Gitlin, A. *et al.* (1984). 'Supervision, Reflection and Understanding: A Case for Horizontal Evaluation', *Journal of Teacher Education*, 35, 3, pp. 46-52.

Gleissman, D. H. and Pugh, R. C. (1984). 'Conceptual Variables in Teacher Training', *Journal of Education for Teaching*, 10, 3, pp. 195-208.

Gordon, D. (1980). 'Is pre-Service Training Really Necessary?', *British Journal of Teacher Education*, 6, 2, pp. 152-157.

Hirst, P. H. (1980). 'The PGCE Course and the Training of Specialist Teachers for Secondary Schools. A Report for the UCET Working Party on the PGCE Course', *British Journal of Teacher Education*, 6, 1, pp. 3-20.

Hirst, P. H. (1983). 'Educational Theory', in Hirst, P. H. (ed.), *Educational Theory and Its Foundation Disciplines*. Routledge & Kegan Paul, London.

HMI (1979). *Developments in the BEd Degree Course. A Study Based in Fifteen Institutions*. DES, HMSO, London.

HMI (1982). *The New Teacher in School*. DES, HMSO, London.

HMI (1983). *Teaching in Schools. The Content of Initial Training*. DES, HMSO, London.

HMSO (1983). 'Teaching Quality.' Paper presented to Parliament by the Secretary of State for Education and Science and the Secretary of State for Wales. Cmnd. 8836. HMSO, London.

Hobar, N. and Sullivan, D. K. (1984). 'Systematic Observation of Instruction: Genesis, Research, Practice and Potential', *Journal of Classroom Interaction*, 19, 2, pp. 26-34.

Joseph, Sir K. (1982). Lecture given to celebrate sixty years of teacher training in Durham. *Durham and Newcastle Research Review*, 10, 50, pp. 38-39.

Karmos, A. and Jacko, C. (1977). 'The Role of Significant Others During the Student Teaching Experience', *Journal of Teacher Education*, 28, 5, pp. 51-55.

Kluender, M. M. (1984). 'Teacher Education Programs in the 1980s: Some Selected Characteristics', *Journal of Teacher Education*, 35, 4, pp. 33-35.

Lothian Regional Council (1984). 'School Placement of Student Teachers', Lothian Regional Council Department of Education, mimeo.

McGettrick, B. J. (1984). 'Report of Working Party on Alternative Procedure, Sub-Committee on First Appointments of Teachers', Joint Committee of Colleges of Education in Scotland.

McIntyre, D. I. (1980), 'The Contribution of Research to Quality', in Hoyle, E. and Megarry, J. (eds), 'Professional Development of Teachers', *World Yearbook of Education*. Kogan Page, London.

McIntyre, D. J. (1983). *Field Experiences in Teacher Education. From Student to Teacher*. Foundation for Excellence in Teacher Education. US Dept. of Education.

McIntyre, D. J. (1984). 'A Response to the Critics of Field Experience Supervision', *Journal of Teacher Education*, 35, 3, pp. 42-45.

McMichael, P. J. and Gilloran, A. (1984). 'Exchanging Views. Workshop Evaluation', Moray House College of Education, mimeo.

McNamara, D. R. and Desforges, C. (1978). 'The Social Sciences, Teacher Education and the Objectification of Craft Knowledge', reprinted in Bennett, N. and McNamara, D. (1979), *Focus on Teaching*. Longman, London.

McNamara, D. R. and Ross, A. M. (1982). 'The BEd Degree and Its Future', School of Education, University of Lancaster.

Moray House College of Education (1983). 'Initial BEd Degree. Submission to CNAA', Moray House College, Edinburgh.

Moray House College of Education with Borders, Central, Fife and Lothian Regions (1984a). 'Principles of Partnership in the New 4-Year BEd Degree', Moray House College, mimeo.

Moray House College of Education with Borders, Central, Fife and Lothian Regions (1984b). 'School Placement of Student Teachers in the New 4-Year BEd Degree', Moray House College, mimeo.

Morris, J. E. (1980). 'A Strategy for the Development of Supervising Teachers', *Clearing House*, 53, 8, pp. 367-370.

Nagley, R. L. and Evans, N. D. (1980). *Handbook for Effective Supervision of Instruction*. Prentice Hall, New York.

Nisbet, J. (1984). 'The Changing Scene', in Dockrell, W. B. (ed.), *An Attitude of Mind*. Scottish Council for Research in Education, Edinburgh.

Peterson, K. (1984). 'Methodological Problems in Teacher Evaluation', *Journal of Research and Development in Education*, 17, 4, pp. 62-70.

Popham, W. J. (1978). *Criterion Referenced Measurement*. Prentice Hall, New Jersey.

Proctor, N. (1984). 'Towards a Partnership with Schools', *Journal of Education for Teaching*, 10, 3, pp. 219-232.

Rowell, J. A. and Dawson, C. J. (1981). 'Prepared to Teach?', *Journal of Education for Teaching*, 7, 3, pp. 315-323.

Schön, D. A. (1983). *The Reflective Practitioner. How Professionals Think in Action*. Temple Smith, London.

Scottish Education Department (1983). 'Report of the Working Party on Primary pre-Service Training.' Scottish Education Department, Edinburgh.

SED/GTC (1978). *Learning to Teach* (The Sneddon Report). HMSO, Edinburgh.

Shulman, L. S. (1984). 'The Practical and the Eclectic. A Deliberation on Teaching and Educational Research', *Curriculum Inquiry*, 14, 2, pp. 183-200.

Smith, B. O. *et al.* (1980). *A Design for a School of Pedagogy*. US Dept. of Education Publication No. E-8-42000.

Smith, R. N. (1982). 'Towards an Analysis of PGCE Courses', *Journal of Further and Higher Education*, 6, 3, pp. 3-11.

Stones, E. (1983). 'Perspectives in Pedagogy', *Journal of Education for Teaching*, 9, 1, pp. 68-76.

Stones, E. (1984). *Supervision in Teacher Education*. Methuen, London.

Stones, E. and Morris, S. (1972). 'The Assessment of Practical Teaching', reprinted in Stones, E. and Morris, S. (1972), *Teaching Practice. Problems and Perspectives*. Methuen, London.

Stout, C. (1982). 'Why Co-operating Teachers Accept Students', *Journal of Teacher Education*, 33, 6, pp. 22-24.

Thies-Sprinthall, L. (1984). 'Promoting the Developmental Growth of Supervising Teachers', *Journal of Teacher Education*, 35, 3, pp. 53-60.

Turney, C. (1982). *Supervisor Development Programmes*. Sydney University Press, Sydney.

Universities Council for the Education of Teachers (1982). *Postgraduate Certificate in Education Courses for Teachers in Primary and Middle Schools. A Further Consultative Report*. UCET, London.

Whalley, G. E. (1980). 'Teacher Education for Primary School Teachers. Two New Courses and Their Evaluation.' University of Leeds School of Education, mimeo.

Wiles, M. M. and Branch, J. (1979). 'University/Public School Collaboration Models in Teacher Education', *The Educational Forum*, 44, 1, pp. 35-43.

Wragg, E. C. (1982). *A Review of Research in Teacher Education*. NFER-Nelson, Windsor.

Yates, J. (1980). 'Teaching Practice and the Supervision of Student Teachers', London, Roehampton Institute, mimeo.

Zeichner, K. M. and Teitelbaum, K. (1982). 'Personalised and Enquiry-Orientated Teacher Education: an Analysis of Two Approaches to the Development of Curriculum for Field-Based Exercises, *Journal of Education for Teaching*, 8, 2, pp. 95-117.

9

Special educational needs

Marion Blythman and Peter Lambert

The origins of Special Education

Special Education in Scotland has a long history, predictable in a country where literacy has always been held in high regard and education seen as the best means of achieving this for the population as a whole. In Scotland the democratic intellectual tradition has clearly had a formative effect on the whole educational system and has influenced the development of special education, although David Petrie, a former HMI, points out: 'A general belief that the problems of the handicapped child could at least be ameliorated by human effort has been slow to develop'.[1] However, by the second half of the 18th century and in advance of many developed countries, private schools for the deaf and the blind had appeared in Edinburgh, largely through the efforts of a few philanthropic individuals and organisations. By the latter half of the 19th century, the education of the mentally handicapped had been pioneered by a Dr. Brodie and his wife in Edinburgh and later at the Royal National Hospital in Larbert.

This was all commendable and within a Scottish silhouette but the essential precondition for any kind of systematic development of special education is compulsory mass education. It is only when all of the children in a country are in the schools that educators become aware of the existence of numbers of children whose educational needs are not being met and who are not making any discernible progress in terms of the school curriculum. In the situation of the 1870s, where the classes were large, and a substantial element of the child population was suffering from poverty and malnutrition and not wholly convinced of the worth or necessity of compulsory schooling, it is easy to understand that the presence of children of limited learning ability was seen by the administrators and teachers as an additional burden. Grants to schools to some extent depended on the standards of performance of the pupils.

These standards were based on rather rigid notions of normality and on a view which tended to equate syllabus with curriculum. Most often this meant that the teacher was required to teach the syllabus in such a way that all children would progress at a uniform rate through the various stages of the school.

Allied to this, and reinforcing the more negative aspects, was a developing view which defined the child with a physical, sensory, intellectual or social disability exclusively in terms of his/her handicap. This suited the climate of the times and helped to create strong but unnecessary stereotypes and role expectations which allowed the school to lay the responsibility for failure on the child. This meant that the school as an institution could proceed as if this group of children were somehow 'different' — later re-defined as 'special' — and therefore not an integral part of the normal school population. In order to understand the development of the system of segregated special education and the problems, issues and debates of the 20th century, it is essential not only to identify these earlier misconceptions but also to understand how powerful they were and consonant with the perceived needs of society at that time. Unfortunately, much of this separation and segregation was legitimised at the turn of the century by the pseudoscientific theories of the geneticists, which are now happily discredited but at that time combined to produce policies and practices which justified separating children from mainstream education and their peers.

The training of teachers: the early years

It was not until after the First World War that it was recognised that there might be grounds for specialised training for teachers of 'defective' pupils. In 1920 the National Committee for the Training of Teachers was set up, following the Education Act of 1918. In the event, this was a large, unwieldy body which met only once per year, but nevertheless by 1922 the *Scottish Education Journal* was able to report that 'the National Committee has come to the conclusion that a beginning should be made to *the adequate and scientific training* of the future teachers of the mentally defective children and submits the proposed scheme in the confident belief that it will receive the support of the Education Authorities in Scotland'.[2]

The real work of the National Committee was devolved on a small active Central Executive Committee (CEC) under the chairmanship of Professor Darroch. '. . . the initiation of new courses and prospectuses was undertaken by the CEC. The new body decided at once to establish a course for teachers of the blind at Moray House and made arrangements to send to Manchester University students training to teach the deaf. It also agreed to combine with the Glasgow Education Committee in providing courses for teachers of mentally defective children.'[3]

The training then established catered for teachers from all over Scotland and although generally speaking it seemed to make little impact on the educational system or on the training of teachers — at least initially — it was for the next 30 years the only course of training for Special Education in Scotland. Special classes and schools for the handicapped were of course legislatively apart from mainstream education at this time.

From time to time Acts of Parliament, beneath their cautious and convoluted phraseology, embody genuine surges of democratic idealism. The Education (Scotland) Act 1945 was one such: its concern to build a brave new educational world embraced the handicapped. To quote the Secretary of State for Scotland in 1966, 'It was not until the passing of the 1945 Education (Scotland) Act that it was *officially recognised that the broad purpose of education was essentially the same for handicapped children as it was for their more fortunate contemporaries . . .'*[4]

However, as Petrie goes on to point out, 'The enunciation of broad legal and administrative principles is one thing; their implementation is another. Education Authorities . . . tended to delegate responsibilities for Special Education to the most junior members of the Directorate and continuity of policy was difficult to achieve as the juniors ascended the promotion ladder.'[5] The Act also laid great weight on the advice given by medical practitioners, thus reinforcing the view of the handicapped child as 'patient' and, while the rights of the parents were protected, this was done in such a legalistic way that in effect they had little power to affect or even influence decisions about the education of their children.

In 1947 the Secretary of State charged the Advisory Council on Education to review provision for pupils suffering from disability of mind or from maladjustment due to social handicap. This was the first comprehensive review in Scotland of the provision for handicapped children. It is interesting to note that the terminology reflected only too clearly a concept which demeaned the children in question and reinforced a pattern of separation and segregation. This Council, under the convenership of Dr. W. B. Inglis, produced seven reports between 1950 and 1952. The writing of these reports, described by Petrie as 'written in an eloquent, magisterial prose',[6] is generally ascribed to Dr. Inglis, who was at that time Director of Studies at Moray House.

Training at Moray House: pre-Warnock

It was not until 1956 that a training course for teachers in Special Education was established at Moray House. This course, which was the first to cater for teachers in the east of Scotland, was initially very similar to that offered at Jordanhill, though it was more psychologically oriented and offered two forms of endorsement, one for mentally and one for physically handicapped children. But as Petrie points out, 'By the end of the fifties, the strategic thinking and the general surveys that had gone on since the end of the war brought home to those responsible for Scottish Special Education the magnitude of their task. Expectations had been raised, areas of uncertainty, ignorance or failure exposed. In civil service planning jargon there were 'roofs over heads' for the more common handicaps; but the roofs, for the most part, were over old-fashioned inadequate buildings. Trained teachers were in short supply.'[7] Not only were the teachers in short supply. They were generally accorded a low status by their peers in the teaching profession, often regarded as 'refugees' from the more demanding work of mainstream education.

About the same time, the assumptions about the pupils with learning difficulties who were still in the ordinary schools came to be questioned. In 1950 backward children had been defined as 'those of limited ability who require special attention in the basic subjects if their whole development is not to suffer'.[8] Retarded children were those 'temporarily unable to make progress'.[9] Where staffing and accommodation made it possible, separate tutorial classes were recommended and over the next 20 years this generally became the pattern of provision in secondary schools, while primary schools where this kind of remedial provision was seen to be necessary appointed teachers to coach small groups withdrawn from ordinary classes for short periods each day.

In 1959 special courses for certificated teachers leading to an endorsement or special qualification to act as a teacher for backward pupils in secondary schools were introduced in four colleges, including Moray House. These courses were designed for 'that small minority of pupils' who were 'so backward in the basic skills' that they required 'remedial treatment', either by 'grouping them under a specialist teacher' or by allocating them to ordinary classes and withdrawing them for 'special remedial treatment'.[10] The courses therefore fitted into the accepted pattern of differentiated provision of the time.

As far as training was concerned, the next fifteen years or so was a period of steady development of the courses, consolidation and expansion of the numbers trained but was not characterised by any kind of radical change, although secondary education had been reorganised and the primary school had seen many changes following the public-ation of *Primary Education in Scotland* in 1965. The special courses became Special Qualifications on the advice of the General Teaching Council in 1970, and in 1972 a similar qualification was offered for primary teachers. 'The reference to "backward children" was finally dropped and the style changed to "remedial teacher" in a primary or secondary school or department.'[11] A course for primary teachers was offered at that time at Moray House and ran up to the point of the introduction of the new style of training in 1981.

Nevertheless, change was in the air, for between 1975 and 1981 almost every education authority, including Lothian Region, in Scotland reviewed its provision for 'slow learners', as the pupils concerned were now deemed. It was typical of the growing strength of the relationship between the colleges of education and the education authorities that Moray House was represented on the small committee responsible for *Could Do Better*, which was the Lothian Region Study Group Report on Provision for the Least Able Pupils in Secondary Schools, published in 1981.

There was clearly, during this period, a groundswell of real concern about the education that was being offered to pupils with learning difficulties. Groups of remedial teachers in various parts of Scotland were beginning to realise the constraints imposed by their traditional roles and not only voiced their disquiet but had a marked effect on the reports which were being issued by the education authorities from 1976-81. These reports highlighted the need for change and made a range of proposals designed to meet the needs of the pupils in question.

At the same time, the Consultative Committee on the Curriculum and other agencies issued a series of major reports concerned with the curriculum in general (Munn, Dunning and Pack) and also with more specific aspects such as Drama, Religious Education, Music, and Health Education. These reports reflected a growing awareness of the need to broaden the curriculum and make it accessible to a wider range of pupils. In each, reference was made to the place of pupils with learning difficulties and the need to view them as an integral part of the total school community. It is also interesting to recall that the Consultative Committee on the Curriculum between 1977 and 1981 had given extensive consideration to the question of the education of pupils with learning difficulties and had on its membership two representatives from the field, one from Moray House itself.

'Another strong influence for change came from the educational sociologists of the sixties who had developed a critique of the social organisation of the school and its effect on pupil achievement. The traditional 'child deficit' models came under close scrutiny which led to many questions about their value both as explanations of school failure and as the basis of provision designed to improve the school experience of the child.

Also during this period, there was an increasing interest in the 'quality of instruction' being offered in schools. The work of Morrison and McIntyre in Scotland had identified a more systematic, dynamic and interactive pedagogy, and this was followed through by Cameron-Jones in a large-scale pedagogics project sited in Moray House.

These developments were reflected in the courses offered by the Department of Special Education at Moray House. In addition, by 1975 the department was making considerable contributions to pre-service courses at both graduate and under-graduate levels although these were still regarded merely as interesting and worthwhile additional elements and not integrated into the courses at the planning stages, and were, moreover, seen as relating almost entirely to the small proportion of children still segregated in special schools, classes and units.

Warnock and after

The situation pre-1978, both in the schools and in the colleges, was thus one of 'countervailing values' and 'dilemmas of action' as Eysenck had put it. The problem was to define a new pedagogy aimed to recognise and value individual difference and to provide an appropriate curriculum for each pupil as opposed to a general education for all.

Two important reports, published in 1978, expressed a need for a broader definition of pupils who experience learning difficulties. The Warnock Report, which covered the UK, proposed a move away from the traditional categories of handicap towards a concept of special educational needs and estimated that one child in five was likely to have special educational needs and would therefore require special educational provision at some point in his/her school career. Later in the same year, the Progress Report of HM Inspectors of Schools (Scotland) made the point that learning difficulties embraced a greater number of pupils than that thought of previously as requiring remedial education: in fact, up to 50 per cent of the total school population could be involved.

It was clear that these reports presented a radical change of educational thinking, one in which members of the staff of Moray House had been involved and one which was consonant with the direction in which the college had begun to move. Both these reports were considered, commented on, and accepted by the Board of Studies and became the foundation of the development of a college-wide policy which was to help determine the form and content of the training to be designed to meet the new requirements for students in training and practising teachers. A series of seminars followed the publication of the Progress Report, initiated by the inspectorate team responsible, and involving education authority and college of education staff. At the same time the Committee of Principals set up a committee, under the chairmanship of Dr. Illsley of Dundee College of Education, part of whose remit was to consider the implications of the Warnock Report and to make recommendations for the training of teachers who would be involved with pupils with special educational needs. Again the Moray House representatives contributed to and influenced the recommendations made by this committee.

In 1980 the Committee of Principals set up an Advisory Committee on Pupils with Learning Difficulties under the chairmanship of the late James Scotland, Principal of Aberdeen College of Education. Its main remit was to consider the implications of the HMI Progress Report for the training of teachers. The work of this committee, which represented a broad range of interests including the colleges, education authorities and teachers' associations, laid down a pattern of course development which reflected the spirit of the times and became a prototype for the future. The Scottish Education Department had set as one of the criteria for the consideration of course proposals from colleges that there should be evidence that, in preparation, due account had been taken of the views of the education authorities and school staffs. At the same time, it became a requirement that colleges had to take all courses for external validation. This all represented an important and innovative development for the Diplomas in Special Education and the Special Qualifications in Scotland generally and in Moray House in particular.

A whole new era of course preparation and planning came about. For each new course a Course Planning Committee was set up, again with representatives of interests within and outwith the college. The deliberations and the outcomes of these planning committees were subject to scrutiny at three main levels. Inside Moray House they went through a democratic committee structure designed to involve the whole college community in decisions about the form and content of the courses. The Scottish Education Department came into the scene with a policy which demanded that each course proposal would meet criteria which involved a formative discussion with the main members of the course planning team at different stages of course planning and writing. Finally, the courses were to be submitted for validation to the Council for National Academic Awards. This proved to be a professionally exciting and stimulating experience, demanding in terms of the public nature of the whole exercise, onerous in terms of the meticulous preparation needed for the validation procedures but, in retrospect, one which proved to be a great learning experience for all concerned, i.e. college staff and representatives of outside interests, particularly those at school and authority level. With hindsight, it can be said that the resultant strains and stresses, rewards and benefits, have developed a sense of public accountability, collaboration and professional maturity which has had a beneficial effect on the personnel and the courses involved.

The same procedures were put into operation for all the Diplomas in Special Educational Needs, and between 1982 and 1984 three Moray House Diplomas in Professional Studies in Education were approved by CNAA, i.e. for Recorded Pupils and for Non-Recorded Pupils (Primary and Secondary).

The contemporary scene

If the Moray House experience is anything to go by, in many respects the whole process which has just been described has helped to bring Special Education and Special Education courses out of the closet and into a more dynamic relationship with other college departments and consequently with mainstream education. Since it is now acknowledged that the education of pupils with learning difficulties is not to be seen as separate, different and 'special' but has to be viewed as a central concern of teachers, schools and colleges, and since it can be claimed that 'The major source of learning difficulty is the curriculum and the way it is presented',[12] there have been two important consequences for teacher-training as a whole.

The first of these is a recognition of the need for pre-service provision for all teachers which will enable them to cope with the much greater range of learning difficulties that they may now expect to encounter. The college's policy statement makes it plain that the importance of this has been thoroughly grasped: 'Moray House policy for all courses is based on a view that there are many factors which affect how pupils learn and perform in school. In the broadest sense these are physiological, psychological, political and economic, which together influence the child, the school, the content of the curriculum and how it is presented. So, rather than concentrate on the child as the only source of the problem of school failure, the training offered should develop in all teachers an awareness of these factors and how they help or hinder pupil progress.' To this end, the Department of Special Educational Needs has greatly increased its contribution to pre-service courses.

The second consequence has been in the field of in-service. There have recently been important developments in the courses for Recorded Pupils in order to prepare teachers for work involving a much greater degree of integration with mainstream education; but perhaps the most striking innovations have been in the new courses for Non-recorded Pupils in both Primary and Secondary sectors, where the college has been breaking totally new ground in several respects. These courses mark a radical departure from all other courses in learning difficulty because, in addition to preparing the practitioner for direct intervention with small numbers of children, usually in separate classes or withdrawal units, they are designed to enable the new diplomates to assist large numbers of children indirectly through the support which they can offer not only to class-teachers and subject departments but to the school as a whole. The diplomates are accordingly trained to fulfil four roles: two of these, involving direct tuition and the provision of special services for pupils with temporary learning difficulties, are roughly speaking on traditional lines; but there is now an emphasis on working co-operatively within the classroom, and this third role adds a new dimension to the training which is necessary — different approaches to diagnosis, to the planning and implementation of programmes and to interpersonal skills involving relationships with colleagues, for example.

Undoubtedly the most significant aspect of the new courses, however, is the consultancy role — 'the hallmark of the new Diploma' — since the diplomate is expected both to give advice on learning difficulties experienced across the whole curriculum, and to take part in the formation of whole-school policy. Clearly therefore the diplomate must have a thorough understanding of the current curriculum models and insight into managerial structures, as well as a considerable knowledge of pedagogy and diagnostic, observational and assessment techniques. These can be taught readily enough. What cannot be taught with the same degree of certainty and precision are the appropriate attitudes of professionalism, respect for pupils and colleagues, and, above all, the ability to form good relationships; it is for this reason that the initial selection of course members has to be undertaken with considerable care and in close collaboration with the seconding authorities.

There have been some interesting consequences of running such demanding courses. Because of the range of areas with which the consultant must have some familiarity there has been a big extension in the variety of contributions made to Special Education courses by other college departments, such as Computer Education and the department of Educational Management and Administration; and the structure of the courses has necessitated much more interdepartmental co-operation, for example, in running shared workshops and symposia. Staff have found this experience most useful and stimulating, particularly since the calibre of the course members is such that learning tends to be a two-way process. Again, it is required by the SED that in these courses the college should work closely with regional advisers, staff tutors and experts in the field, not only in their planning but in their day-to-day running; the assistance which has been received has taken many forms, and it has given to all concerned a greatly enhanced idea of the potential of such co-operation for future courses both within and outwith the college. Finally, because of the wide experience and maturity of the course members, there have been important developments in the ways that 'student' participation can be invoked — not only in setting up workshops and presenting seminar papers, but in such spheres as self-evaluation and negotiated assignments; and there have been particularly helpful discussions with staff on ways of assessing the effectiveness of co-operative teaching and consultancy; the relevance of all of this to the college in the whole context of assessing placements is obvious.

These consequences have been described in the context of the courses for Non-recorded Pupils, but most of them are strikingly replicated in the other courses with which the department is concerned. It is unfortunate that lack of space precludes a discussion of the other work of the department, which includes some important research, the planning of further courses such as that for the visually impaired, and a considerable amount of agency-based in-service work. Enough has been said, however, to indicate something of its scope, and to bring out the point that the college is not only forging stronger links with the field, but is also enriching its own staff.

Conclusion

Since the Second World War and particularly over the last decade or so, the volume of legislation relating to pupils with learning difficulties is unparalleled at any point in the history of Scottish education. There have been major surveys such as the one which underpinned the Progress Report, major reports such as those produced by the Melville,

McCann and Warnock Committees and the Scottish Inspectorate, all of which have combined to produce far-reaching changes in how pupils with learning difficulties are both regarded and treated within the educational system as a whole. Moray House College of Education has accepted the spirit and philosophy of these and accepts further that, if they are to be translated into action at a practical level, then the same spirit and philosophy should inform and pervade all the courses offered at pre-service and in-service level. It would be facile and specious to claim that this has come about or is even going to be achieved in the foreseeable future. But if we also accept that the integration of all children into the mainstream of education is, like education itself, 'a good thing', then we should also accept the implications and relate them to Booth's definition of integration 'as a process of increasing children's participation in the educational and social life of comprehensive primary and secondary schools', and acknowledge that colleges of education like Moray House have an important and unique contribution to make to that process.

References

1. Dockrell, W. B., Dunn, W. R. and Milne, A. (eds) (1978) — *Special Education in Scotland*, SCRE, Ch. 1.

2. (2 June 1922) — *Scottish Educational Journal*, Vol. 5, p. 380.

3. Cruikshank, Marjorie (1970) — *A History of the Training of Teachers in Scotland*, SCRE, pp. 163-4.

4. Dockrell, W. B., Dunn, W. R. and Milne, A. (eds) (1978) — *Special Education in Scotland*, SCRE, Ch. 1, p. 2.

5. (1978) — Ibid., p. 3.

6. (1978) — Ibid., p. 4.

7. (1978) — Ibid., p. 9.

8. Scottish Education Department — *The Primary School in Scotland*. A Memorandum on the Curriculum. HMSO, para. 541.

9. Scottish Education Department — Ibid., para. 535.

10. Scottish Education Department (1978) — HMI Progress Report, *The Education of Pupils with Learning Difficulties*, p. 7.

11. Scottish Education Department (1978) — Ibid., p. 7.

12. Scottish Education Department (1979) — *The Roles of the Remedial Specialist* (Appendix A), para. 21 (iii).

10

Educational management
Edmund A. Ewan and John E. A. Havard

Early developments

The department of Educational Management and Administration in Moray House College was formally established in 1968. Work in this area had begun in the college the preceding year when a member of the directorate joined the college staff. For some time before then concern had been growing about certain aspects of the management of education at both national and local authority level. Standards of provision among the then 35 education authorities varied widely in a number of respects, and in none more than staffing.

No agreed or even common pupil–teacher ratio applied nationally, and secondary schools were staffed on an astonishingly variable basis, each authority setting its own criteria and standards. Besides the obvious inequity of such arrangements, there was, in an era of critical staff shortages in many subjects, the further problem of defining just how many teachers were required both in individual subjects and in the secondary system as a whole. While one authority estimated its shortages on an assumed pupil–teacher ratio of nineteen to one and another used a much more favourable ratio of, say, fifteen to one, the Secretary of State, whose responsibility it was (and is) to ensure that adequate numbers of teachers were trained to meet the requirements of the system, had no rational basis on which to make decisions about entry to training.

At that time, too, there were many uncertificated teachers working in secondary schools, in some schools as many as 50 per cent being unqualified, but again it was impossible meaningfully to state how many additional staff were required to enable the nation to dispense with their services. Different types of secondary schools were also common, ranging from junior secondary organisations, sometimes with a creaming off to a more academic institution at the end of year two, through traditional rural all-age multilateral schools to selective senior secondaries. And while actual pupil–teacher ratios did vary somewhat among schools of different types, they varied even more among schools of similar organisational pattern. Similarly, while certain parts of the country could superficially be identified because of notorious instances of shortage as much worse off in staffing terms than others, further investigation demonstrated that even in areas of apparently desperate privation there was great inequality of provision from school to school. Overall shortage was in fact seriously compounded by gross maldistribution of available staffing resources.

Against this background the earliest efforts of the department of Educational Management and Administration were concentrated on information-gathering about issues of staffing complement and deployment and the evolution of techniques to facilitate more efficient and even utilisation of existing staff resources in the secondary sector. The close scrutiny of secondary school timetables which this approach involved led naturally to attempts to develop useful measures of the ways in which both staff and accommodation were being used. Pupil–teacher ratio clearly provided a convenient and intelligible measure of staff availability. It soon became evident, however, that schools with similar pupil–teacher ratios were in fact deploying their staff very differently in terms both of numbers of periods taught and of the sizes of pupil groups they dealt with. This led to the development of the concept of pupil–teacher contact ratio — a rough equivalent of the average size of class taught. From this approach there quickly developed the idea of using the number of pupil contacts per teacher and per subject to provide further interesting data about how schools used staff and suggest means of evaluating teacher loads.

Work in these areas was carried on both at national level in the Scottish Education Department and in the college. A national survey of staffing in secondary schools largely concerned with pupil–teacher ratios was published in 1969. This led in turn to the idea of using a series of norms of pupil contacts per teacher per week as an indicator of teacher loads and a basis of comparison of teacher utilisation from school to school.[1] Moray House's parallel studies of the staffing requirements of differing sizes and types of secondary school indicated that very considerable economies in staff accrued as school size increased to around 1,300 with an optimum figure of some 1,800 pupils, assuming a common comprehensive curriculum and organisational pattern in each case.

From these studies it quickly became apparent that different strategies and techniques of timetabling made a marked difference to the staffing required to implement a given curriculum. The college set up a Timetabling Research and Advisory Unit with the help initially of two early-retired headteachers. Besides doing a great deal of research, developing a series of techniques to facilitate efficient timetabling, mounting a series of national courses and providing an emergency help and consultancy service, the unit also undertook feasibility studies of the Scottish Education Department model prescribed in the 'Red Book' of 1973.[2]

Scottish Centre for Studies in School Administration (SCSSA)

Whilst the college retained a national interest in the timetabling sphere, the Scottish Education Department decided to set up in conjunction with Moray House a new national centre to concentrate on training for Headteachers, Depute and Assistant Headteachers in Secondary Schools. Accordingly, the Scottish Centre for Studies in School Administration was established in April 1972. This occurred shortly after the publication of the Scottish Education Department's Green Paper, *The Structure of Promoted Posts in Secondary Schools in Scotland* (1971).[3] This proposed a substantial increase in the number and range of promoted posts in order to meet the then changing needs of schools which had increased considerably in size and range of functions. In particular the paper proposed the introduction of a level of assistant headteachers, the number of which depended on the size of school. This was to meet the increased complexity in the school, particularly in the area of curriculum management, and to enable headteachers to delegate more of their management and administrative duties. It was also recognised that the introduction of a further level of senior staff provided an opportunity for more teachers to obtain the training in management and administration necessary for further promotion.

The SCSSA was established to assist schools in carrying out these objectives. To this end the Centre has developed four main purposes:
(a) to study and co-ordinate information on the application of basic management principles in the school;
(b) to collect and study current views on curriculum design and innovation;
(c) to appreciate and evaluate the work of the school, social and economic, in the regional and national setting; and
(d) to develop courses and other means of disseminating such information to improve the efficiency and effectiveness of management in secondary schools.

The first Director was a Chief HM Inspector who was joined in 1974 by a soon to retire secondary headteacher as Associate Director. The first Director retired in 1976 and since then the Director has been the only professional member of staff. He is assisted by an administrative officer, an executive officer seconded from the Scottish Office. The Centre has offices in Moray House College and is able to make use of their support services, such as secretarial staff and reprographic facilities, but in order to recognise the Centre's national responsibility and need for independence it is not represented in the college's committee structure. From the beginning it was agreed that the Moray House College Department of Educational Management and Administration would play an important part in the work of the Centre and that extensive use would be made of visiting staff to draw on a broad range of specialist expertise.

The Centre is guided by an Advisory Committee consisting of representatives of the Association of Directors of Education Scotland, the Headteachers' Association Scotland, HM Inspectors of Schools, a representative of Secondary Assistant Headteachers, a representative of Lothian Region, and college staff. Thus this committee is a professional body representing the interests of Scottish education across the nation and has been influential in the development of the Centre's policies and practices.

From time to time consideration has been given to the establishment of a fully staffed and separately accommodated Educational Staff College and this has been strongly argued. It would still appear to be a natural development for Scotland in line with current developments in different areas of England and Wales, though it is probable that such a development would require an improved financial climate for the education services.

Recent developments such as the publication of the NCITT Report on Staff Development,[4] the HMI Management Report[5] and the introduction of the Scottish Education Department's specific grants for management courses have led to a substantial increase in the demand for the Centre's courses in support of curriculum and management developments in schools.

Between 1972 and 1978 the Centre offered between eight and ten residential courses a year on management and curriculum; since then the number has increased sharply until in 1984 sixteen courses were offered and a similar number are planned for 1985. This is likely to be the largest number that can be tackled within the limits of present staffing.

From the beginning the Centre has offered short residential courses, most commonly between two and six days' duration with a membership drawn from all parts of Scotland. From the 460 secondary schools in all the regions of Scotland over 80 per cent of Heads, about 50 per cent of Deputes, and a third of Assistant Headteachers have attended at least one course. Very few schools have not been represented at all and a number have been able to send all their senior staff on at least one course at different times. It is unusual for a new headteacher to be appointed who has not attended.

The content of courses has changed over the years from an emphasis on lectures and discussions and a 'systems' approach to management to one that depends more on participants' activity and experience. The Centre does not assume a prescriptive role, but rather aims, through a programme of lectures, debates, case-studies, small group discussion, visits and projects, to promote the exchange of ideas and experience so that members may select the elements they consider desirable or essential for their particular schools. Courses have never been compulsory, but there is no doubt that they add to the education of the members in management and curriculum as they are exposed to the witness, beliefs, experience and prejudices of a wide variety of visiting speakers drawn from school, college, univeristy, and other sources in both Scotland and England.

In each course, usually limited to about twenty members to obtain maximum involvement, the Centre designs a programme of high standard. It has been crucial for Headteachers and Deputes to see the importance of what was offered and to appreciate the significance of the provision. The success of the programme may be evaluated by the continuing demand for places on courses, favourable reports from course members and employers and the evidence of beneficial changes in the operation of schools.

The influence of the Centre on the management style in many schools is now becoming apparent through greater participation of the staff, more thought in planning, delegation, communication and control, and an awareness of the school's accountability to the public and to their employers. The demands of current curriculum developments have themselves assisted staff to develop and, often, to increase their professional development and satisfaction.

Courses have regularly been evaluated by participants, by their employers and outside visitors. Results have been correlated and published and are regularly used for the development of new course programmes.

The Centre has developed strong links with other agencies involved in Educational Management. It has regularly had course participants from Europe through the Council of Europe Bursary Scheme. These individuals have learned something of the work done in Scotland and have been able to contribute information about their own educational systems. Participants have attended from the Moray House College Scottish Centre for Education Overseas and the Director has contributed to a number of their programmes. In addition the Centre contributed to a major report on school leader training sponsored by the Council of Europe and the Director has attended three of their conferences. He has also been involved in the International Schools Improvement Project of OECD and a report on heads training prepared by the EEC Commission. Individual contacts have been made with Educational Administrator trainers from Sweden, Holland, South Africa, Papua New Guinea, New Zealand, Australia, the United States, Canada, India, Sri Lanka, and Thailand.

The Centre has a regular consultancy role with individual schools and authorities who approach them about issues concerned with school management and administration and it publishes a series of occasional papers which are issued to every secondary school and to Educational Administrators on topics such as 'The Teacher and the Law', 'School Accounts', 'The Cost of Running the School', 'Computers in School Administration', 'The Role of the Assistant Headteacher', 'Staff Development', and 'Grievance and Discipline Procedures'.

The HMI Management Report, *Learning and Teaching in Scottish Secondary Schools: School Management* (1984) commented: 'For its size and scope, the Scottish Centre for School Administration, based at Moray House College of Education, makes a commendable contribution to the national training programme in School Management' (para. 2.4.5).

The management triangle

In the early activities described above the perspective on the explicitly management side was clearly an effectiveness/efficiency one in precisely measurable terms. At the same time the department of Educational Management and Administration was pursuing studies in broader aspects of educational management. Two levels of school management, namely, the positions of headteacher and head of department, were the prime focus in the late 1960s, and with the help of a number of experienced practitioners at both levels critical problem areas were identified and courses organised with the explicit aim of improving practice. Such an emphasis in educational management was somewhat unusual at that time. While in Britain the study of Educational

Management and Administration had never quite adopted the rigorous academic stance current in the US and Canada, for example, there was quite definitely a thrust in England, particularly in those early years, towards a substantially theoretical research-based approach which looked somewhat askance at efforts to make a direct impact on practice. To some extent this was a reflection of two factors: the university/polytechnic base of the earliest work, and the understandable desire not to rush to prescription before due study and analysis. From the start the Scottish approach was more rashly pragmatic. It was, however, gratifying to be able to see quite clearly identifiable changes and improvements in management practice associated with these Scottish initiatives in both primary and secondary schools.

The basic ideas underlying these general management studies were developments of the three fundamental irreducibles of the management process. These ideas and their interrelationship are conveniently shown in the management triangle:

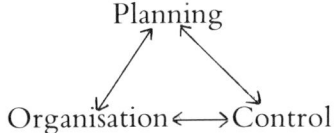

In applying these to the management of education the stance was accepted that there is common ground in the management process in a whole range of fields from industrial and commercial through to service enterprises like hospitals and education. It was a question of modification and adaptation rather than an attempt to create a totally unrelated model for education. For example, the study of the planning function brought into focus aspects of objectives as a guide to management action. While Management by Objectives as a developed general management package was recognised as having little to offer the educational manager, certainly at institutional level, the ideas of using objectives in management were found to illumine the task at many levels by focusing on the need to think clearly about what precisely the organisation's activities were designed to achieve. With the move away from the clearly defined academic aims of the selective school to the much more diffuse and pervasive purposes of the comprehensive institution, clarifying and making explicit these purposes were crucial not only for managers but also to help all staff towards an understanding of the changed nature of the task of the school and to facilitate some organisational cohesion.

It is when organisational questions are approached without a sense of what the arrangements are designed to achieve that difficulty is most likely to arise, particularly with a professional staff. Failure to recognise this danger led to much frustration and disillusionment in academic schools facing the transition to a wider role. Changes such as mixed ability groups and common course patterns were often resented at least in part because teachers had not been given to appreciate clearly the purposes they were intended to further. Application of the management triangle approach allows the organisational arrangements to follow logically or at least consonantly from the explication of what it is they are supposed to be designed to achieve, and so to generate at least a measure of legitimation.

This last concept opens the door to a wide-ranging study of organisational factors which influence the ongoing life of corporate institutions, and it was in this area that the Moray House approach to management drew most heavily on the very extensive academic literature of organisation theory. For the most part, however, the stress was on seeking to use these studies and throw light on actual management situations and problems rather than presenting them as a detached academic activity to form a general part of the educational manager's training. In fact this approach often resulted in the stimulation of interest of practitioners in the further study of such questions. In the same sort of way while headteachers and other educational managers might frequently be heard to express considerable scepticism about the relevance of general management theory to education, it was quite remarkable how often these same groups would find contributions to courses by either practising managers in industry or university business school staff highly stimulating, and with little effort be able to identify the parallel situations in education.

There is little doubt that education is generally weakest at the third point of the triangle — the managerial control activity. Traditionally there have been much testing and many examinations, and even of late a great surge of interest in a whole range of new assessment techniques. Only very recently, however, has much attention been devoted to the overall management control aspects of the educational enterprise — questions such as, 'What is the school achieving as a whole?', 'Is it doing what it ought to be doing?', 'Are there other ways, and perhaps more effective ways, of doing what the school is trying to do?'. Many education authorities throughout Britain are now taking this function seriously and have issued a whole galaxy of instruments to help schools evaluate their work in terms of both political and professional accountability. For the most part these are of the checklist type, but more rigorous objectives, criteria, standards approaches have also been tried.[6]

Changing perspectives

Much play has been made in the literature of education management as well as general management of this observable progression from classical management theories through human relations approaches to an emphasis on human resources management. A parallel progression is observable in the major Scottish Education Department initiatives as reflected in the key Green Papers and reports issued in the management field over the last 15 years. First came the 1969 Paper on Staffing already referred to, following through to the 'Red Book' of 1973. Next came the 1971 Green Paper *The Structure of Promoted Posts in Secondary Schools in Scotland*. Focus at present is on the long awaited School Management report in the Learning and Teaching in Scottish Secondary Schools series eventually published in 1984. Efficiency is the concern of the first, and the emphasis is on information collection, analysis, and application to develop more efficient techniques of management and administration of resources, As indicated by its title the 1971 Paper moves on to questions of structure and organisational patterns as the means to securing more effective as well as more efficient management. Clearly underlying its argument are assumptions about the ways in which effective management can be facilitated or frustrated by matters of senior staff deployment. Job descriptions come to the fore and there is a strong feeling that things will improve if only we get the system right and operate with a degree of sensitivity to people's needs as well as the organisation's. It is true that the 1984 School Management report incorporates a wide-ranging review of the management systems evolved from the 1971 Green Paper and begins its conclusions with the words, 'The case for a quite radical redistribution of the posts . . . is clear from events and from the need to manage change'. Nonetheless, it is much concerned with questions of responsibility, effectiveness, and the dynamics of management.

Recent moves in the management of the colleges of education reflect a not dissimilar pattern over a considerably shorter timescale. Efficiency was clearly a prime value in the rationalisation, reorganisation, and closure programme of the late seventies and early eighties. Subsequent calls for each college to submit to the Scottish Education Department its proposed management and organisational structure correspond to the second schools phase above. Current extensive involvement in new course development, participative procedures and external validation highlights emphasis on responsibility and effectiveness of management in a situation of change.

Current issues

Educational management at both central and institutional level faces quite a range of common issues. Apart from the general constraints of the accountability movement reflecting a whole spectrum of differing interests demanding a say in decision-making and providing an ever-widening context for the activities of the educational manager, there are the steadily increasing pressures from above. Even at the very highest level, education is subject to the Treasury. Viewed from this standpoint then even the senior educational manager appears as combining with his 'top' role a middle management role as well — a feature of the job scarcely calculated to reduce ambiguity and uncertainty. At school level this is most critical for the headteacher, who must be at one and the same time manager and leader of his staff and also an executive arm of the education authority. Tensions between professionalism — i.e. concern with the interests of the professionals as a group — and professionality — i.e. the promotion of personal and professional standards of work[7] — is a further aspect of the complexity of the managerial task particularly at a time of serious unrest among staff, and forces the educational manager, however much against his will, to come to terms with industrial relations types of questions.

These matters are not, however, simply to do with regulations and practices, grievance and disciplinary procedures: leadership and management styles are of critical importance. Consideration has to be given to the manager's personal propensities, the characteristics of the staff, and the nature of the task and situation. Contingency studies of leadership suggest strongly that it is not a matter of the leader finding the right style and improving his capacity to perform in that way. Rather he must increase his sensitivity to the requirements of the situation and his ability effectively to adopt whatever style is most appropriate for the occasion. Such an approach demands an enhanced professionality of the manager himself, a reflective as well as performative capacity. Of late such uneasy problems as the management of contraction have turned the minds of many educational managers to such considerations with deepened interest.

Contraction is, of course, but one aspect of change, albeit a particularly acute one. The 1984 Inspectorate Report on School Management referred to above focuses sharply on the general problems of the management of change as of key significance for the senior and middle management in schools. Here, the effective manager must be sensitive to such issues as the balance between innovative, thrusting leadership and counter-productive drovership; carrying staff along with real commitment and understanding and pushing ahead with an all-consuming zeal that leaves them confused and disillusioned, or even disaffected, far behind; the impressive short-term impact and the substantial longer term development. Real educational leadership must be concerned with professional development and hence the issue of participation is not a purely academic management style question. In education this is the more important, inasmuch as effective implementation is so dependent on the staff. In the words of Lao Tsu, the ultimate aim of the genuine educational leader will be so to lead that when the task is done the staff will say, 'We did this ourselves'. For this kind of reason the Swedish School Leader Improvement Project concentrates almost exclusively on issues of leadership, personal relations, group skills and motivation in the compulsory two-year programme for all secondary headteachers.

Espousal of one particular school or phase of educational management thought has never been a feature of the Moray House approach. And so it is not inappropriate to turn from essentially human resources ideas back to an important plank in classical management theory which is still of great importance and concern at all levels in the system today, namely the matter of delegation. In the 1971 Green Paper on the Structure of Promoted Posts, the Scottish Education Department voiced its concern that there was inadequate delegation in the schools, and still in 1984 that concern remains in such statements as 'Headteachers . . . have often failed to make clear the high expectations they have of promoted staff, or failed to follow through these expectations by insisting that promoted staff should regard themselves as fully accountable for what they do, or fail to do.'[5] This is simply the perennial problem of delegation and control, yet another instance of the need for balance, this time between subordinate initiative and manager interference. The border between delegation and abdication is a fine one, and it is control that marks the line.

This paper offers few if any prescriptions — and mades no apology for the omission. Its view of management prohibits such a posture. It sees the role of the manager in education as a complex one demanding a range of skills and sensitivities, and the task of management education as chiefly attempting to develop these skills and sensitivities, while not ignoring certain specific knowledge and techniques that may be necessary to help him exploit them effectively. Perhaps none has framed a more perceptive list of these requirements than March. He identified five critical administrative skills:

    The Skill of Dealing with Experts
    The Skill of Building Coalition

The Skill of Making Decisions in Conditions of Great
   Ambiguity and Uncertainty
The Skill of Allocating One's Own Time
The Skill of Analysing Data, not for Research, but for
   Managing[8]

While the relative significance of each may differ a little from institution to institution and situation to situation, there is no doubt that, even a decade after it was written, this information epitomises particularly aptly the requirements of the educational manager today.

References

1. SED (1969)   'Circular 714'.
2. SED (1973)   *Secondary School Staffing* ('Red Book'). HMSO.
3. SED (1971)   *The Structure of Promoted Posts in Secondary Schools in Scotland.* HMSO.
4. NCITT (1984)   *Arrangements for the Staff Development of Teachers.* National Committee for the In-service Training of Teachers. Scottish Education Department.
5. SED (1984)   *Learning and Teaching in Scottish Secondary Schools: School Management.* HMSO.
6. Ewan, E. A. *et al.* (1975)   *Assessment of Effectiveness of School Guidance System.* Moray House College of Education.
7. Hoyle, E. (1974)   'Professionality, Professionalism and Control in Teaching', *London Educational Review*, 3.2.
8. March, J. G. (1974) 'Analytical Skills and the University Training of Educational Administrators', *Journal of Educational Administration*, 12.1.

11

Guidance and counselling in school and college

Margaret Jarvie and Nicholas Tate

Introduction

Within education, concerns about personal, curricular and vocational guidance are not new. Though often with different assumptions and objectives, educational thought has always been concerned with more than just the intellectual development of students. It is nonetheless true that one of the most significant shifts in emphasis in Scottish education during the last quarter of a century has been the growth of awareness and interest in these other aspects of education. What has changed is that the concerns have become more overt and have been formalised within new structures. The aim of this chapter is to comment upon the contributions to these developments being made by Moray House College of Education, both through the training of teachers for guidance in schools and through the provision of an advisory and counselling service for students.

Training for guidance in schools

In 1968, in a publication which is now referred to as the 'Orange Paper', the Scottish Education Department (SED, 1968) noted that, because of changes taking place both within and outwith schools, young people were being subjected to stresses which earlier generations had not experienced. Their recommendation was that schools should respond to this situation by offering all pupils curricular, vocational and personal guidance. They defined guidance as 'the taking of that personal interest in pupils as individuals which makes it possible to assist them in making choices or decisions' (ibid., p. 3).

Fifteen years later, in their report to the Committee on Secondary

Education, the Scottish Central Committee on Guidance wrote that, although circumstances had changed considerably since the publication of the 'Orange Paper', the need for guidance was as great as it had ever been (SCCG, 1983). This view appears to be shared by the Inspectorate who, even more recently, declared that, in spite of falling rolls and the need to economise:

> the evidence strongly suggests that a reduction in the proportion of guidance posts would be undesirable, and is reinforced by the fact that all pupils are likely to meet crucial decision-making points . . . more frequently than ever before (HMI, 1984, p. 33).

The indications are, therefore, that the contribution of guidance to the development of pupils is being recognised as worthwhile and that, as Anne Fletcher expresses it, 'guidance has become an integral part of education' (Fletcher, 1980).

Although guidance has become an established part of education, not all of the implications of this situation have been fully resolved. Some of these implications relate to the question of training. The importance of training is widely acknowledged and, like other colleges of education, Moray House offers a wide range of courses in guidance. The provision of such courses does not, however, by itself remove all the problems. A major remaining problem concerns the voluntariness of such courses, there being no requirement on anyone taking up a promoted post in guidance to undertake training. Echoing the feelings of most authorities on this matter, the Pack Committee declared the state of affairs to be unsatisfactory and urged that steps be taken to alter it (Pack Committee, 1977). The Scottish Central Committee on Guidance also recommended that 'all teachers should have appropriate guidance training' (SCCG, 1983, p. 11). Such recommendations have not yet been acted upon. The voluntary nature of training is, of course, by no means the only issue which impinges on the work of the college in this area. Some of the issues currently being addressed within Moray House will be discussed under the following headings: pre-service training of secondary teachers; Certificate course in guidance; advanced qualifications in guidance.

Pre-service training

While there is general agreement that all teachers in training should be informed about guidance systems in schools, there is disagreement about the extent to which some of the constituent parts of guidance training should be incorporated into pre-service courses. Those who oppose the latter approach mainly do so on the basis that these parts of guidance training are only pertinent to those who are taking up posts in guidance. Commenting on this issue, the National Advisory Committee on Guidance drew a distinction between learning *about* guidance and being trained *in* guidance and suggested that, at the pre-service level, the need was for students to learn about guidance. However, they did add that:

> Nevertheless, there are basic techniques of communication, relationship building and helping others which are common to guidance work and to teaching in general, and it would seem to be essential that all students should have some opportunity to learn some of these skills in a structured way (NACOG, 1981, p. 24).

The skills mentioned here are not exclusive to guidance but they are inherent in it and, as such, have been focused upon in guidance training. In the past they were not emphasised in the training of secondary teachers but, because the committee with responsibility for organising workshops within the postgraduate secondary course agree with the opinion expressed by the National Advisory Committee on Guidance, they are now being emphasised within the current course. The innovation is being monitored and future developments will depend on the final evaluation.

Though there is a strong argument for providing all teachers with opportunities to develop communication and relationship-building skills, it is not the only one which may be advanced in favour of including some training in guidance, as well as about guidance, at the pre-service level. A compelling justification is that there are aspects of guidance, like pastoral care and social education, which are the concerns of all staff in schools and not exclusively of guidance teachers.

Two of the distinguishing features of the Scottish approach to guidance are (i) the belief that guidance is about normal development and is, therefore, for all pupils; and (ii) the emphasis on promoted guidance staff spending some time teaching their subject. These features reflect the aim of making guidance part of mainstream education and not an adjunct to it. In Scotland, guidance is regarded as a function of the whole school and, therefore, requires the efforts of an extended guidance team which is comprised of other members of staff as well as guidance specialists. The Scottish Central Committee adopted the term 'first level guidance' to denote teachers who are in daily contact with a group of pupils and who have a pastoral role, whether or not they are in a promoted guidance post. The same Committee recommended that training should be provided for first level guidance teachers. Moray House responded to this by running in-service courses for this group of teachers but the recognition that a high proportion of students will be involved in guidance at this level has given rise to seeking ways of introducing some preparation for this work in pre-service courses. One of the ways in which a contribution is being made is through workshop activities within the course for secondary graduates.

A similar argument may be put forward on the basis that personal and social education are inherent parts of education. In his note of reservation on the Report of the Munn Committee, Gordon Kirk, the present Principal of Moray House, presented persuasive arguments for the inclusion in the curriculum of a compulsory core component aimed at developing the social understanding of pupils. His contention was that the recommendations of the Munn Committee did not go far enough in that although they took account of the need to involve pupils in 'the consideration of the political, economic, industrial and environ-mental aspects of life in contemporary society' (SED, 1977, p. 69), they neglected the associated need to 'engage pupils in an analysis of human behaviour and of the factors which influence their behaviour' (ibid., p. 69). Furthermore, the proposals did not acknowledge the need for qualified specialists to undertake this work over and above the contributions that could be made by every teacher. Although his proposal was rejected by the Committee, the tenor of his comments was not.

In their research into the position in Scottish schools, the Scottish Social Education Project team found that 'the day-to-day teaching of guidance/social education tends to lie with guidance staff' (MacBeath et al., 1981, p. 5). NACOG's explanation for this is that the responsibility has devolved on to guidance teachers because of the similarity of philosophies underpinning guidance and social education, but they go on to point out that the concept of social education is inextricably tied up with the work of subject departments. A similar view is expressed in the Position Paper of The Consultative Committee on the Curriculum, 'Social Education in Scottish Schools'. This Committee is of the opinion that:

> social education should permeate everything in a school and most of all the classroom where teachers and pupils spend most of their time. The formal curriculum is, therefore, the most important channel for social education, which should be conveyed through both curricular subject and special programmes, the former an increasingly flexible resource as modules, short courses and inter disciplinary courses take their place beside the traditional structures (CCC, 1984, p. 1).

They further advocate that 'all teachers should assume responsibility for contributing to this element of pupils' education' (ibid., p. 1). If this is to happen, then, as Douglas Weir has pointed out, 'a wider range of skills will have to be offered in teacher training than has been in the past' (Weir, 1981).

For the reasons stated above, what is offered to students in pre-service courses at Moray House College of Education goes beyond informing them *about* guidance. Attempts are being made to redress the imbalance, bemoaned by Kenneth David (1983), in which personal and social aspects of education are not sufficiently emphasised at the pre-service level. Incorporating elements of guidance training into pre-service courses is one of the ways in which students are equipped with skills and encouraged to focus on ways of advancing the all-round development of pupils. Capra (1983) has claimed that the emerging paradigm is one which stresses holism and interrelatedness. This idea is also advanced by Marilyn Ferguson (1981) who quotes evidence to substantiate her claim that this paradigm is beginning to be the dominant one in education, as well as in other spheres of society. Within Moray House, students are being encouraged at the pre-service level to examine this paradigm, to consider its implications for their teaching role and to familiarise themselves with the skills which the paradigm demands.

Certificate course in guidance

In 1978 the Committee of Principals set up the National Advisory Committee on Guidance and gave it a remit which included scrutinising and commenting upon training courses in guidance and making recommendations concerning them. At the end of their three-year period of office the Committee suggested that:

> The new one-term or one-term equivalent course should
> become the basic course for newly appointed or recently
> appointed Guidance staff who have now made a career choice
> (NACOG, 1981, op. cit., p. 36).

There is some evidence that this is happening. For instance, some education authorities sponsor teachers to come on one-term equivalent courses, which are commonly known as Certificate courses. Indeed one authority, Central Region, requested that Moray House make special provisions to enable staff from that Region to attend Certificate courses. Again, in a recent notice advertising a guidance post it was stated that preference would be given to applicants who held the Certificate in Guidance.

One of the tasks undertaken by NACOG was the scrutiny of the content and structure of Certificate courses with a view to encouraging the emergence of and maintenance of national standards. Moray House's one-term equivalent course was approved by NACOG in 1978. As the course is a basic one it is general in nature and covers the whole range of activities entered into by guidance specialists. It, therefore, contains standard components but as guidance is evolving the course is by no means a static one. Information gleaned from course evaluation spawns innovations for future courses as do changes taking place in the field.

One of the current concerns being addressed in Moray House relates to the weighting given within the course to training in counselling. In their early publications on guidance, the SED made it clear that in Scotland the emphasis was to be on guidance and not, as in England, on counselling. Guidance teachers were to be concerned with the personal development of pupils but they were not to be full-time counsellors. Most guidance teachers accept this but, nonetheless, find that they are better equipped to fulfil their role if they are able to exercise counselling skills.

Part of the confusion regarding the place of counselling in schools stems from the semantic difficulties associated with the term 'counselling'. It is sometimes used to refer to therapy in which psychoanalytic techniques are used to restructure the personality of an individual. This kind of counselling requires lengthy, specialist training and is beyond the remit of teachers. However, counselling may also refer to the process whereby an individual is helped to arrive at a decision having reviewed his rational and emotional responses to the alternatives open to him. It is in this latter sense that counselling may contribute to guidance. Speaking at a National Course on Developments and Priorities in Guidance, Professor Fulton put forward the view that 'guidance' and 'counselling' were not mutually exclusive alternatives. He defined 'guidance as the fundamental concept and counselling as the activity through which guidance goals can be achieved' (Fulton, 1978). There is an awakening of the realisation, among teachers and others, that the choices which pupils have to make in the curricular, vocational and personal spheres are so complex that personal counselling must precede guidance. Not only does counselling provide an opportunity for each pupil to be known individually and to have his needs recognised and understood, it also increases their independence because the developmental process of counselling is aimed at helping pupils to deepen their understanding of their situation, to review the alternatives available to them and to select the one which is most appropriate for them. Experiencing the process and learning from it is an educational exercise geared to facilitating the autonomy of the individual. The balance of the components in the Certificate course in Guidance offered by Moray House reflects this aspect of the changing demand which is coming from practitioners in the field.

Another change which has been incorporated into present courses is that part of the curriculum is negotiated. While it is true that there is a commonality of needs among the teachers who come on the courses, it is equally true that their needs greatly vary. They come from a range of school backgrounds in which they have different responsibilities and, as individuals, their personal careers and experiences are also different. As the course aims to increase their professional and personal development, the introduction of a negotiated curriculum component enables account to be taken of these variations and makes the course sufficiently flexible to meet the needs of individual members. It has additional advantages, one of which is that it engages the teachers in self-assessment. One can only identify one's needs by examining one's strengths and weaknesses in the context of the goal for which one is striving. Another advantage is that it encourages the course members to take responsibility for their own learning; and a third is that, as the aims of guidance in schools are reflected in the functions of a negotiated curriculum component, it allows the teachers to experience a *modus operandi* which serves as a prototype for some aspects of their work in schools. In this way, the inclusion of a negotiated curriculum component into the Certificate course contributes to the professional and personal development of course participants.

One of the characteristics of the negotiated curriculum component within the Certificate course is that we are endeavouring to extend it to encompass the group situation as well as the individual one. Course members do undertake a programme of study related to their individual concerns but, in addition, they are given responsibility, as a group, for planning the timetable towards the end of the course. This not only allows the group to fill in any residual 'gaps', it necessitates their negotiating with each other, deciding on priorities for topics to be covered, choosing the form sessions should take and making the appropriate administrative arrangements. As they are asked to reflect on their experience of being in a group which has been given this task, the exercise not only allows them to increase their knowledge in chosen areas, but also advances their understanding of group processes.

These are some of the innovations which have been introduced into the Moray House Certificate Course in Guidance. The developments are being carefully monitored as are all aspects of the course.

Advanced qualifications in guidance

No training establishment in Scotland offers courses in guidance at an advanced level. Anyone wishing to pursue their training beyond the level of the Certificate course must do so in another country. The disadvantages associated with this are obvious. There is, therefore, general agreement that there is a need to provide courses which would enable guidance teachers to pursue their interests and specialisms to a greater depth than is possible at present. However, there is less agreement about how that need should be met. Moray House's response to the debate has been to set up a working party to investigate and evaluate the possibilities. As the deliberations of the working party are continuing it would be premature to make any statements concerning outcomes but the thinking of the working party is sufficiently well advanced to enable some general comments to be made.

The need is for a structure which provides a coherent framework which will enable teachers to build on their existing qualifications. It must, therefore, be a tiered one. In their crystal ball gazing into the future, NACOG considered and rejected the notion that there should be a one-year diploma in guidance. Their consideration was 'that such a step would not be to the best advantage of teachers or of Guidance at present' (NACOG, 1981, p. 37). What they did recommend was that there should be an advanced course 'constructed on a modular basis of varied course units from which different groups of teachers might choose out nationally acceptable patterns for their own particular career or interest purposes' (ibid., p. 37). The thinking of Moray House's working party has led them to a similar conclusion. They are opting for a modular based course constructed in such a way that course members would be able to take either a general qualification in professional studies in secondary education or a specialist one, depending on the modules selected.

A modular based course also facilitates the creation of a framework within which entry to some modules may be made dependent upon the completion of others and it makes exit possible at different levels. It is also economical in that it allows teachers who may be following different specialised courses to come together to study components which are germane to several specialisms. This has the additional advantage that it facilitates communication among personnel from different sectors of education. As has been demonstrated by the Moray House-based project 'Pathways to the Professions' (McMichael and Gilloran, 1984), much is to be gained from bringing together in training participants from various professions and from different sub-sections of the same profession. Sharing viewpoints with non-guidance teachers is potentially productive for guidance teachers who, paradoxically, wish both to become specialists and, simultaneously, to encourage their colleagues to participate in guidance in order that the concept of the school as a caring community is put into operation. A modular-based, tiered system, therefore, would meet the needs of guidance specialists. It could incorporate basic training, such as is currently offered in Certificate courses, and allow anyone who wished to cease their studies at that level to do so; it could also provide opportunities for those who wished to progress to a more advanced level in their chosen specialism of guidance; and, without detracting from the emphasis on the specialism, it could facilitate the development of understandings and relationships with others who are not in guidance but who share an interest in, and concern for, education. Such a course would be a major and welcome development.

Guidance in higher education

As in schools, those in higher education concerned with the provision of guidance and counselling are often conscious of operating within a context of attitudes and institutions that are the legacy of educational situations in some ways very different from those of today. The personal tutor system that forms the backbone of pastoral support in many areas of British higher education has its origins in a former Oxbridge world in which the roles of undergraduate and (moral) tutor were ones, respectively, of *in statu pupillari* and *in loco parentis*. Some of the well-documented inadequacies of the present system may well arise from the way in which it has been grafted on to an educational environment now lacking in many of the attitudes that once gave it support. The solution to the dilemmas created by such disparities lies, however, not in any revolutionary clean sweep — the organisational separation between teaching services and student personnel services, for example — but in a cautious adaptation of institutions to situations for which they were not originally designed. The dangers of the revolutionary clean sweep are apparent in recent developments in US higher education, where faculty advisement programmes over the past decade have been designed, to a large extent, with the aim of restoring some aspects of student assistance to the tutor (Pashley, 1974). In Britain swings of the pendulum have been less violent, with cautious modifications of an established system the usual pattern of change. Developments over the last 15 years have adapted the traditional personal tutor system in a number of important ways, most notably through the appointment of trained (or untrained) student counsellors or through the formation of teams of tutors with an expertise or interest in personal counselling. Alternative sources of advice and counselling had always of course been available, though rarely in a form that was both confidential and completely separated from the exercise of a disciplinary role. In general, however, the characteristic features of the personal tutor system — the involvement of personal tutors in the teaching and assessment of their students, the lack of training, and the non-voluntary nature of the job — persist much as before.

Such persistence might be seen as indicating not so much institutional ossification as the existence of consensus about the system's value and about the lack of realistic alternatives. Such a consensus — the belief that the personal tutor system represents 'a fundamentally good idea' — coexists, however, with a widespread acceptance of its inadequacies as frequently operated in practice. These inadequacies were highlighted during the 1970s by the researches of Risby (1972), Williamson (1972) and Rees (1977) into the personal tutor systems of a number of English colleges of education. To some extent they are inadequacies which are the likely result of the structures and pressures of the educational environment in which the system functions or to which the system itself, given its essential features, is inherently prone. Williamson's two most striking conclusions were, firstly, the disparity between the public aims of the system and its operation in practice and, secondly, the differing perceptions of it manifested by students, tutors and college administrators. Though designed with 'personal' as well as 'academic' development in mind, the system appeared to be providing little service with regard to the former. To many students their personal tutor was not a particularly important person, one who was often seen very rarely and in some cases not at all. The system also suffered from having a large number of sometimes conflicting demands made upon it. The fact that it satisfied certain demands more effectively than others helped to account for the varying ways in which it was evaluated by the three groups involved. Of these groups — students, tutors and college administrators — Williamson found that it was the final group that regarded the system with most favour. To those primarily concerned with the smooth running of the college's academic administration the personal tutor system was above all an administrative tool, useful as a channel of communication, an agent of discipline and social control, an early warning system, as well as a source of information on individual students. The parallel with the situation in schools is very close. As in schools, few would suggest that most of these administrative concerns were unimportant. It may also be the case that personal tutors, as well as acting as academic tutors, vocational guides and confidantes, are the best people — if only in the interests of students — to perform these tasks. The juxtaposition of such varied duties requires, however, more thought about the aims and the functioning of the system than either Williamson or Risby encountered in the course of their surveys. Risby indeed identified as one of his main criticisms of pastoral care in colleges of education that 'the aims behind their counselling arrangements do not appear always to have been clearly thought out and agreed by all the staff'.

Aware of these research findings and realising the weaknesses in its own arrangements, Moray House recently set about the task of investigating, defining and improving its own provision with regard to pastoral care. For a number of reasons the college had a very varied set of arrangements for guidance and counselling. Some of these reasons were of a historical nature, comparable courses sometimes having markedly different arrangements as a result of their origins or their varying links with outside bodies. Other reasons related to the differing aims and objectives of the college's courses — social work courses, for example, traditionally placing greater emphasis on counselling, if only in part because it constituted an exemplar of an important professional skill that students themselves were also concerned to develop. The task of compiling a policy document that recognised the demands of diverse courses but at the same time provided precise and useful guidelines and that also took due notice of the *status quo* while moving in some respects radically beyond it was not an easy one. Bramley's wise words were noted and acted upon:

> If the personal tutor system, however elegantly designed and
> efficient, descends from some central committee or august
> personage in the college it may well be unconsciously sabotaged
> by those who are intended to implement it or derive benefit
> from it. For if individual and sectional needs and interests have
> not been taken into account, and if people do not feel identified
> with the system, it is not going to work properly, even when all
> procedures are adhered to on paper. Obviously no tutoring
> system can be policed even though subtly coercive means do
> exist to ensure that tutors will give 'personal tutorials' or produce
> wastage statistics and so on. But a tutoring system which really
> results in better inter-personal relationships between staff and
> students works because tutors are highly motivated. This means
> that tutors should be a party to the system's creation as well as to
> its implementation. (Bramley, 1977).

'Central committees' and 'august personages' may well have been involved in the formulation of Moray House's new policy paper, but so, too, were most members of academic staff, both through attendance at a staff conference devoted to these issues and through membership of one or other of the college's boards and sub-boards whose opinions on these matters were sought. A particularly helpful feature of some of these meetings was the presence of students who gave their own frank views both on existing arrangements and on how these arrangements might be improved. The sharing of viewpoints among tutors from different departments in a large multi-purpose institution, as well as by staff, students and academic administration, was more useful in clarifying aims and procedures than anyone perhaps could have imagined. The continual testing of ideas by those who, in a wide range of situations, would be responsible for the success of their implement-ation helped to ensure that the final form taken by the policy paper was, to a much greater extent than might otherwise have been the case, free from the 'quite impossible recommendations' by which, according to Bramley, such documents are often characterised.

Topics discussed ranged from fundamental aims to the minutiae — though important minutiae — of accreditation, timetabling and room allocation. Opinion varied about the extent to which personal tutors (or advisers as, consensually, at the end of the day they came to be known) should also be involved in the compilation of the student's final report or profile. This was existing practice in some courses, though not in others, and there was a strong minority view that giving personal tutors responsibility for reporting might inhibit students in discussing confidentially matters that they feared might adversely affect their final report. The majority opinion, however, was that — in the students' interests — the personal tutor was the best person to collate a report that would do justice to their strengths and abilities over the course as a whole. It was agreed, though, that the principle of open reporting should be accepted in all college courses and that there should be experimentation — in areas of the college previously unfamiliar with such procedures — with a more negotiated form of profiling. This, it was hoped, would both lead to fuller and more accurate reporting and at the same time reassure students that the purpose of the system was to encourage self-evaluation rather than to assess, to assist in their academic, professional and personal development rather than to discipline or control.

However carefully planned in advance, the success or failure of any personal tutor system will obviously depend on the provision that is made for continuing support once it has got under way. Though it is still too early at Moray House to assess the impact of the college's new policy with regard to advising and counselling, it is already clear that its effectiveness will be determined to a considerable extent by the arrangements that are made in the following four areas: (i) publicity within the student body, (ii) staff development, (iii) staffing and resource allocation, and (iv) evaluation.

The importance of publicity, both for the personal tutor system and for the college's supplementary personal counselling provision, was highlighted at the time of the recent revision by the realisation that substantial numbers of students were unaware of the facilities for advice and information already on offer. Though unable to mount a campaign of 'intrusive' publicity on the scale of the one described by Appleton (1983), the use of posters widely displayed throughout the college and its halls of residence, the issuing to all students on registration of a leaflet listing available services, together with talks to groups of new students during the first week of the year, have all helped in raising levels of awareness within the college concerning the help that is available. Almost equally important has been ensuring that all tutors are similarly well informed, especially with regard to new arrangements for careers and personal counselling, in order that there should be no difficulty in referring students to the appropriate source of help whenever the need might arise.

Keeping tutors well informed, however, is only a small part of the much wider need for a staff development programme for those involved in guidance and counselling. Williamson's survey suggested a connection between the inadequacies of the personal tutor system in colleges of education and the fact that 'most personal tutors seemed to be untrained for the job'. His criticism is still valid today and might also be applied to many of those in colleges whose function is to provide a personal counselling service. Training can take many forms: full-time secondment in order to acquire professional qualifications, attendance at conferences, the forging of professional links with colleagues in neighbouring institutions, staff development days and, of course, regular meetings of personal tutors in which those involved share their experiences and transfer their expertise. It is hoped that all these will play a part in the continuing development of guidance and counselling in Moray House. One aspect of the personal tutor's work singled out for particular attention in the immediate future is the promotion of appropriate study skills. Personal tutors may recognise the potentially important role they are able to play in this part of their students' lives, but in many cases may also be aware that they lack the knowledge necessary for effective study skills teaching. It should be one of the aims of staff development to communicate to tutors the research findings of recent years with regard to study skills, both the nature and aetiology of the problems and — in so far as there is any agreement about these — the most effective ways of tackling them.

In order to give public recognition to the work of the personal tutor and counsellor, staff development must be closely linked with appropriate arrangements for staffing and resource allocation. In committing itself, within its externally prescribed staffing quotas, to the principle of accreditation for the work of personal tutoring, Moray House has attempted to demonstrate to those involved in the system that this is an integral part of their work, and not just some cosmetic extra that need not be taken very seriously. The constraints of these staffing quotas are likely, however, to inhibit further necessary development, making difficult or impossible secondments, realistic time allocations for the work performed, or the appointment of full-time student counsellors from outside the academic staff. It is hoped that due attention will eventually be given to the well-attested cost-effectiveness of counselling provision in reducing student drop-out rates. As in schools, too blinkered an approach to the making of economies can itself be financially costly (Frank and Kirk, 1975).

The final *sine qua non* of any effective counselling system, whether at Moray House or any other institution of higher education, is adequate provision for continuing evaluation. This will be an essential part of the institutional self-analysis to which Moray House is already committed. Such evaluation, it is hoped, will be linked to descriptive and analytical research into what is actually being provided — often the province of myth and stereotype — and will involve students, tutors and outside review bodies. The beneficial effects of such evaluation are a striking feature of the findings of recent research into US faculty advisement programmes (Kramer, 1983; Hines, 1981; Appleton, 1983).

An effective personal tutor system is of course in itself — as in schools — a medium for the continuing evaluation of the institution as a whole. As Stander (1974) observed in the mid-1970s with regard to the 'new polytechnics':

> The aggregate of student difficulties are susceptible to
> amelioration through reform of the structure and practices of the
> institution; information regarding felt needs and wants can be
> fed into the decision-making system of the institution by tutors
> and counsellors. Although confidentiality is crucial if individual
> students are going to feel free to come forward to use counselling
> facilities provided, the range and nature of student problems
> could be identified and clarified, leading to progressive

improvements in the institutional structure . . . [Counsellors and tutors] may thereby contribute significantly to dynamic policies of development and change.

In promoting ends such as these, Moray House's new arrangements for guidance and counselling should make a valuable contribution to that tentative, but determined, institutional improvement that the college, as illustrated elsewhere in this symposium, is attempting to pursue on many fronts. Above all, however, guidance and counselling — in schools as well as in higher education — are concerned with individuals and with relationships between individuals. In many ways the school and college community is a simulacrum of the wider world, both personal and professional, which our students will one day join. If in improving the quality of experiences and relationships within this simulacrum the outside reality for which it is a preparation can also itself be improved, then all the effort that has been put into this aspect of our professional work will be more than justified.

From the above it will be seen that changes are occurring both within our teacher training courses and in the provisions we are making for the pastoral care of our students. These changes have widespread implications for the institution. Richards (1983) draws a distinction between 'closed systems' and 'open systems'. The former are systems within which adaptive processes mould individuals to conform to the needs of the institution; the latter are systems within which individuals are encouraged to pursue personal development while recognising and voluntarily accepting parameters. In Moray House we are striving for an 'open system' and we recognise that this requires constant vigilance, continually reviewing our activities and the involvement of all members of staff in extensive staff development programmes. Establishing and maintaining caring communities requires a high level of commitment from the whole college staff and not just from those who act as advisers or directly participate in teacher training. Like Maurice Craft, we recognise that 'guidance and counselling ... treads an extraordinarily difficult path (but) . . . there is every reason for moving on with this exciting new development' (Craft, 1969, p. 23).

References

Appleton, S. (1983). 'The Impact of an Academic Advising Program: A Case Study', *NACADA Journal*, 3/1, pp. 57-63.

Bramley, W. (1977). *Personal Tutoring in Higher Education*. SRHE, Guildford.

Capra, F. (1983). *The Turning Point*. Fontana Paperbacks, London.

Consultative Committee on the Curriculum (1984). *CCC News*, 19.

Craft, M. (1969). 'Guidance, Counselling and Social Needs', in Lytton, H. and Craft, M. (eds), *Guidance and Counselling in British Schools*. Latimer, Trend & Co. Ltd., Whitstable.

David, K. (1983). *Personal and Social Education in Secondary Schools*. Longman for Schools Council.

Ferguson, M. (1981). *The Acquarian Conspiracy*. Granada Pub. Ltd., London.

Fletcher, A. (1980). *Guidance in Schools*. Aberdeen University Press.

Frank, A. C. and Kirk, B. A. (1975). 'Differences in Outcomes for Users and Nonusers of University Counseling and Psychiatric Services: A 5 Year Accountability Study', *Journal of Counseling Psychology*, 22/3, pp. 252-258.

Fulton, J. F. (1978). 'Guidance and Counselling: Some Conceptual Considerations', *Developments and Priorities in Guidance: Proceedings of the National Course in Guidance*. Dundee College of Education.

Hines, E. R. (1981). 'Academic Advising: More than a Placebo?', *NACADA Journal*, 1/3, pp. 24-28.

HMI (1984). *Learning and Management in Scottish Secondary Schools: School Management*. HMSO.

Kramer, G. L. and Peterson, E. D. (1983). 'Utilizing an Accreditation Model to Evaluate Academic Advisement', *NASPA Journal*, 2033, pp. 42-50.

MacBeath, J. *et al.* (1981). *Social Education: the Scottish Approach*. Jordanhill College of Education, Glasgow.

McMichael, P. and Gilloran, A. (1984). *Exchanging Views: Courses in Collaboration*. Moray House College of Education, Edinburgh.

National Advisory Committee on Guidance (1981). *The Development of Guidance Training in Scotland*. Joint Committee of Colleges of Education in Scotland.

Pack Report (1977). *Truancy and Indiscipline in Schools in Scotland*. HMSO.

Pashley, B. W. (1974). 'Pastoral Support for University Students — *in loco parentis* or Functional Necessity?', *Universities Quarterly*, 28/2, pp. 179-208.

Rees, W. D. C. (1977). 'Counselling in Colleges of Education', *British Journal of Guidance and Counselling*, 5/1, pp. 65-72.

Richards, K. (1983). 'Pastoral Care: Open or Closed?', *Pastoral Care*, June.

Risby, J. (1972). 'Counselling and Guidance in Some British Colleges of Education', *The Counsellor*, 12, pp. 8-17.

Scottish Central Committee on Guidance (1983). *Report to the Committee on Secondary Education*.

SED (1968). *Guidance in Scottish Secondary Schools*. HMSO.

SED (1977). *Structure of the Curriculum in the Third and Fourth Years of the Scottish Secondary School, Munn Commission*. HMSO.

Stander, S. (1974). 'Student Counselling and the New Polytechnics', *Universities Quarterly*, 28/2, pp. 197-208.

Weir, D. (1981). 'More Learning, Less Teaching', *Times Educational Supplement*, 20 November.

Williamson, G. R. (1972). 'Personal Tutors — How Personal?', *Universities Quarterly*, 27/1, pp. 66-73.

12

Multicultural education

John Landon

The Scottish Tourist Board slogan 'Scotland's for me' has been used on a series of posters to promote multicultural education.[1] The posters show Chinese, Pakistani and Sikh children involved in activities in their Scottish schools. In a purely descriptive sense, the posters declare that demographically Scotland is a multicultural society. Many different ethnic and cultural groups have settled within Scotland throughout history.[2] Most recently, settlers from the New Commonwealth have made Scotland their home, making up approximately 1 per cent of the population. Scotland *is* for them, in that, for one reason or another, they have come to live in the country.

If we look at the situation more critically, however, we would have to question Scotland's commitment to a multicultural society. On the one hand, there is the rising number of incidents of racial harassment and abuse committed by individuals or groups, reported in the annual statements of the regional community relations councils.[3] On the other hand, there is the institutional response to cultural and racial diversity. A society which practises a policy of cultural and linguistic assimilation, however covertly, towards members of minority cultural or linguistic groups must be guilty of discrimination in favour of the majority population. Thus we can interpret the term 'multicultural' either descriptively or critically. These two interpretations underlie the developments and debate in multicultural education in the past 15 years in Scotland. They can be seen in provision and policy in Moray House. On the one hand, there has been education to meet the specific needs of members of ethnic minority groups in terms of language and culture. We might call this 'education *in* a multicultural society'. On the other hand, there is education of the whole community for cultural and linguistic diversity and towards racial equality — 'education *for* a multicultural society'. On the whole, the focus of the educational establishment has been upon the former. The latter, more comprehensive view, is, however, gaining increasing prominence and is beginning, in a number of schools and colleges, to affect curricular planning and classroom practice.

Multicultural education — the deficit focus

Multicultural education began as a response to a demographic emergency. Children were arriving in the sixties and early seventies in Scottish schools with little or no English. A 1983 Inspectorate Report mentioned that in 1965 there were 800 immigrant pupils in Glasgow schools, but that within two years that number had doubled.[4] This situation, although on a smaller scale, was repeated in Edinburgh, Dundee and Aberdeen. By the late seventies, there were an estimated 6,500 to 7,000 pupils in Scottish schools whose ethnic origins were outside the United Kingdom.

The response to this situation has been the establishment in many Scottish regions of language centres to which children for whom English is a second language can be withdrawn from the mainstream school or class for the whole, or part, of the day. These centres are often classified under Special Educational Needs, or, in one or two regions, are under the purview of the educational psychologist. Thus, multicultural education began with a deficit focus. The aim of specialist language teaching was to make up the deficit, so that children could be returned to the mainstream classroom where they could begin to benefit from the mainstream curriculum.

There are serious problems with this deficit view, both perceptually and procedurally. One perceptual problem concerns the failure to regard the ethnic minority child as a potential bilingual. The emphasis is upon the lack of English, not upon the already acquired first language. The child's early social and conceptual development has been mediated through that first language. Yet, upon entry to the school, the language and all that the child has gained through it, has to give way to another language and another set of cultural assumptions.

There are two results. One is a possible hiatus in conceptual development until the second language reaches a stage at which the child will be able to use it to negotiate the primary school curriculum. This hiatus is particularly likely in situations where the child is withdrawn from the mainstream primary classroom. In withdrawal classes, the focus for the child is more likely to be upon language learning in isolation from more general learning. Recent Canadian research[5] has shown that it takes at least five to seven years on average for pupils arriving in the country at age 6 or later to approach grade norms in English vocabulary. Social facility in the second language is, however, gained much more rapidly. However, if the child's home language were used as a medium of instruction, or support for learning, in the early primary school years, at least transitionally, this discontinuity in learning could to some extent be mitigated.

The other result is the denial to the child of the proven cognitive and social benefits of a well-developed bilingualism. As one language is phased out in favour of a second, with all the implications of differential linguistic status, the child is denied the opportunity within school of developing the first language beyond a narrow domestic usage. Indeed, so low may be the perception of the first language, that the child may well be unwilling to speak it at all, even at home.[6] The loss for the child is not only social, in the distance that this creates from the child's family and community. It will also lead to the diminution of cognitive benefits, such as higher levels of divergent thinking and greater language awareness, which recent research[7] has shown to accrue from balanced bilingualism. The argument is not that access to English should be withheld, but that the child's mother-tongue or community language should be maintained right through the school system. If mother-tongue provision is not introduced, the community is denying itself a potentially rich linguistic resource, and is also acting discriminatorily towards the linguistic minority population.

The common rationalisation for such obvious discrimination is the argument that the maintenance of the first language will interfere with the learning of English. There is no empirical evidence for this view. On the contrary, the findings of a recent research project in Bradford,[8] in which children learning entirely through their second language, English, were measured against children learning half through English and half through their first language, Punjabi, suggest that there is no significant difference in the degree of acquisition of English amongst children taught bilingually. However, the bilingual group, as well as performing far better in their first language than the English-only group, also seemed to read in English with greater understanding and perform better in mathematical tests and in certain tests of cognitive functioning. Another reason given for not making bilingual provision is the shortage of teachers suitably qualified in the community languages. Perhaps this difficulty results not from the fact that members of the ethnic minority populations do not have teaching qualifications — many of them do have, but yet cannot be registered to teach in Scotland — but that registration and training procedures are not flexible enough to respond to such an obvious need.

If failure to support the pupil's bilingualism causes one kind of disadvantage, current procedures for teaching English as a second language may well aggravate the situation. The emergency situation of the sixties and early seventies, and the consequent emergence of a cadre of experts in teaching English as a second language, led to the conviction amongst many class teachers that their skills were not sufficient to meet the second-language learners' needs. The mystique of the specialist de-skilled the mainstream teacher and validated the practice of withdrawal. Although arguments against extraction have been well rehearsed for pupils with learning difficulties, extraction for part of the day is still the norm for many ESL learners.

One result of withdrawal is that language is taught largely in isolation from the needs of the mainstream curriculum, and from the benefits of interaction with native-speaking peers during the conduct of learning activities. Research into second-language acquisition[9] has shown conclusively, however, that children learn language most effectively in a meaningful environment. The mainstream classroom provides such an environment, if there is opportunity for the second-language learner to come to terms with meaning in a context which is supportive both visually and psychologically. Activity-based learning is the ideal setting for language learning to take place.[10]

An alternative role for the specialist ESL teacher might be co-operative teaching within the mainstream class. This is being attempted in a number of schools, but is extremely expensive of manpower. The challenge for trainers is to build into all courses an understanding of the role that the mainstream teacher has as a language teacher, not through the acquisition of additional skills and techniques, but through the improvement of approaches already used for maximising pupil interaction and for increasing the meaningfulness of learning tasks. Thus, teaching English as a second language comes out of the closet — literally in some cases — and takes its place within the whole-school language programme.

Whilst policy with regard to language was one of subtractive bilingualism[11] (phasing out one language in favour of another), policy with regard to culture was one of cultural assimilation. The school was perceived as the agent of social cohesion, imparting a culture which was broadly British. The implication for the white British child was of the superiority of British culture, accompanied by disdain, or at best a mild curiosity, towards more 'exotic' cultures. The child from an ethnic minority group could either yield to the pressure to assimilate, only to find in the playground or on leaving school, that colour or culture was a barrier to complete acceptance. Alternatively, he or she could seek refuge in the home culture. In some cases confusion resulted, or alienation from the majority culture.[12] The response of educational policy-makers was to add to the deficit focus, which had largely concentrated on language provision, a focus which concentrated on cultural diversity. The deficit view, however, has remained, and still influences language provision and referral procedures in many schools.

Multicultural education — the diversity focus

The evidence of alienation and under-achievement by many black children in inner-city schools required action. The response was to build aspects of the pupils' home culture into the school curriculum, either as discrete areas of study, for example, Black Studies, or as integral parts of topic development or subject study. Further support for inclusion of aspects of a child's home culture within the curriculum came from research into the black child's self-image.[13] Denial of the child's home culture, or presentation of the child's country of origin in the emotive terms employed by the aid agencies or in the stereotypic fashion of many children's educational books, produced within the ethnic minority child a loss of self-esteem. Within children from the majority population too, there is likely to have developed a strong set of preferences for their own groups, and distrust and dislike of other groups, especially people from alien cultures of the third world, and of ethnic minority populations in Britain, by association.

Thus, the multicultural movement developed, with the commitment, on the one hand, to develop a sense of respect for self, especially amongst children from ethnic minorities, and to build a respect for others amongst the whole population. Jeffcoate[14] produced a taxonomy of objectives which itemised areas of knowledge which all pupils should cover: the basic facts of race and racial difference; the customs, values and beliefs of the main cultures represented in Britain and of those forming the local community; and reasons for immigration. In order to gain respect for self, pupils should know the history and achievements of their own culture and what is distinctive about it. Further, skills developed through a multicultural curriculum should enable pupils to detect stereotyping and scapegoating in what they see, hear and read; and to evaluate their own cultures objectively. Underlying these cognitive objectives is a set of affective objectives which inculcate an acceptance of common humanity, cultural validity, tolerance, and a commitment to the principles of equal rights and justice. In order to achieve these objectives, he proposed a review of the selection of learning experiences which would eschew ethnocentrism, stereotyping and bias, and would accurately represent the diversity of British society, and Britain's place within an independent world.

For Jeffcoate, multicultural education is primarily affective, being concerned with attitudes and dispositions, and only instrumentally cognitive. There are, in this relationship between cognitive and affective objectives for multicultural education, two underlying problems. The first is the nature of the facts imparted to children. The second is the relationship between facts and attitudes in real practice. If knowledge of one's own culture and the cultures of the major ethnic groups represented in Britain is one of the cognitive objectives, we have the problem of defining what those cultures are. James[15] makes the point that 'culture is not transmitted from one generation to another in fixed and permanent forms: rather it is broken down, reinterpreted and made the source of new growth, like the organic matter of physical life'. Therefore, there is a problem of identification for those teachers who wish to 'locate' a child's culture in order to validate or celebrate it. The danger is that the teacher might seek cultural examples in exotic stereotypes, or in crude presentations of aspects of culture in the countries of origin of pupils' families.

Further, there is the problem for the teacher of accessibility to this culture, when faced by the ambivalence of many ethnic minority schoolchildren towards their 'own' cultures and languages. On the one hand, the teacher might be felt to be breaking the child's cover in a society which is exerting pressure to assimilate, and to which pressure the child has yielded. On the other hand, the child who has adopted the defensive position of alliance to the home culture in face of the onslaught of insecurity and racism may well feel that the teacher's use of the home culture in class is an attempt to colonise and to exert control. In other words, cultural difference handled purely descriptively, with no reference to the pressures which society exerts on that different culture to conform, and with no account taken of historical causes for negative and hostile attitudes towards black minority groups in particular, is misleading for all children, and confusing for the ethnic minority child. In effect, the choice offered by the school to view selfpositively is no choice at all, when the option to proceed in that way is denied by society at large.

Hence we come to the second difficulty with Jeffcoate's assumption, that there is some sort of equation between cognitive and affective knowledge in this area. A knowledge of the food, customs, religious beliefs, dress of a particular ethnic minority group, could furnish the majority child with a thousand good reasons for hostility towards that group, or a sense of superiority, especially if difference is presented in isolation from a rationale for difference,[16] or if the multicultural topic or insert is not supported by a whole curriculum or school system committed to inter-ethnic respect, justice and equality. The danger of so much practice that goes under the name of multicultural education is that it is tokenistic, and that comparisons (expressed or implied) with Western culture are odious. As James[17] puts it in his critique: 'all non-Western cultural forms are judged as more or less successful attempts at doing what white men have (by implication) done best, while avoiding at the same time the storms that blow up when we attempt to present the truth about inequality and injustice (within Britain and the whole world) without implying that the victims are to blame or that their exploitation is inevitable'.

The diversity focus is clearly simplistic since it leaves out the question of power. It is describing difference in an anodyne and unproblematic way; it is not attempting to challenge or remove inequalities within society which are often drawn along lines of difference – racial difference, gender difference or class difference. As the London Borough of Brent's strategy paper for multicultural education, *Education for a Multicultural Democracy*, states:[18] 'If children are exhibiting "poor self-images" it is time to examine the institutional mirrors in which they are constructing those images.'

Multicultural education — an anti-racist focus

The diversity focus, as expressed in the multicultural approach, contains superficial presentations of cultural epiphenomena and attempts to undermine prejudice through its affective objectives. The presentation of features of ethnic minority cultures alone, especially in many of the all-white schools in Scotland, is a nonsense, if it is not associated with teaching against prejudice. However, innovation is curriculum design needs to go beyond that. As a recent discussion paper of ALTARF[19] (All London Teachers against Racism and Fascism) states: 'Those who would like to use a multicultural approach to alleviate tension in the short term, rather than articulate it, are in danger of overestimating the power of ideas, and of assuming that the right attitudes can wish away material inequalities and the resentment they cause.' In other words, the curriculum needs to concern itself not only with prejudice, but with institutionalised forms of prejudice which 'imply the inherent inferiority of people with different colour, culture, or ethnicity'[20] and their manifestations in terms of structural inequalities and injustices, racially based distortions of facts and opinion, and racially motivated incidents of harassment and abuse. The purely descriptive and affective approach of multiculturalism must give way to a more highly critical exposé of racism at all levels, and consequently move away from any implication that the black population is the problem, to a position which sees the problem as white racism.

There is, as a social sciences teacher, Angela Mukhopadhyay,[21] reports in a survey of Schools Council projects in multicultural education, 'a caution and reticence in discussing race in any way other than a superficial commonsense discussion of the existence of prejudice and discrimination and attempts at government amelioration'. This reticence partly results from fear of unleashing a torrent of racist claims, and assumptions within the class, or from the fear of being accused of bringing politics into school. The first fear is justified. Classroom discussion must be handled carefully and sensitively. The second fear is unavoidable, as the whole anti-racist position is a challenge to entrenched institutional responses and a historically based power imbalance still acted out in white/black or north/south terms.

There are two main models for the anti-racist teacher to follow: the historical approach, which examines incidents of racism in the past, and in other societies, and redresses the balance of traditional Western historical reporting by showing minority* resistance to majority domination. The second, more direct, approach confronts racist arguments made both in the British and global context, by a critical examination of rationalisations of racism and racist distortions.

The historical approach can be developed in environmental studies in the primary school or within History, English or Modern Studies. For example, the Institute of Race Relations has produced materials which link the theme of racism with a study of slavery, colonialism and imperialism.[22] In the English classroom also many African novels or novels dealing with the ethnic minority experience can be used to raise the issue of race. In subjects like Mathematics and Science, opportunities can be found to show how, throughout post-Renaissance history, the contribution of non-Western cultures to mathematical thought and scientific progress has been distorted or dismissed.[23]

A look at current manifestations of racism can be included in subjects like Biology,[24] where physiological bases of racial difference can be explored. In Geography[25] the debate can be extended to an analysis of inequalities and structural imbalances on a global scale, and tie up with the concerns of Development Education and World Studies. Such analysis should end with action, where pupils consider

---

*Minority is here used as a term of power, rather than of population.

what they might do to counter racism and injustice at a local, national or global level.

Clearly, content which stresses the righting of power imbalances within society should have a profound effect upon the power structures existing within the classroom and school. Thus, the ILEA Guidelines on Multi-ethnic Education in Schools[26] include the whole ethos of the school, the question of teacher–pupil partnership in learning and the school's openness to the wider community in matters of consultation and decision-making. The school is seen not just as a transmitter of the cultural or political *status quo* — a clear shift from the assimilationist position inherent in the deficit focus — but as a transformer of society. Pupils too, are not the passive recipients of the majority culture, language or world-view, who are rendered powerless by their inability effectively to choose which way to take. Instead, they are given skills to explore the various avenues and points of view that they might adopt. Pupils from the majority white population are taught to see situations through the eyes of those who hold power as well as from the viewpoint of the oppressed.

Policy and practice in multicultural education at Moray House

The evolutionary stages in the development of multicultural education which have been outlined in the previous section have been clear in practice at Moray House over the past decade. Concern to train teachers to meet the needs of ESL learners, and to develop an awareness of ethnic minorities groups and their cultures in training for social work and community education, can be traced back to the early seventies. At about that time, too, students, through the Students Representative Council, began to demand inclusion of a multicultural element in all courses of training. The focus was upon ethnic minority needs.

In 1975 the college became the first institution in Scotland, and one of the first in the UK, to offer a course leading to a qualification in teaching English as a second language. This qualification, the Royal Society of Arts (RSA) Certificate (now Diploma) in Teaching English as a Second Language in Multicultural Schools, was soon informally accepted as a prerequisite to a career in TESL, and was in demand from specialist teachers in Edinburgh and Glasgow, and later in Central, Fife and Tayside Regions. Moray House was the co-ordinating centre for courses held in each of these areas. As a result, the college was given a national remit in the area of TESL and multicultural education, to be exercised through a post established in the Scottish Centre for Education Overseas, whose staff had previously been overseeing the

RSA course. The language-related work has changed significantly since the inception of the TESL course, as it has been realised that ESL learners require support, preferably in the mainstream classroom, far beyond the initial stages. Consequently, the RSA course has moved away from being a qualifying course for specialists only, and now chiefly attracts mainstream teachers who have ESL learners in their classes. Rather than adopting a narrowly language-focused approach, the current course considers second-language development in the context of a whole-school policy on language and multicultural education. Or perhaps one should say 'policy on languages' as it is being recognised increasingly how important it is to maintain and support learners' mother tongues or community languages within the mainstream school.

In order to train community language teachers, for work either in supplementary community-based schools or within the mainstream (as has begun to happen in a few Glasgow and Edinburgh secondary schools), the college was approached in 1982 by the RSA to pilot a Diploma course in teaching Community Languages. In the two years that this course has run, firstly in Edinburgh and then in Glasgow, teachers of five community languages have undertaken basic training in language-teaching methodology and in the principles underlying bilingualism and bilingual education. The existence of this course, along with the strong demands from ethnic minority communities for increased provision in their languages, is encouraging regional authorities to consider bilingual provision.

The phenomenological approach to other cultures, characteristic of the diversity view, also found its way into Scottish schools. The college's early attempts at in-service work in this area frequently led to projects which tended to present a stereotypic view of another culture. In schools with an ethnic minority population the 'culture' presented was often unfamiliar to the children, or disowned by them. In all-white schools, the avowed rationale of enriching the curriculum was obviously overturned when the project seemed only to reinforce children's hostility and sense of cultural distance. As a result, project development in a school has increasingly been preceded by a period of in-service training aimed at making teachers aware of their own attitudes and prejudices, and of the objective of the class project to challenge prejudice and racism.

One such project piloted with a P6 class in a primary school in Central Region is built around the subject of Barriers.[27] The aim is to investigate the nature of physical and social barriers, and to consider ways of overcoming barriers between people. Through mathematical tasks, the children explore the nature of classification. They then investigate the idea of a barrier as a means of protection (to keep things out) and as a means of control (to keep things in). The next stage is for children to make a sociogram of the school playground during break. The children discuss why they play with certain people, and why certain groups are formed. The concept of 'in-group' and 'out-group' is developed, and extended to a consideration of groupings according to wealth, class, age, gender, race, or language and the barriers which might be formed to protect a group's interests and identify its members. The question of overcoming barriers is raised through drama. The children improvise a play about two families who live next door to each other, separated only by a large wall between their two houses. The families are neighbours but they do not speak to each other, because of prejudice. The children get to know each other through a hole in the wall, and discover the distortions which they have been fed about the other family. They act as the means of bringing both families together, and finally the wall is dismantled. The project draws upon a number of curricular areas, and seeks to develop attitudes within the classroom, and an atmosphere within the school, which can be described as anti-racist.

Affective objectives such as those realised through the Barriers topic, as well as a concern to raise student awareness of the multicultural nature of British society and the implications such a society has for educational planning and provision, underlie the college's policy statement on multicultural education, adopted by the Board of Studies in June 1983. The statement commits the college to a policy of permeating all courses, in theoretical and practical components with pluralistic and anti-racist concepts. A start has been made with implementation in the planning of the Primary BEd degree, validated by the Council for National Academic Awards.

The institution of multicultural policy at college level, and within the regions, brings with it massive staff development implications. In order to co-ordinate this development programme, and to initiate and disseminate examples of good practice, with a corresponding pro-gramme of in-service training at regional and school levels, the college's research and development committee established a Multicul-tural Resource and Development Unit within the college in 1984. The Unit brings together members of staff involved not only in school education at primary and secondary stages, but also staff involved in social work and community education training. The aim of the Unit is to develop and pilot resources which can be fed into new course developments within college and can also be available to support regional policy initiatives. In social work training, programmes and resources have begun to be worked out to meet the demands of Curriculum Paper 21, the multicultural policy statement of the Central Council for Education and Training in Social Work (CCETSW).[28] In community education, discussions have started with community workers to seek to discover the most effective ways of introducing anti-racist teaching into informal education. In pursuance of its national remit, the college is also called upon for advice and help with staff development by other colleges of education. To this end, a national Training the Trainers initiative in multicultural and anti-racist education is being launched in 1985 in which each of the colleges is invited to participate.

Prospect

Although a start has been made, it must be admitted that the college is a long way from permeating all its courses with multicultural and anti-racist principles. At an institutional level, also, a good deal of groundwork has to be carried out to ensure that admission procedures, staff–student and inter-student relationships, accountability to the whole community, recruitment policies, course provision and the college's relations with national and governmental bodies are dictated by a commitment to multiculturalism and anti-racism. This is not a complaint but a recognition that a thoroughgoing implementation of a multicultural and anti-racist policy will affect not just the curricular content but also the teaching methodology and institutional structures of the college, and will take time.

It has been said[29] that the black presence in Britain has acted in much the same way as a barium meal. It has added colour to the picture of society's infrastructure and has revealed a deep-seated disease. An anti-racist approach should expose power imbalances within society which act against certain sections of the population. Traditionally, we have been aware of these imbalances at the level of class difference. More recently, we have been concerned about discrimination according to gender difference. A multicultural and anti-racist approach to education looks at race, sex and class. One question which needs to be considered seriously is the extent to which race, sex or class differences affect entry into the teaching, social work or community education professions. If it becomes clear that they do, entry procedures require to be changed, or pre-training access courses need to be instituted.

In view of the racial, gender and class differences of those seeking training, we need to look at training procedures. We need to examine classroom techniques to see whether a top-down process of teaching is operating, with students receiving the 'wisdom' of the person in a power position, but being given little or no opportunity to reinterpret or oppose this 'wisdom' from the point of view of their own experience. In assessment, we also see students' views judged by an examiner who may well not share the student's experience of the world, but who has no recourse to the student for an interpretation or defence of the student's position. Such practices could well prove discriminatory, with students from a variety of backgrounds being constrained to assimilate to the views of the lecturer or examiner.

A multicultural and anti-racist perspective thus brings into question many of the previously unquestioned bases of our training procedures. We need to ask whether such practices are still appropriate or tenable in a society characterised by diversity, as Scotland is. We should debate whether many of our taken-for-granted assumptions militate against the pursuit of fairness and justice. Multicultural education, far from being a marginal issue in the education debate, is, in fact, central to the provision of an appropriate education and training for all.

Notes and References

1. The posters are produced and distributed by the Multicultural Education Centre, Leith Walk Primary School, Brunswick Road, Edinburgh.
2. There has been a black presence in Scotland for the past 400 years. See Fryer, P., *Staying Power: The History of Black People in Britain*, p. 4. Pluto, 1984.
3. See, for example, 1983 Annual Report of Lothian Community Relations Council.
4. Scottish Education Department, *The Education of Ethnic Minorities in Strathclyde Region: Inspectorate Report*, 1983.
5. Cummins, J., 'Psychological Assessment of Immigrant Children: Logic or Intuition?', in *Journal of Multilingual and Multicultural Development*, Vol. 1, No. 2, 1980, p. 101.
6. See University of London, Institute of Education, *Linguistic Minorities in England: a Report from the Linguistic Minorities Project*, pp. 80, 81. Tinga Tinga, 1983.
7. See Skutnabb-Kangas, T., *Bilingualism or Not*, pp. 227-233. Multilingual Matters, 1981.
8. Fitzpatrick, F. and Rees, O., 'Mother Tongue and English Teaching Project', in *Disadvantage in Education*, Vol. 3, No. 1, 1983.
9. See Dulay, Burt and Krashen, *Language Two*. Oxford, 1984.
10. Hester, H., Bulletins of Schools Council Project: 'Language in the Multiethnic Primary School.' Institute of Education, London University, 1983.
11. Lambert, W. E. 'Culture and Language as Factors in Learning and Education', in Wolfgang, A. (ed.), *Education of Immigrant Students*. OISE, 1975.
12. Lambert, W. E. 'The Effects of Bilingualism on the Individual: Cognitive and Sociocultural Consequences', in Hornby, P. A., *Bilingualism*, p. 1527. Academic Press, 1973.

13. See Milner, D., *Children and Race: Ten Years On*. Ward Lock, 1982.
14. Jeffcoate, R. 'Curriculum Planning in Multiracial Education', in James, A. and Jeffcoate, R. (eds), *The School in the Multicultural Society*, p. 4. Harper & Row, 1982.
15. James, A. 'The "Multicultural" Curriculum', in James, A. and Jeffcoate, R. (eds), p. 24 op. cit.
16. An alternative approach to syllabus design which seeks to provide a rationale for difference can be found in 'Primary School Projects: A Multicultural Approach', in AFFOR, *Issues and Resources: A Handbook for Teachers in the Multicultural Society*, pp. 38 ff. AFFOR, Birmingham, n.d.
17. James, A., op. cit.
18. London Borough of Brent Curriculum Development Support Unit, *Education for a Multicultural Democracy*. Book 1, p. 12. Brent Education Committee, n.d.
19. ALTARF. *Teaching and Racism*, p. 3. ALTARF, n.d.
20. Inner London Education Authority. *Race, Sex and Class: 2. Multiethnic Education in Schools*, p. 16. ILEA, 1983.
21. Mukhopadhyay, A. 'Social Sciences', in Craft, A. and Bardell, G. (eds), *Curriculum Opportunities in a Multicultural Society*, pp. 44 ff. Harper & Row, 1984.
22. Institute of Race Relations. *Roots of Racism* and *Patterns of Racism*. IRR, 1982.
23. Hemmings, R. 'Multi-ethnic Mathematics II', in *Multiracial Education*, Vol. 9, No. 1, 1980.
24. Vance, M. 'Biology', in Craft, A. and Bardell, G. (eds), *Curriculum Opportunities in a Multicultural Society*, pp. 151 ff. Harper & Row, 1984.
25. See Gill, D. 'Education for a Multicultural Society: the Constraints of Existing O Level and CSE Geography Syllabuses', in Association for Curriculum Development in Geography and the Commission for Racial Equality, *Racist Society: Geography Curriculum*. CRE, 1983.
26. Inner London Education Authority. 'Race, Sex and Class: 4', *Anti-Racist Statement and Guidelines*. ILEA, 1983.
27. I am indebted to Anna Mackay of Moray House Multicultural Resource and Development Unit and Ann Coulter of Larbert Village School for the development of this topic.
28. Central Council for the Education and Training of Social Workers. *Curriculum Paper 21*. CCETSW, 1983.
29. Sheppard, D. *Bias to the Poor*, p. 10. Hodder & Stoughton, 1983.

13

Educational television

R. J. McCann

In April 1984, in a major statement to the Educational Television Association, the Hon. Peter Brooke, Parliamentary Under-Secretary of State at the Department of Education and Science, heralded the dawn of a new era in communication, an era which will hold profound implications for society in general and for education in particular. Specifically, he focused upon the onset of the 'cable' revolution, the advent of direct broadcasting by satellite and the emergence of video as one of the principal constituents of information technology. These elements are destined to spread, initially 'entertainment-led', into fields of application with unlimited potential. By providing many more channels and outlets, they will stimulate a much increased demand for television material, including that relating to education. In turn, this will identify a much increased need for the universities, colleges and polytechnics to construct and contribute many of their more specialised television productions.

These are the thresholds of information technology upon which we stand, thresholds shared by all members of the Educational Television Association, not least Moray House College. And it is fitting that the story of the development of the Department of Educational Television within Moray House should be told in parallel with the development of the Association, for when in 1967, HMI James Edwards issued a simple invitation to those educational institutions interested in using television to form themselves into an association, Moray House was among the first to respond.

The Educational Television Association

From a small gathering at County Hall in the Inner London Education Authority there was formed the National Educational Closed Circuit Television Association — later to become the Educational Television

Association — with Derek Holroyde, Director of Television at the University of Leeds, elected Chairman. As membership grew, three regional groups were constituted, the Scottish, Northern and Southern regions, and some time later the Western group became the fourth region. To this and other Association developments, Moray House has been a major contributor, having held the key chairmanships of the Scottish region, the Conference Committee and the Editorial Board of the *Journal of Educational Television*. Today it holds the Chairmanship of the Association itself.

By addressing the Educational Television Association, the Minister was acknowledging the leading role played by its members over the last 17 years, the period in which the educational centre of the Association, supported by its broadcasting and commercial wings, tackled successfully the complex task of establishing television in education. Therefore, before commenting on issues raised in the Minister's statement, it is profitable to consider how the relevant institutions, in particular colleges of education and universities, grappled with the problem of making television effective in education at an acceptable cost, the principal issue of the early years.

The creation of an Association was an important development. Up to that point, institutions had tended to operate in isolation, unable to share experiences of equipment utilisation, production techniques, research and development. Indeed, development had been little more than a random association of ideas, liberally sprinkled with hope. James Edwards understood that a synthesis of ideas was required and a sharing of experiences necessary to indicate more clearly the way to proceed, particularly in a world which was largely alien to the development of information technology. His solution was to encourage educational institutions to establish a vehicle for greater co-operation and the Association was formed.

What were the aims of the Association in 1967? Seven were identified, with three reflecting the hopes, aspirations and even uncertainties of the time:

—to establish appropriate educational and technical standards for educational television;

—to promote working contacts between producers and users of television at different levels of education;

—to foster contact and co-operation with overseas organisations and research centres concerned with educational television.

Although positive, these aims tended to encompass the feeling of being part of a movement which was unproved, of low status in education, and isolated from it. James Wykes, then Director of the Television

Service for the Inner London Education Authority, put the position clearly: 'We wanted to make our presence felt, to get it across to the teaching force and general public that television was viable as an educational tool. The problem was partly untrained staff and partly inadequate equipment and some of our early efforts were primitive.'

There were exceptions, of course. The ILEA itself started to recruit staff from the broadcast companies and in 1968 began transmitting high-quality educational television programmes to some London schools, with the service expanding to meet the needs of other London schools by 1970. During this period, Glasgow developed a similar educational television service and Hull and Plymouth smaller ones. Sadly, none of those developments was to survive intact the savage financial cuts of later years — an ironic situation as we prepare to receive in 1985 a substantial cable operation, planned to cover eventually the major centres of population in the United Kingdom.

Colleges of education

College of education members of the Educational Television Association were to fare much better. One of the earliest initiatives saw Avery Hill College in south-east London and a primary school in nearby Eltham linked by cable. With two cameras in the classroom transmitting down the line to the college, large numbers of students were able to study teaching skills and styles by means of the television monitor. Moray House, in common with other Scottish colleges, developed television in a similar way but did not transmit live to students, preferring instead to record material on videotape. Although losing some spontaneity, this had a two-fold advantage. Firstly, it allowed the college tutor to select the most appropriate school for the exercise, irrespective of location, and secondly, it gave the tutor opportunity to preview the material before using it with students, strengthening preparation and promoting effectiveness. The principal clients for this service at Moray House were tutors in the Primary Methods Department, and the Television Unit, still in the early stages of development, was based there.

This was development work on the very edge of education and technology. Almost without exception, teachers, when being recorded, were put under considerable strain as they grappled with unfamiliar hardware in the classroom, and children were often distracted by television cameras and microphones. And echoing the words of James Wykes, some of the early recordings were barely adequate as untrained personnel wrestled with the problems set by equipment still in its technological infancy. Membership of the Educational Television Association was particularly fruitful at this time, as members pooled their experience and learned of operational procedures which successfully circumvented the more acute technical and production problems.

Perseverance is often rewarded and this recording of teachers 'in action' was the forerunner of a use of television which today has become so well established that some degree courses in teaching have their methodology based firmly upon the identification of teaching skills through the analysis of videotape. Material of this kind, produced at Moray House, now forms an important part of the theory and practice of teaching component in the new BEd degree. The same material, modified to meet local needs, is also used in other colleges in the United Kingdom, in Holland, South Africa and Australia.

In the sixties, however, television was still attempting to establish its position in education. A credibility gap existed between television producer and educator and the portrayal of teaching skills was only one way of filling this gap. A second was in the production of programmes explaining the radical educational thinking of the day, including that of Plowden and Newsom and the implications of ROSLA. A third initiative taken by television was microteaching.

Microteaching, using videotape recording for immediate feedback, is a teacher education technique developed by the School of Education at Stanford University, USA,[1] and was first applied there as a combined training and diagnostic tool in the teacher intern programme in 1963. At Moray House, the Scottish Centre for Education Overseas has been using microteaching extensively since 1971 in pre-service and in-service programmes of training for teachers of English as a second or foreign language.[2] This has been a successful development and staff of the Centre have repeated this success in more intensive short courses in Sri Lanka, Argentina and Thailand.[3]

Widespread use of microteaching heralded a decade of rapid expansion for television in other areas of education. Several factors contributed to this, the two most important being an improvement in the quality of the product and a growing realisation by the academic world that technology did not pose a threat but was part of the communication revolution, influencing not only education but the whole of society.

Departments at Moray House responded to the improved service, placing heavy demands on the Television Unit, and in 1974 the attachment to the Primary Methods Department was severed and the Department of Educational Television created. Operating in colour, with two studios and an outside broadcast unit, a comprehensive television service was provided for all departments. Demand continued to grow and a third studio was added to the complex in 1979. Development on this scale is something few educational institutions have enjoyed and tribute must be paid to the staff of Moray House for the many and varied ways in which they proved television to be effective — from microteaching, simulation and role playing, production courses, school broadcasting, to more complex television exercises such as the exemplification of teaching skills and research in the British Sign Language, Discussion Development, Pedagogics and other projects.

Of course, a prerequisite of a relevant programme of successful television is adequate funding and the Department of Educational Television, acknowledging that no academic institution is ever given the inalienable prerogative of unlimited finance, has always received financial support from college and the Scottish Education Department. The latter, aware that television is a long-term investment, provides funding on a scale which, although on the same specified terms for all colleges of education, gives scope for individual idiosyncrasies and circumstances.

Universities

Not all Association members have been so fortunate. In the last few years, some institutions, particularly the universities, entered a period which marked the end of reasonable funding. University authorities, under pressure to cut costs, challenged television departments to prove their cost effectiveness. Indeed, there were some university senates whose members seemed to await the inevitable collapse of educational television — the logical conclusion of anticipated severe internal pressure from academic departments. Initially, television struggled to preserve a viable production operation as financial cuts were implemented. Justifiably, salvation came, not through the efforts of television departments alone, but from support given by those university departments whose members had profited from a long-standing excellent television service. Vigorous protests by the teaching staff flatly contradicted the implicit intentions of some university authorities and forced them to reaffirm their commitment to television.

In one respect the financial stringency which initiated the rigorous examination of university television services carried with it the final seal of approval for television in education. Demand from academic departments emphasised that television was no longer sitting uneasily outside education but comfortably inside and an integral part of it. The three principal aims of the Educational Television Association had been realised. It had developed from a small committee to an influential organisation, with a distinguished Journal, an international Conference and a developing research group; it provided a comprehensive service in training, design and technical matters to all members and it enjoyed formal links with British Council, CET, DES, SED and others.

Cable and direct broadcasting by satellite

Turning, then, to the present day, the most intriguing of the issues raised by the Minister is that of 'cable'. In 1981[4] the Government considered the potential of 'cable' as a provider of entertainment and interactive data services, and in February 1982 the 'Cable Systems' report proposed a substantial expansion of 'cable' throughout the country. The keyword 'expansion' may come as a surprise to some, because it is not generally known that cable systems have been in existence for television and radio in this country since 1950. Those operations have been small scale, sometimes but not always to serve communities living in 'shadow' areas inaccessible to UHF signals.

To 'cable' must be added direct broadcasting by satellite. As the name implies, DBS[5] refers to the utilisation of a space satellite sufficiently powerful to broadcast television programmes, including those of other European countries, direct to receiving points in the United Kingdom — the home, school, etc. — where the receiving points are equipped with dish aerial technology. The connection between DBS and 'cable' is that a cable company could have its own powerful dish aerial receiving signals from the satellite in order to relay them as authorised satellite transmissions to all its cable subscribers.

The Government, aware that a proliferation of 'cable' could attract promoters of material questionable in both technical quality and content, set up a committee under Lord Hunt to consider issues about wider public interest, including the safeguarding of public service broadcasting and a supervisory framework for expanded cable services. The committee duly reported and preceded a Cable and Broadcasting Act, with 11 pilot franchises awarded in advance of the creation of a Cable Authority. Two Scottish companies were successful in their application for a franchise — Aberdeen Cable Services Ltd. to operate in the Aberdeen area, and Clyde Cable Vision Ltd. with north Glasgow its area of responsibility.

If this early development in 'cable' seems small in the number of companies selected and narrow in the extent of area covered, it must be emphasised that, in the first instance, each franchise holder was to be restricted to communities of 100,000 homes/institutions for a period of 12 years. This period has already been extended. Moreover, as the Cable Authority evaluates the operation, it may recommend expansion by enlarging the number of units to the original franchise holders and by granting new licences to companies planning to operate in other centres of population.

DBS development is less clear but the BBC is to have a 50 per cent investment in a satellite expected to be operational by 1987-88, with ITV and other commercial organisations each holding a smaller interest. This investment is slow-moving and whilst the United Kingdom dithers other European countries take positive action. One example of successful co-operation in satellite broadcasting of educative material has been demonstrated by five French-language television organisations — Télévision Suisse Romande, Radio-Télévision Belge de la Communauté Francaise and the French television networks TF1, Antenne 2 and FR3.[6] Using the ECS satellite, those organisations have created a television service with the principal aim 'to disseminate French culture and the French language'. The development is identified as TV5 and has established a new format in broadcasting and communication.

This initiative is education in its widest sense but the educational potential of DBS cannot be challenged, with European commitment to satellite broadcasting clearly stated in the EEC paper on transmissions across European frontiers. This emphasises 'new information and communications services' and pinpoints satellite technology as 'one of the main factors accelerating the transition to an economy that will in large part be based on ready access to information and to rapid methods of communication'.

Similar claims have been made for 'cable' on a national basis but the principal aim of cable operators is to succeed financially. This implies an 'entertainment-led' business, with cable operators enticing subscribers by offering them programme channels of 'guaranteed' popular television such as feature films and sport.[7] The hope is for large viewing audiences, high ratings and huge profits; the more realistic expectation is of slow growth and a modest return on capital. Placed against this business acumen, the world of education is in disarray. One major problem is that the Cable and Broadcasting Act did not stipulate an educational channel. Therefore, the educationist has been compelled to negotiate with the cable operator in every franchise area. In this, leadership has already been given by the Educational Television

Association, which issued a policy document for education in response to the Government White Paper. Three important points should be noted:

—All cable operators should be required to offer at least one free channel for education purposes. The various providers of continuing education — universities, colleges and LEAs — should be encouraged to use the various cable systems in order to expand their course provision to those members of the general public not already benefiting from this — the housebound, shiftworkers and the disabled.

—Colleges of education, universities and LEAs should be encouraged to use cable systems for the distribution of materials for school-based in-service training. This could make a significant contribution to the raising of teaching standards at a time of declining school roles and of limited recruitment of new entrants. It would require all schools, colleges of education and universities to be linked to 'cable', either without charge or at favourable rates.

—In education, the multi-channel cable system should provide opportunity for interactive education and not concentrate on traditional and formal teaching techniques. This ought to include the facility for the learner at home to work with locally produced video material . . . and the facility to link the microcomputer at home with mainframe computers in educational establishments.

To date, as cable operators proceed towards the new system's launch there are hopes that channels will indeed be provided for educational purposes but little indication that any finance will be forthcoming for programming. The technology will probably be there for interactive services, if not at the outset, certainly when demand is established. But is education capable of taking advantage of the opportunities presented? Comprising a number of disparate sectors, education seldom speaks with a united voice. This reduces its influence and may encourage the cable operator to lean heavily on the indigenous television resource to provide the principal education input, and in Scotland that would mean Aberdeen and north Glasgow. Unfortunately, this approach is flawed. Certainly, local needs must be met but if 'cable' is to be used to help resolve educational and social problems which are national in scale the initial impetus must take on a national dimension. Education must project itself in Scotland as a single establishment, harbouring the power and capacity to provide a comprehensive cable television service which would be meaningful, interesting and attractive to potential consumers, investors and sponsors.

Co-operation in Scottish education

This would require co-operation on a scale hitherto unknown in Scottish education but evidence exists to suggest such co-operation is possible. For example, education in Dundee enjoys a television service where the local colleges of education, technology and art combine in resource utilisation. Moreover, the Scottish colleges of education have already demonstrated their capacity to co-operate in television matters, particularly in association with outside partners.

Recently, in order to give a fresh impetus to the use of broadcast material in schools, the Scottish colleges took part in a major staff development exercise conducted by broadcasters under the aegis of the Scottish Council for Educational Technology. The exercise consisted of an extended series of meetings between broadcasters and college staff to measure the strengths and weaknesses of schools broadcasting, to apprise each other of problems and to consider solutions. It was also a statement by both parties of their determination to improve the use of an outstanding resource and to take account of its changing nature as it prepared to meet the challenge of an education undergoing major curriculum surgery.

Partly as a result of this exercise, Moray House has responded by introducing educational broadcasting as an important constituent of the Resources for Learning Course in the initial BEd degree. The beneficiaries of the course, which includes the educational rationale, design and implementation of information technology based materials, are students in training and one of the expectations is for the increasing and more effective use of television in schools. This has already been realised in a mathematics project involving varied use of pre-prepared video material as part of the ongoing work of primary school classes, the value of the video material being clearly evident in the subsequent work of the children.

Broadcasting and adult education

The contribution of broadcasting to education is not confined to schools television. In a recent article,[8] Don Grattan, former Controller of Educational Broadcasting at BBC, discusses changes in broadcasting to meet the needs of the adult population through continuing education and the Open University. He points out that the broadcaster has had to respond to the changing curriculum in adult education by linking educational broadcasts to appropriate agencies in the community. Issues concerning the economy, alternative employment, health, new technologies and the complex nature of society form the basis of this new broadcast curriculum and Grattan underlines the essential link with outside agencies for well-designed follow-up activities 'or educational broadcasting will fail or be relatively ineffective'.

One effective use of broadcasting is that made by the BBC and Open University partnership,[9] even if the impression enjoyed by the general public of the student gaining a degree by viewing 30 minutes of television each day must be dispelled. The printed word is still the premier means of communication on all courses, with broadcasting comprising a smaller but important proportion of the total package. Dr. J. H. Horlock, present Vice-Chancellor, makes the point that Lord Perry, as founding Vice-Chancellor, was at least as much concerned with improving teaching methods of conventional universities, through Open University innovations, as he was with 'alleviating any deprivation in the adult population'. In the event, he did both, with more than 62,000 earning a degree and many more taking advantage of shorter courses.

The future

A major by-product of Open University development has been the significant research completed, particularly now in interactive technology where, with London University and University College, Cardiff, it leads development work. 'Interactive Video' — the harnessing of computer and video technologies — is one of the most interesting and exciting developments in information technology. The emergence of videodisc systems has brought forth a remarkably flexible audio-visual device which, under computer software control, is proving to be an ideal technology for the delivery of computer-aided learning materials. Aware of the educational implications, Moray House, through the Computer and Educational Television Departments, is planning to produce one of the first educational interactive videodiscs in Scotland.

Addressing itself to the new technologies — 'cable' through the Educational Television Association and 'interactive video' more directly — the Department of Education Television is proving the Minister's words to be prophetic and in considering the future two other developments must be noted.

The first is in the Criteria of Teacher Selection Project, which is investigating selection practice in Scottish colleges of education. In an extension of this work, it is proposed that television will be used to:

—explore differences in performance on a practical teaching task of teachers (or potential teachers) at different stages of their career with a view to identifying factors which discriminate between differing kinds of skilled performance; and

—orientate assessors to their role in the different elements, such as interviewing, in a full-day selection programme.

The second development encompasses all colleges of education in Scotland. Since 1982, colleges have co-operated in the free exchange of television material and, in this, have largely eliminated programme duplication. It is now proposed to extend this systematic approach to programming to include developments in the curriculum at a national level. Therefore, from October 1985, the Department of Educational Television at Moray House, together with television departments from the other colleges, will allocate a proportion of time, technology and expertise to the production of material based on national priorities and developments. Each college will take a proportion of the work and make the product available to the widest possible market in education.

The most positive votes of confidence a service can gain are those of continued resource provision and increased demand for services. In agreeing to the provision of resources to support and enhance curriculum development at a national level, education is recognising the effectiveness of television as a communicator; in moving it to the centre of curriculum development it is paying television the compliment of extending its already wide influence. The last two decades have seen a steady growth in what might be called applied television in education. The next decade is likely to see the new pivotal position of television even more exploited and will thus provide opportunities and challenges greater than ever before.

References

1. Allen, D. W. *et al.* (1967)	'Micro-teaching: a Description.' Stanford University, USA.
2. Carver, D. and Wallace, M. J. (1981)	'SCEO Microteaching Papers.' Moray House College.
3. Wallace, M. J. (1979)	'Micro-teaching and the Teaching of English as a Second or Foreign Language.' Moray House College.
4. Pragnell, A. (1983)	'Future UK Cable Development: an Examination of the Government's Proposals.' *EBU Review*, Vol. xxxiv, No. 5.
5. Howkins, J. (1983)	'The Potential of Cable and Satellite.' London.

6. Peyre, P. (1984)   'TV5: a French Language Satellite Television Service.' *EBU Review*, Vol. xxxv, No. 3.

7. Murray, J. (1982)   'The Future of Educational Broadcasting.' SCET.

8. Grattan, D. (1984)   'This Moment in Time.' *Media in Education and Development*, Vol. 17, No. 2.

9. Horlock, Dr. J. H.   'A University without Walls.' *Media in Education and* (1984)   *Development*, Vol. 17, No. 2.

14

Computing

Peter Barker

Early developments

With High Street shops displaying computers in their windows, advertisements for home computers and small business systems on television and in the newspapers, and radio and TV programmes devoted to home computing activities, there must be few members of the public today who are not aware of the existence of the computer and of its profound impact on our society. Computers are probably unique in providing more and more facilities for less and less money as time goes by, and it is the introduction of relatively cheap machines offering a wide range of facilities which has brought about the current state of affairs. But computers have actually been around in fair numbers for more than thirty years and the British Computer Society, the premier society for computer professionals, has been in existence for over twenty-six years and was granted its Royal Charter in 1984.

The first school in the UK to acquire a computer took delivery of a machine in 1965[1] for some £15,000, obtaining a system with a lot less power than can be had for £1,000 today. At that time the introduction of computing to schools depended upon a thinly scattered band of enthusiastic teachers although there was some co-ordination of their work through the formation of the Schools Committee of the British Computer Society. There was a fairly heavy orientation towards hardware, many schools manufacturing bits of electronics to demonstrate aspects of the working of a computer. Any real computing done by the schools had to take place on machines in higher education establishments or on those of local businesses who were prepared to offer some time on their machines to education. Only in one or two isolated cases was there any formal recognition by local authorities of computing work being done in their schools.

In 1967 the Scottish Education Department set up a committee under the chairmanship of Mr. B. T. Bellis, then headmaster of Daniel Stewart's College in Edinburgh, with the remit 'To consider the implications of computers for the schools and to make recommend-ations'. This committee published an interim report which gave the initial impetus to the introduction of computing in Scottish schools.[2] The report recommended:

1. An elementary course in Computer Studies (the Introductory Course) should be provided for the great majority of pupils.
2. The teaching of the Introductory Course should be undertaken by teachers of various subjects and not only by teachers of mathematics. Pre-service and in-service training of teachers should be provided.
3. As a measure to help in the provision of instruction for teachers and of access to computing facilities for schools, three educational computer centres should be established.
4. Local education authorities should continue to develop and expand facilities for computer education for school pupils.

As a result of these recommendations the Centre for Computer Education at Moray House was set up, soon to be followed by others at Jordanhill, Dundee and Aberdeen colleges of education. The Moray House Centre was not, however, the first centre to provide a computing service to schools in Scotland since Glasgow Corporation opened its first schools computer centre a few months before Moray House.

For some time after the start of operations there was no computer at Moray House. The Edinburgh Regional Computing Centre, which provides computing facilities to Edinburgh and other universities in Scotland, generously offered to process schools programs free of charge, and in the early days the programs written by pupils would arrive on coding sheets, be punched on to cards which were collected by a van service, to be processed at the Regional Computing Centre. The output was returned by van and posted from Moray House to the schools. It was recognised by the college that the support from the Regional Computing Centre could only be a temporary measure and negotiations were entered into between the college and neighbouring local authorities for the acquisition of a computer system and provision of the service direct from Moray House. These negotiations took place before regionalisation and were therefore conducted between the college and the old county authorities, most of whom agreed to make a financial contribution which would help towards paying the rental on a small computer system. As a result an IBM 1130 Computer was installed at the college in 1971.

The Bellis Committee subsequently published a final report[3] reiterating their original recommendations and also commenting on the potential of the computer as an educational tool in many subject areas. As a result of the publication of this report and the moves towards the provision of computing facilities, Scotland was at that time regarded as being in the forefront amongst European nations in having a national policy relating to the promotion of computing in schools.

This optimistic start, however, did not result in a rapid growth and the reason for this can be found in another of the recommendations of the Bellis Report: 'computer studies should not become a separate specialist subject at school level'.

This was accepted by the Consultative Committee on the Curriculum and became part of the national policy. Whilst the Committee had good reasons for making its decision, the effect in the schools was different from what they had intended. The construction of school timetables tends to be based around the examination requirements and therefore non-examinable subjects are relegated to minority time slots. In most schools, therefore, computing was not regarded as an essential part of the curriculum and it was introduced by enthusiastic teachers who managed to obtain an allocation of a few periods to teach computer topics to their pupils. The volume of work from schools being processed at Moray House gave a very good indication of the differing levels of activity and it was even possible to detect work moving from one school to another when a particular teacher changed his employment.

At about the time the final Bellis Report was published the Scottish Computer Education Group was formed. This was largely at the instigation of Mr. Bellis himself and he became its first Chairman. The Group consisted of about fifteen people drawn from local authorities, colleges of education, schools and further education. Their objective was, and remains, to promote the use of computers as an educational tool and the study of computing as a subject within the school curriculum. For several years the Group organised annual conferences where about 150 teachers would gather to see the latest in hardware and software, hear papers presented, and engage in discussion. These conferences undoubtedly helped to build up the level of interest and enthusiasm in schools throughout Scotland.

It is interesting to contrast the situation in Scotland with that south of the border during this period. There were of course many similarities. As in Scotland the enthusiastic teacher was the main element in maintaining and developing interest in computing, but because of the different examination system there it was possible for teachers under CSE Mode 3 to propose assessable computing courses, and it was through this route that large numbers of children in schools in England and Wales were able to take computing as an examinable subject. Eventually the pressure grew for 'O' level and 'A' level examinations and these have now been offered for a number of years by several Examination Boards in England and Wales. The Scottish Computer Education Group became aware of these developments and took the view that computing would never attain its rightful place in the curriculum in Scottish schools unless there were examinations here as well. Associated with this proposal was one that there should be a teaching qualification in computing for secondary school teachers.

Examinations introduced

The effecting of a U-turn in official policy is not an easy thing to achieve, but the rapidly increasing number of pupils taking computer examinations south of the border and the growing demand within Scotland eventually brought about the acceptance of the idea that there should be an 'O' grade in computing. The piloting of this course began in 1982 and the first pupils took the examination in 1984. Meantime, however, Munn and Dunning developments indicated that there would be no long-term future for an 'O' grade examination although it has now been made available to all schools. There was, as might be expected, some criticism of the content of the 'O' grade course and the introduction of a Standard grade under the new arrangements provided the opportunity to revise a number of ideas about course content and the method of teaching various topics in computing, in particular programming. The programming language COMAL, originally developed in Denmark, was selected as being the most appropriate vehicle for schools to teach good programming practice, while at the same time allowing pupils without any special aptitude for computing to do worthwhile work.

Another factor which added considerably to the pressure for examinable computing was the arrival of the microcomputer. At last schools did not have to rely on a rather slow postal service to a possibly remote centre but could do computing on the spot with pupils actually getting their hands on the machinery. And a prerequisite for schools wishing to be involved in the 'O' grade pilot was that they should have an adequate number of microcomputers. Such a stipulation is hardly required as far as Standard grade is concerned because most secondary schools in Scotland now have a number of machines — the average at the time of writing being at least ten.

Computers across the curriculum

Accompanying the developments in computing as a subject for study there has been a corresponding growth in the use of the computer as an aid to teaching across the curriculum. The Government offer of half-price computers led to the installation of a large number of school microcomputer systems at a time when there was very little educational software. At the same time there was an explosive demand for introductory courses, at first for secondary teachers and later, when the offer was extended to primary schools, for primary teachers. It would be impossible, and inappropriate, to make every teacher into a computer programming expert. What the teacher needs to know is how to connect up a microcomputer system, and how to load and run programs. Once these skills have been acquired the much more important topic of the evaluation of computer-based teaching materials can be addressed.

Introductory courses offered at Moray House are of ten two-hour sessions. During the course teachers can examine a range of software available to schools, and methods of introducing computer techniques into their teaching are discussed. This is not to say that there is an adequate supply of good-quality software. The upsurge in demand has stimulated the production of a large quantity of programs, and the problem for teachers is to select suitable material for purchase from a very modest budget. The college also offers courses on the design of computer-based packages. This has not produced a spate of new material, but it has done much to help the teacher with the evaluation process.

A further demand for in-service courses has come from teachers who have developed an interest in computing and want to achieve a fairly high level of expertise. To cater for them the college offers a two-year part-time course leading to a Diploma in Professional Studies in Education (Educational Computing) validated by the CNAA. The course has been taken by teachers from primary, secondary and further education and by college of education staff. Secondary teachers who obtain the diploma can go on to acquire a Teaching Qualification in Computing.

The introduction of Standard grade will not bring to an end the debate on what a computer studies course should consist of. Microprocessors are only just beginning to have a real impact on the range of functions offered by all kinds of machines from tape recorders to motor cars. Profound changes will come in the field of communications, both commercial and domestic. The Schools Committee of the British

Computer Society has continued to review the situation and has published a paper 'Curriculum for the Future' in which are discussed many of the issues raised by these developments.[4] The document contains many useful guidelines and raises important questions which all teachers should be aware of.

Research activities

From its inception the Centre has been involved in research activities, both in a support role to members of the college staff and directly in the investigation of the use of computers in teaching and learning. As part of the National Development Program in Computer-Aided Learning, which operated from 1973 to 1977, the Centre was involved in a project to move a computer-managed learning system from a computer in the south of England to a different machine in Moray House. In addition, with the co-operation of Lothian Region, trials of the system were carried out in some Lothian schools. The project demonstrated the effectiveness of computer-managed learning to route pupils through a large number of modules of learning materials so as to individualise the learning process. This was found to be particularly beneficial in mixed-ability classes. The use of this system did not continue after the initial trials and there were several reasons for this. On the one hand, the imported teaching materials did not exactly fit the Scottish curriculum, and on the other the cost of producing new modules was very high indeed. The fact that the system could be operated only by using a fairly large minicomputer meant that results had to be processed on a central computer, and there could therefore be no immediate response to the pupil and the teacher. Nevertheless, the introduction of the microcomputer has revived interest in computer-managed learning, and funding is being sought for further work in this area.

Another major project with which the Centre has been involved is School Based Assessment using Item Banking. A suite of computer programs was developed at Moray House allowing an APPLE II computer to be used in the classroom for the marking and reporting of multiple-choice tests. The reports generated by this package, called SCRIBE, provide diagnostic as well as summative assessment information, and although the project ended in March 1985, a number of schools continue to use the package as part of their regular assessment procedures. The final part of the project involved moving data from the microcomputers to the college mainframe so that overall statistics could be accumulated for the test questions. The project also examined ways in which the computer might help to provide an achievement profile for the pupils. A further package called SCOPE was developed on the APPLE microcomputer, and was used to produce reports across several tests. Its use throughout a whole course is possible but cumbersome because of the amount of floppy disc manipulation involved. The mainframe exercise demonstrated that, given enough computing power, profiling with the SCOPE package is a practical proposition. These packages might therefore be worth investigating as possible tools to help with Standard grade assessment.

There are still a number of applications for which mainframe computing power is necessary. One of these is the JIIG-CAL careers guidance system, which involves the production of voluminous reports from large files of information. The Centre was involved with early trials of this system in Lothian Region, and now provides a regular service to Lothian schools. New devices using microchip technology are continually appearing on the market, and some of these have potential as educational tools. One of the most promising is the laser scanned videodisc, which can hold a very large amount of information including text, still and moving pictures, all with sound and colour. The control of one of these machines by computer opens up some interesting possibilities. The hardware is not expensive, nor is the reproduction of the discs. On the other hand, the collection and preparation of materials to go on the disc involves a great deal of work. To justify this effort any disc produced for education would need to have a potentially large market. A research proposal has been submitted by a member of the Computer Centre staff to investigate sources of materials, and prepare a module using a computer-controlled videodisc.

The unintelligent machine

Over the past 20 years the amount of computing power available for a given sum of money has approximately doubled every two years, and it looks as if this trend will continue in the foreseeable future. On the other hand, the fundamental logical design of computers is much the same as at the beginning of this period. The revolution has been one of scale and cost rather than a change in the kinds of things which computers can do. One might have expected therefore that by now we would know the best way in which computers can be used to help with the educational process.

In the early sixties, programmed learning was looked on as the pathway to mechanise the learning process. But teaching machines of the time were inflexible and unresponsive. It was soon recognised that computers provide a much higher level of interaction with the student. Responses need not be restricted to multiple-choice button pushing, but can involve the recognition of words or numbers related to the context of the subject.

In order to present information and questions to the student and to provide for appropriate branching, depending on the response, some form of programming language is required. COURSEWRITER and later PILOT are 'author languages' which allow someone without technical knowledge of computing to prepare programs of this kind. Text and graphics can be displayed, responses analysed, and appropriate action taken.

A tool such as this might seem to put considerable power in the hands of the teacher and yet such systems are hardly used at all in our schools. One reason is that the preparation of course materials using an author language is, like that for videodisc systems, a very time-consuming business. A figure of 60 to 100 hours of preparation is quoted for each hour of student time at the computer. Such an investment is only worthwhile if the material can be used by a large number of students, and that assumes that the necessary resources in time and hardware are actually available.

There is a more fundamental reason for lack of progress in computer-based tutorial systems and this relates to the fundamental lack of 'intelligence' on the part of the computer. It is easy enough to generate drill and practice exercises which test a student's ability to produce a predictable response. It is quite another matter to provide useful advice if the response is wrong. The human teacher has a mental model of the student and can make a reasonable estimate of why a particular wrong answer has been produced. The longer the teacher has been in contact with that student the better he or she is able to offer constructive advice. The kind of system discussed above has no such model of the student on which to make decisions, nor does it have access to the large body of subject knowledge which is held by the human teacher. Its responses therefore must be stereotyped and unintelligent.

Further evidence of the lack of machine intelligence is the failure to make computers 'understand' natural language. We talk about 'programming languages' for computers, but these are not languages in the ordinary sense. They are just systems of coding which provide a highly stylised way of writing down the solutions to particular sorts of problems. The fact that programs in these languages, although made up largely of English words and some well-known mathematical symbols, are unintelligible to the lay reader indicates the gulf which still exists between the kind of verbal instructions which can be given to another human, and the coded instructions required by the computer. In his 1984 Reith Lectures for the BBC, Searle has argued that the construction of an intelligent machine is a logical impossibility.[5] Many researchers in this area would dispute such a claim, but so far they cannot provide the essential demonstration to the contrary.

The development of 'expert systems', which can provide advice and information on the basis of human experience which is fed into them, is one step in the direction of machine intelligence. However, such systems are limited to knowledge in a tightly defined domain, and cannot operate outside this area. Nevertheless, there may well be something here for education, and the Centre may seek support for research in this area also.

The computer in the classroom

Where does this leave the computer as a tool for the teacher? Clearly we have to exploit its strengths rather than complain about its weaknesses. However dull much drill and practice material may seem, children will often work at it for a considerable time without losing concentration. Rote learning is rightly out of favour in most educational contexts, but there are certain things which it is convenient to be able to recall instantly, and the computer can help us to remember them. The school pupil soon learns that the computer never gets tired, never loses its temper, will always respond almost instantaneously to any input, does not display the pupil's ignorance to other people, and these factors help to provide a micro-environment within which the pupil is stable and secure.

The introduction of computers into primary schools has concentrated the minds of educators on the use of the machine as an aid to the teacher, without the distraction of computer studies as a subject in its own right. The computer is very good at storing and rearranging information, and the introduction of simple database manipulation packages has allowed teachers to present their pupils with the opportunity to collect information which is of interest to them, to structure it appropriately, and to store it on the computer. From the files thus produced various reports can be generated. These packages can be used in a variety of areas of study, from history to science, and an introduction to them is now an important part of teacher education in the use of computers. Computers can also simulate various dynamic situations, and a number of packages exploit this ability. Even the adventure games, which are sold for amusement to home computer users, can be turned to advantage if the problem-solving aspects are emphasised and the pupils' activity is appropriately structured.

LOGO

The LOGO programming language was invented by Seymour Papert and some colleagues at the Massachusetts Institute of Technology. Their aim was to produce a new type of problem-solving environment for children in which they could program the computer to perform a number of interesting tasks. The most familiar part of LOGO is Turtle Graphics where, using a few simple commands — forward, back, left, right, penup, pendown — a small robot can be made to crawl around the floor producing drawings. Many schools have to do without the Turtle robot, but drawings can be produced by the same commands on the computer video screen, and reproduced on the computer printer if the school has one. The Turtle environment undoubtedly motivates children, and Papert puts forward LOGO as a means for bringing about a revolution in education[6]:

> My own philosophy is revolutionary rather than reformist in its concept of change. But the revolution I envisage is of ideas, not of technology. It consists of new understandings of specific subject domains and in new understandings of the process of learning itself. It consists of a new and much more ambitious setting of the sights of educational aspiration.

Much work has been done at Edinburgh University by Dr. Jim Howe and his colleagues at the Department of Artificial Intelligence on the use of LOGO both with pupils and serving teachers. It certainly has benefits to offer, and with the advent of LOGO systems for the small computers currently used in schools we can look forward to its wider introduction. Turtle Graphics are already being used extensively in Moray House for introducing students to the use of LOGO in primary schools.

Learning from our pupils

Persons of maturer years often feel nervous about approaching new technological devices. One of the principal objectives of in-service courses is to demystify the computer. No such problems occur with children, who approach the machine without any inhibitions. Many of them, with computers at home, are accustomed at a very early age to connect up the machines and run programs. Programming abilities can also be discovered and developed long before any formal computer studies courses are encountered. Teachers have to reconcile themselves to the fact that, as far as computers are concerned, some of their pupils are going to be ahead of them in their use and understanding of the machine which they have in the classroom. If this leads to a recognition that the teacher is not the fount of all knowledge, and that everyone in the classroom has something to learn, it can only be to the good of our educational system.

References

1. Broderick, W. R. (1968)   *The Computer in School*. The Bodley Head.

2. Curriculum Paper 6 (1969)   *Computers and the Schools*, p. 9. HMSO.

3. Curriculum Paper 11 (1972)   *Computers and the Schools*, p. 4. HMSO.

4. Samways, B. (Chairman) (1984)   'Curriculum for the Future.' The British Computer Society.

5. Searle, J. (1984)   '1984 Reith Lectures, No. 2.' *The Listener*, Vol. 112, No. 2884, 15.12.84.

6. Papert, S. (1980)   *Mindstorms*, p. 186. The Harvester Press Ltd.

15

The future context of professional education

Gordon Kirk

Introduction

Do colleges such as Moray House have a future? In view of the evidence adduced in this volume of papers that question might appear otiose. It has been maintained that the professions which the college serves have an incontestably important contribution to make to human well-being and to people's capacity to choose and exploit lifestyles which they find amenable; it has been claimed that the quality of these professions depends crucially on the quality of the training their entrants receive and the level of support they are able to enjoy subsequently in enhancing their professionalism; and it has been demonstrated in various ways how the college continues to respond to changing professional needs and remains resolutely committed to improving the quality of the training and support it provides as well as extending our understanding of how professional activity itself can be improved. If it is granted, then, that the functions currently performed by colleges of education must continue to be performed, questions might still be asked about the institutional context in which these functions are conducted. Are these functions best conducted in separate, independent and self-governing institutions known as colleges of education? This chapter seeks to explore that question in the light of the establishment of the Scottish Tertiary Education Advisory Council (STEAC) and of the review it is currently conducting into the structure of higher education in Scotland.

The establishment of STEAC

There were several factors that pointed to the need for a review. The demographic trends showed a significant decline in the size of the relevant age group and naturally questions arose as to whether there should be a corresponding reduction in the provision of higher education facilities. The possibility of such a reduction was bound to merit serious consideration at a time of fiscal stringency, especially by a Government that was pledged to securing reductions in public expenditure. However influential these considerations might have been in the establishment of the review, a strong case for such a review could be made on quite separate grounds.

Higher education in Scotland is an untidy and inadequately co-ordinated collection of institutions. These institutions are not consistently differentiated according to function; they stand in no obvious relationship to each other; they are funded, differentially, by different agencies — the University Grants Committee, two separate divisions of the Scottish Education Department, and regional authorities; and they operate in accordance with four different sets of management procedures and regulations. In all of these ways they provide evidence of haphazard and piecemeal growth rather than of a rationally planned and structurally coherent system.

The establishment of STEAC itself, with terms of reference which imply the necessity for co-ordinated planning on a national basis, is a move in the direction of a coherent system of higher education. It would be surprising, indeed, if STEAC did not recommend the institution of a central agency to undertake strategic planning for higher education in Scotland, to conduct a detailed analysis of manpower and higher education needs, to identify priorities for development, and to generate and maintain a comprehensive plan for higher education. The merit of a single central planning agency, with responsibility for resource allocation and for the operation of an equitable and rational system of funding, is an essential precondition of a national system. Institutions, for their part, would need to be regarded as national institutions in the sense that they are directly funded by central government; they should have constitutional parity, in that they stand in the same relationship to central government; they should be subject to central planning procedures; and they should be free to recruit students from all parts of the country. Unless institutions are national in all of these senses there can be no genuine improvement on the unco-ordinated and haphazard developments that characterise our existing arrangements.

The creation of a rationally ordered system of this kind is such a self-evident social imperative that it is inconceivable that STEAC will fail to endorse it. The only difficulty concerns whether or not the universities should form part of the national system and be subject to the national funding and planning procedures. While the universities have recently been critical of their treatment at the hands of the University Grants Committee, and while they wish to emphasise that their status as Scottish institutions requires special recognition, it is unlikely that they would all agree to their full integration into a coherent structure of higher education for Scotland. In their defence, they claim to be part of the structure of higher education in the UK and indeed to be members of an international academic community. On the other hand, it is difficult to see how the universities can be excluded from the national planning of higher education in Scotland. The objective is to relate provision to needs and that cannot be achieved if the major range of resources and facilities that are represented by the universities are subject to separate and independent planning.

Higher education provision: the 'concentration' thesis

In its analysis of higher education in Scotland, STEAC is bound to consider whether a coherent system is to be achieved by concentrating a very large number of small and medium-sized institutions into a smaller number of larger units. Several arguments have been adduced in support of the concentration of higher educational provision in this way. It is claimed in the first place that large institutions are in a better position to switch resources from one field of activity to another in response to rapidly changing needs and demands. Secondly, since the facilities required to sustain higher education are expensive it is considered that these are best located in a restricted number of centres, where they can be fully exploited. Thirdly, the education of students is thought to be most appropriately fostered in institutions in which there are concentrations of academic expertise in each of the available fields of study, thus allowing diversity of perspectives to be made apparent and a climate of intellectual questioning to be generated for the benefit of the students' intellectual development. Fourthly, the larger institution is able to attract substantial intakes of students, thus allowing a full range of option programmes and a variety of different pathways — the kind of provision which small institutions are not in a position to offer. Moreover, in the large institution the existence of a diversity of programmes makes it easier for students to switch courses according to their progress or to changes in their vocational aspirations. Besides, the formal and informal interactions that take place in a context in which there is a wide diversity of courses with different career outlets is thought to have a liberalising effect and to confer other related educational advantages. Finally, the large institution of higher education, with its extensive range of disciplines, is considered to sustain an authentic academic culture which the smaller institution cannot rival. Indeed, where that small institution is geographically remote from other centres it may well find itself academically isolated.

Higher education provision: the 'pluralist' thesis

To counter the arguments advanced in support of the concentration of higher education facilities in a limited number of centres it is not necessary to demonstrate, as some have claimed, that large institutions tend to be mere aggregates of departments with very little communication between them, or that they have the impersonality of 'degree-factories'. Nor is there any point in maintaining that there should be no large institutions or that all higher education provision should be as widely dispersed as possible. The thrust of the argument must be to show that the 'concentration' model has its weaknesses and that some of the arguments adduced against small and medium-sized institutions are invalid. There are five factors that need to be taken into account.

The first concerns the values of a pluralist society. In such a society, it is argued, power should not be concentrated at the centre or in large monolithic institutions but should be heavily decentralised to allow individuals to play a major part in decisions that affect their work and their way of life. In such a society, with its commitment to participative democracy, there is a need to create and preserve institutions which secure the maximum involvement of ordinary citizens in decision-making. That principle would extend to the ordering of educational institutions.

Secondly, an efficient and coherent system of higher education does not require institutional conformity. A national system certainly requires planning and resource allocation on a national basis but it does not require that every institution should operate as an identikit version of every other. Indeed, many would consider it to be essential in such a pluralist society as ours that higher education was characterised by diversity of provision in which institutions displayed features that rendered them distinctive rather than those which rendered them uniform. A pluralist system would tolerate a variety of different institutions of varying size, each making its distinctive contribution to a varied and responsive structure of provision.

Thirdly, there is ample room in that variety of provision for institutions which make no claim to comprehensiveness of academic or intellectual coverage but which have a distinctive and specialised professional function to perform. A college such as Moray House

would be an institution of this kind. Its whole tradition has shaped it as
an agency for teaching, research and development and professional
education. The centrality of that preoccupation with professional
activity does not weaken the institution: on the contrary, it is the source
of the institution's strength, providing a focus for individual, interdepartmental and institutional activity. Besides, the relatively restricted
range of its academic and professional coverage helps to maintain the
quality of the academic environment, to sharpen the sense of institutional purpose and to provide a powerful source of student
motivation.

Fourthly, the centralisation of higher education in a limited number
of centres would weaken access and would reduce the capacity of
higher education to respond to needs that are local. Colleges of
education have a central role to play in providing continued professional support for teachers, social workers and community educators
already in post. In the years ahead, as the members of these professions
begin to assert their entitlement to continuing professional education,
colleges will be under even stronger pressure to provide that support.
However, that support can only be provided if institutions are
sufficiently dispersed to ensure that professionals can have reasonable
access to continuing professional education.

Finally, the alleged relationship between size, geographical location
and academic isolation is surely questionable, given the resources for
communication in modern society. If, in spite of these resources, an
institution began to look in upon itself and to show signs of withdrawing from the international community of scholarship and professional
activity, the cause is more likely to be found in the quality of its staff
than in its size or its proximity to the nearest large-scale institution.

Possible lines of development

Each of the models discussed allows two lines of development. On the
'concentration' model the first would involve colleges of education in
establishing close links with the universities, if not being incorporated
by them. Clearly, there is nothing new or unusual about locating
responsibility for the professional education of teachers and others in
universities. Universities perform these functions in other countries and
the newest Scottish university has become a major centre for education
and teacher education. There are many staff in colleges of education
who would see a move of this kind as a natural development and as a
way of recognising the quality of their work over the years. They
envisage the current responsibilities of a college of education being

transferred to a neighbouring university and discharged possibly through a faculty of education.

The success of such a transfer would depend on how effectively the 'host' university could accommodate the professional ethos which colours all college of education work. For example, the new wave of BEd degrees introduced in 1983–84 differs strikingly from the traditional BEds that have been operating since the mid-1960s following the publication of the Robbins Report. The most striking difference is that while the new degrees attach high value to academic and intellectual accomplishment they attach equal value to professional accomplishment — that is, to the capacity to engage in appropriate professional action in a real setting. The old BEds did not always attest to achievement of appropriate professional standards: achievements of that kind were assessed independently by the colleges of education and were recognised by the award of the certificate conferring a licence to teach. Unless professional achievement can be granted the same recognition and status as academic achievement currently attracts, the incorporation of colleges of education into universities would endanger the full professionalisation of teaching in Scotland.

An alternative scenario also derives from the 'concentration' model and depicts two major sectors of higher education — the universities on the one hand and all other institutions of higher education, including colleges of education, on the other. According to this version of the 'binary system', in each major area of population there would be two large institutions — a university and an amalgamation of existing central institutions and other colleges. Those favouring such an institutional arrangement see value in encouraging non-university institutions to pool their resources to enable them to compete with the universities and to offer in the public sector a quality and range of course provision that seeks to match what the universities can offer. Whether or not institutions flourish in such a climate of competition, it has to be questioned whether the distinction between public and private sector institutions is any longer sustainable. All institutions, insofar as they rely for their survival on public funds, are public institutions; they ought all to be concerned to respond energetically and resourcefully to the various demands that are made on the system. Indeed, any institution which, invoking claims to autonomy, refused to demonstrate that responsiveness could make no claim on public funds. While it is conceivable that colleges of education might form part of such institutional amalgamations the 'binary' proposal itself is incoherent.

The two possibilities deriving from the 'pluralist' model seek to retain the identity of existing institutions but to bring them into much closer relationship with other parts of the system. The first of these might take the form of federations of institutions. According to this proposal there would be established in each significant area of population a federation in which the constituent institutions retained their identity but nevertheless engaged in close and continuing collaboration. While the precise nature of that collaboration would call for a detailed analysis of management and organisational practicalities, the central feature of the arrangement would be that in each area there would be a spectrum of institutions, each with its distinctive functions to perform, but contributing to a comprehensive range of courses and supported by a national system of awards. There need be no necessity for each federation to incorporate every single type of specialist institution, for an analysis of national needs might demonstrate that there was a limited need for certain specialist agencies. At the same time, some institutional reorganisation would be required, particularly when, as at present, there is a clear duplication of function by institutions only a few miles apart.

Such a system of federations, underpinned by a coherent structure of courses and a graded structure of national awards, would constitute an extremely powerful educational resource. The credit transfer/credit accumulation model would form an essential part of the system and would enable federations to respond with the necessary flexibility to needs at the undergraduate or initial training stage as well as to the changing professional needs of people in post. It could also accommodate changes in career aspirations and would strongly facilitate course transfers. Undoubtedly, a system of institutional federations such as has been sketched would create at the national and regional levels a co-ordinated and systematic structure of provision in which institutions are clearly and consistently differentiated according to function and in which duplication of provision is avoided. However, that arrangement clearly involves a considerable curtailment of institutional autonomy as well as extensive rationalisation of activities and neither of these is a feature that is likely to win the enthusiastic support of institutions in the present climate.

The second line of development in a pluralist system would include most of the features of the federation system just described but would allow colleges of education to develop particularly strong links with regional authorities. The justification for forging such links is that already in present circumstances colleges of education and regional authorities cannot escape the need to co-ordinate their activities. Both are at present involved in consultations about the size of the intake to colleges of education; they collaborate on selection procedures and in the planning and evaluation of courses; they each organise and support major programmes of professional development for local authority staff which require careful collaboration in order to ensure that resources are used to best effect; and, of course, colleges and regional authorities must engage in close partnership with regard to placement activities, for these take place in agencies which belong to the regions and not to the colleges. In all of these ways collaboration takes place at present. However, special arrangements have to be made to create the context and the structures for collaboration. Why not abandon such *ad hoc* arrangements in favour of a constitutional position in which colleges of education were fully integrated into the regional structure to serve as their professional education and development agencies?

The establishment of such centres would strongly facilitate many current developments in professional education. It would institutionalise the pioneering work in placement supervision currently being undertaken at Moray House and in the regions; it would bring the advisory service and college staff into full instead of partial collaboration in the provision of professional support; it would enable much freer exchanges of staff between colleges and schools and other agencies; and it would provide a focus for curriculum development, research and professional support. What is more, while these centres would themselves conduct curriculum development, research and professional development work, they would also have responsibility for stimulating and sustaining such work in the region's schools and other agencies, thus strengthening the region's commitment to professional education and development and its capacity to provide it.

Critics of such a development will question whether it is really compatible with the federation principle earlier discussed and will insist that the advantages that are thought to lie in the strengthening of links with regional authorities can only accrue if colleges of education are transferred to local authority management. In that case, the argument would run, the colleges of education would cease to be national institutions performing national functions and would become local or regional institutions, thus frustrating the emergence of a national system of higher education that is subject to national planning procedures.

Conclusion

This chapter began by asking whether the present functions of colleges of education should be performed in separate independent and self-governing institutions. The answer is by no means straightforward.

Those who favour the concentration of educational resources in a limited range of centres maintain that position not simply on the grounds of economic efficiency but also because they believe that such institutions would offer a richer educational experience for students and confer maximum flexibility of course provision. Those who support the existence of smaller and more specialised institutions invoke the principle of social pluralism and insist that such specialised institutions create a purposeful and professionally stimulating environment for teaching and research. In our present dilemma, there is a danger that, in the interests of creating an efficient and coherent structure of higher education, a solution will be adopted which, instead of strengthening the commitment of colleges of education to professional activity and professional education and development, makes the pursuit of these critically important tasks even more difficult to sustain.

List of Contributors

All contributors are on the staff of Moray House College of Education.

J. Callan Anderson, Director of the School of Community Studies

Wilson Bain, Lecturer, Department of Education

Peter Barker, Director, Centre for Computer Education

Marion Blythman, Head of Department of Special Educational Needs

M. Cameron-Jones, Senior Lecturer, Department of Education

Edmund A. Ewan, Vice-Principal

John E. A. Havard, Director, Scottish Centre for Studies in School Administration

Margaret Jarvie, Senior Lecturer, Department of Sociology

Gordon Kirk, Principal

Peter Lambert, Lecturer, Department of Special Educational Needs

John Landon, Lecturer, Scottish Centre for Education Overseas

Robert J. McCann, Head of Department of Educational Television

Alexander McLellan, Director, Scottish Centre for Education Overseas

Hugh Perfect, Assistant Principal and Director of In-Service, Research and Development

Nick Tate, Senior Lecturer, Department of History

John D. Wilson, Head of Department of Education